A Revolution in Education:
Scaling Agency & Opportunity for All

Chris Unger

ISBN 978-1-312-33422-9

Dedication

for Emily, Chloe, Sienna, my dear grandson "Bub" and
new grandson Anakin, and all those youth and adults who
continue to suffer the design of our public school ecosystem.
And all my good friends, colleagues, and comrades in arms
in pursuit of a Revolution in Education!

Let's GO!

Table of Contents

Foreword

Remember Apple's 1984 Superbowl commercial? It introduced the Macintosh. It was the same year Ted Sizer organized The Coalition of Essential Schools (CES) around a dozen small progressive schools – the education revolution against "Big Brother." The Miracle in East Harlem was underway – Seymour Fliegel's Center for Educational Innovation had created 42 small schools including Central Park East led by the incomparable Deborah Meir.

A Nation at Risk, published a few months before the 1984 Superbowl, sparked a state policy reform movement that included academic standards, standardized tests, and accountability systems. By the mid-1990s almost every state had enacted a version of the policy trifecta in a top-down effort to fix failing schools and close the achievement gap.

Simultaneously, new school developers were organizing learner-centered project-based schools coast to coast. In 1991, Expeditionary Learning was sponsored by the New American Schools initiative. One of the first charter schools, Minnesota New Country, opened in 1993. Big Picture Learning launched a small high school in the Rhode Island Commissioner's office in 1995. Napa New Tech opened in 1996. A few years later Larry Rosenstock opened High Tech High in San Diego.

While testing became reductionist and accountability fueled a 'back to basics' push, these new schools invited students to use their minds well, to exercise voice and choice, to do work that mattered for a public audience. Ron Berger invited us all to show students examples of excellent work. Dennis Littky and Elliott Washor reminded us of the power of rigor, relevance and relationships. Larry Rosenstock reminded us that good schools have always had a common intellectual focus and about 100 students per grade.

While states were enacting standards-based reforms and school developers were opening new schools, the web exploded. In 1994,

Time Magazine wrote about "The Strange New World of the Internet." The Apple IIe in the back of classrooms was replaced by laptops. Maine put Apple laptops in every high school. Microsoft sponsored Anywhere Anytime Learning, an early network of 1:1 schools. Virtual schools opened coast to coast and expanded full and part-time options.

With the turn of the century, new schools exploded in membership networks and managed networks and district improvement efforts. New York City closed failing schools and opened more than 400 new schools. Like Urban Assembly, most were Coalition inspired with a focus on meaningful work. Some charter networks chased test scores and college acceptance and scaled 'no excuses' models while others leaned into blended learning hoping for efficiency and effectiveness. The new school revolution unfolded through the 2010s on multiple fronts ranging from classical to progressive – all small and personalized, mission-focused and coherent.

The last 40 years of American public education were marked by the strange collision and interweaving of standards-based reforms, progressive pedagogy, networked new school development, and technology integration. However, none of the change levers worked as well as advocates had hoped. Testing and tech swamped progressive pedagogy resulting in worksheets over workshops, and coverage over challenge. Forty years into the information age, math teaching and testing remains fixated on hand calculations – multiplying fractions and factoring polynomials over data science and math modeling.

But there is good news. Despite the continued constrictions of the testing industrial complex, the learning revolution continues around the edges powered by four new change forces.

Unbundled learning exploded during the pandemic building on the 20-year expansion of open education resources (OER) and learn-anything platforms including Wikipedia, Khan Academy, and YouTube, as well as subscription platforms such as Udemy, Master Class and Outschool, and higher ed platforms such as EdX, Coursera, and Udacity. Despite much of the structures and practices of schooling remaining the same, expanded access to anywhere anytime learning is making it easier to create new learning pathways and making learners more demanding.

The platform economy has reduced barriers to employment (for example, Uber and Upwork) as well as entrepreneurship (Shopify, Amazon, and Angi) making it easier to produce, publish, and sell anything to anyone. Scaling efforts in education has become easier with platform networks inclusive of shared resources for learners and teachers (e.g., NAF, New Tech Network, Summit Learning, and Project Lead The Way). During the pandemic, platform networks like Prenda and Wildflower went direct to consumer. Platform networks and direct-to-family funding in a quarter of the states made it easier to launch a microschool.

New pathways are connecting more learners to opportunity – and they are accelerated, applied, and supported. New employer, community, and higher education agreements are supporting blends of work-based learning and accelerated skill building with progress being made with the development of digital credentials and shared learner records.

Artificial Intelligence was ubiquitous in corporate computing by 2017 but the explosive entrance of generative AI into the consumer market in 2022 is making it very clear that learning will change forever. New pathways and platform networks will soon incorporate AI incorporating co-authoring, AI tutoring, and AI advising.

The revolution in learning will be expressed as new models that rebundle resources with new platforms and pathways using AI to help learners string together powerful experiences linked to opportunity. The best of these new models will blend personalized pathways with advisory cohorts and project teams into a sequence of social learning experiences. They will connect with place – local and global – to help learners understand themselves and their world. They will expand the ways learners can contribute to the world designing solutions and making an impact.

For the last 20 years, Chris Unger has been a leading champion of experiences and environments that change lives – schools that invite learners into work that matters to them and makes a difference in their communities. Unger is a provocateur on the frontier of learning. He calls us back to the principles Sizer and Meier taught us. He calls us forward to a sense of possibility through the design of new schools inspired by what "fellow revolutionaries" are doing across the county. Unger is a modern Johnny Appleseed spreading seeds of deeper learning.

In *A Revolution in Education*, Unger curates pictures and stories from schools leading the way forward. Some are old favorites that are more relevant than ever, some will be new to most readers. Unger outlines how we could potentially move forward in the revolution in education, providing ways each of us could play a role in that revolution, no matter who you are. Classroom educator, school or district leader, community member, policy actor, or other. In the end, it will take us reconsidering what the purpose of school is and reimagining what school can be, as well as rebuilding our learning ecosystems that build agency and expand opportunity for all.

Thanks to readers that have been fighting for deeper learning as long as Unger. For those new to the most important work in the world, welcome to the Revolution!

Tom Vander Ark
CEO of Getting Smart

Preface

We have been doing "school" pretty much the same for a LONG time, even though our world has changed, the interests and aspirations of our youth have changed, and the need for a better humanity throughout the world has changed. In short, we are stuck. The very design of our education ecosystem is ultimately doing a gross disservice to our youth, the adults attempting to serve them, our communities, and the world. The good news is that there are educators around the world that are pursuing new "images of possibility," learning communities and practices that far better provide youth with what they need as well as inspire and empower them to make a difference in the world. Our educational ecosystem, by virtue of its history, continued policies, and funding architecture maintains the status quo when, in reality, we need to reimagine what is possible in how we work with youth. We need to reimagine how we think about teaching, learning, and schooling in order to support continual innovation that truly benefits our dynamic and ever-changing world.

In the pages ahead, I not only clearly share how broken our education system is but also provide numerous examples of what teaching, learning, and schooling could look like. Beyond that, I present ideas for HOW our education system could be redesigned to incentivize the transformation of educational opportunities for youth and how such transformations could be proactively created.

As Chris Dede said in a recent podcast, "Innovation is not the issue. Scaling is the issue."[1] But both are true. We do have truly innovative practices for supporting the development of youth and learning communities that are far better focused on developing the skills, competencies, and agency of youth. But these innovations are typically the result of a small few doing what they can either in the outskirts of schooling or outside our system of public education altogether. And rarely do they scale – as they should.

In this book I offer some specific recommendations for what you can do no matter your place in our system of education or your community. What YOU can do to contribute to a revolution in education. Most of us feel stuck, not seeing where "I" can make a difference. When, in reality, there is much you can do.

For me, the need for a revolution in education is not unlike the need for the civil rights movement in the 50s and 60s – recognizing that this need continues today. The ways that political and social perspectives, mindsets, and laws perpetuated social injustice in the the 50s and 60s I argue continues today. We see it every day in the rhetoric of politicians, actions of citizens, and the outcomes perpetuated by the very design of our systems and the espoused ideology and actions of our politicians. If our social and educational systems were designed to provide everyone with the opportunity to pursue gainful employment and lives, we would not have what we have today.

This will not be an easy read because I clearly point to the significant shortcomings of our education system today. At the same time, I point to some hope. I point to educators, communities, and networks that are pursuing the revolution in education, offering us new images of possibility. What is possible, and how. And I offer concrete recommendations as to how each of us can "pursue the revolution!" Each one of us individually and as a collective.

If after reading this you should wish to connect with others in the revolution and/or connect with me, contact me. It is only our collective will, effort, and relationships with one another that can make the revolution a reality.

As I like to say ... Onward!

– 1 –

Why Write This?

Over the last 25 years, I have been seeking out, learning about, and reaching out to schools that grabbed my imagination. Schools that have acted, behaved, and worked differently from others. But not different in just in any way, different in particular ways.

How are these schools different? They engage students in exploring and pursuing their interests and passions and foster their students' agency by supporting them in making a difference in the world and the ways they want to be in the world. They actively nurture students' identity and sense of possibilities in healthy and generative ways. They work with youth in ways that have a profound impact on their future lives. And they embrace who their students are and while building sense of personal agency and possibilities.

Then there is the last twelve years, where I began to dig deep into the design of our education system and how it did, or did not, work to support if not create schools toward these same ideals.

Assuming that this book will just be a cool and nifty way to learn about these schools would be a significant underestimation of the book's purpose. While I will be pointing to a number of schools that simply do school differently, more important than that is how we see, value, and think about education. The current paradigm of teaching, learning, and schooling in which our current system is now grounded is ultimately doing more harm than good – for our youth, the adults serving them, our society, and the world. This paradigm is so unconsciously influential that most educators, policy makers, and parents don't even see it as a lens by which they can critically examine the issues present in our current public schools and from there begin to consider new possibilities.

In this book I attempt to pinpoint many of the central issues in our education system today, and then link that directly to how we are failing our youth, communities, and society.

The numbers are startling when we step back to consider the tremendous impact of our education system. Its very design is currently shaping the lives of the 50 million plus youth it now serves, and in reality has had and continues to have a tremendous impact on the lives we live them.

Besides impacting the 50 million plus lives of youth currently enrolled in in our public school system, the system and its design is also impacting the lives of the adults working in the system. Over 3.5 million educators across 15,000+ communities working in 13,000+ school districts, ranging in size from 100 to 1 million students, from Arvada, Montana to New York City, respectively. Ultimately, the design of our education system from the federal and state level down to our local communities reinforces how our schools operate. In some districts, how they "do school" is impacting the current and future lives of hundreds of thousands of youth. For the better?

District	# of students
Los Angeles	~635,000
Broward (FL)	~270,000
Chicago	~380,000
Houston	~216,000
Miami-Dade	~360,000
Hillsborough (FL)	~214,000
Clark County (Vegas)	~330,000
Orange (FL)	~200,000

In short, our education system and how it functions makes a significant difference in the experience and shape of our lives. Our future education. Our professional pursuits. Our employment. Even our happiness. Are we doing what we love to do? Are we meaningfully and gainfully employed? Do we feel empowered to pursue work that matters to us, and are we able to contribute to our communities and humanity in ways we are proud of?

How we and our youth are educated impacts our future – our personal actions, professional pursuits, and community contributions. Our lives are shaped by how our schools operate, starting with the expectations for learning, expectations of teaching, and the structures and practices of our schools and school systems.

Given this reality, the first intent of this book is to show how the design of our current education system is actually doing a substantial disservice to our youth, our communities, and our society by virtue of how we "do school." The second purpose of this book is to show how the paradigm by which we do education constrains the possibilities of how we could be doing education. The third purpose of the book is to showcase how education and "schooling" could look different, far better serving youth to lead purposeful and meaningful lives. The fourth purpose is to present how educators, policy actors, states, and the federal government could incentivize and facilitate the proliferation of schools that far better serve our youth, communities, and society than they do now. Finally, the fifth purpose of the book is to offer suggestions as to how each stakeholder in our education system – educators, parents, school board members, community members, and local, state, and federal policy actors – could press for and pursue "a revolution in education" that increases agency and possibility for all.

So, as you read this, please keep an open mind to what I am saying and, please, if you are a classroom educator or school or district leader, keep in mind that I am not attempting to put the singular blame on *you*. Rather, I am wanting to show how the system by its very design continues to perpetuate the status quo of schooling as we now know it. It isn't your fault. You are part of a system that reinforces how we do school – and as an educator, you too are a victim of the system as much as is true for most of our youth. Then for parents, I want you to be able to see how the system is designed and how that design is limiting the possibilities for your children. As for employers and community members, I want you to see how our education system is impacting you as well – limiting the skills and competencies of your local workforce and how your local graduates can give back to your community.

Of course, I can point to numerous issues in our current system, but how useful is that? To just point to these issues and offer no other possibilities is easy, and really doesn't help, does it? So for the greater part of this book I offer new possibilities. I share numerous examples of how some educators across the country *are* doing school differently, and to what end. I also offer *how* these schools got started, including the circumstances that facilitated their start-up, hopefully providing some insight as to how more of these schools – learner-centered and future-focused – could take root and grow in your community and proliferate nationally.

What are these schools? How are they serving youth differently? How are they impacting the lives of youth not only today – but their future?

Beyond that, I offer specific recommendations as to how our education ecosystem – perspectives on learning, models of schooling, and policies and funding – could be different and result in the proliferation of learning environments such as the ones I showcase. Schools that yield greater agency and opportunity for all. Beyond that, I offer specific actions each of you reading this book, whether you are a classroom educator, school or district leader, community or school board member, policy actor, parent or student, can take. Actions you can take in support of the revolution we need. Actions that could be taken in support of a revolution in education.

There are Other Possibilities

It is in this way that the book pursues a specific focus: How can we reimagine the purpose of schooling and the means by which we can reach those ends?

Luckily, we already have a great number of creative educators who have been able to create schools and learning programs across dozens of communities that offer us some new "images of possibility" – how we could engage our youth to better ends. Having these new images of possibility is invaluable because reimagining the purpose of school without ideas on how to pursue these new ends would leave us wanting. Fortunately, we have educators who have pursued both – new visions of the purpose of school and the redesign of school that assists students towards those purposes.

So, we have a jumping off point. We have examples of possibilities. Or what I like to refer to as "images of possibility." Not just in how we can rethink the purpose of school but how we can *do* school. Because this is where the rubber hits the road. How can we do school differently, with greater outcomes that we value, true to what we believe is important. For me, the question is: What designs can we create that truly inspires and empowers our students to pursue the lives they want to live, and hopefully contribute back to our humanity too.

Having been around the block, I remain disheartened when seeing students in classrooms where their "fire" is not lit. Of course, my disposition is to worry about this. My passion is to inspire and empower others to think differently about what school could be, and then support them in considering how they can pursue change, influenced by my own early experiences of school.

The first half of third grade I went to a Montessori school, where I was able to do what I wanted – playing, creating, making, and doing things that I was moved to do because I was, quite frankly, moved to do it. I wrote poems. Built structures. Role played with peers.

The last half of third grade I found myself in a desk in a row of desks, facing a teacher, where I was being told how to tell time (which I already knew), and where I had to remain seated. This was foreign to me as I had previously become accustomed to doing as I wish and learning through my own design: self-determined exploration, play, and creative activity. This distaste for traditional school structures was further deepened when I ended up in a large middle school where I was bullied and tried, simply, not to have my head knocked off. Little if any learning. Just going through the motions and trying to get by.

Fast forward, I didn't arrive at my focus on the need to change schools until I worked hard at finding alternative school designs. In doing so I learned that there were already educators who had not only been thinking about how school could be different but were doing school different.

Learning about the initial Big Picture schools that Dennis Littky and Elliot Washor created in Providence way back in 1995 was an eye-opener. To think that two individuals had created a school where the focus was students' interests and providing an opportunity to work with adults in the community with that shared interest was a huge deal for me. The focus of their school was NOT typical school content – such as history and physics, algebra and biology – it focused on finding ways to connect students to others in the community based on their interests. This blew my mind. To think that they did this by not having classes and not having kids move in prescribed blocks of time from one room of 30 students with one teacher to another fed my imagination.

As I had been hired by the Seattle Public Schools to support the development of their high schools, I had started to look for alternative school models and practices. Finding the Big Picture schools (bigpicture.org) opened my mind to the idea that school did not have to operate as I had always assumed it had to operate. That schools could, in fact, act very differently and toward a very different end. Just as important, ends and ways that resonated with me.

Focusing on their students' interests and help them to find ways to explore their interests resonated with me. Why? I look back to my days at the Montessori school prior to being dumped in a desk in a row of desks listening to a teacher tell me how to tell time, and I think ... What?

I finally began to question why schools needed to be designed as they were, and why most schools looked all the same and "did" school the same.

At this time too, and as a result of my opportunity to work with high schools throughout Seattle, I began to see how much the design and culture and focus of schools played such a huge role in the experience and support of youth.

This became very apparent to me when I started working with two very different high schools in Seattle. Probably the two most disparate and different schools in the district.

One school, Nova, considered itself to be the only truly democratic high school west of the Rockies, Nova. Working at Nova (novaroots.org/nova-high-school) was incredible. Occupying an old elementary school building made of wood (not concrete!) with huge open spaces and classrooms with tall ceilings and large sun-filled windows was a welcoming space. I didn't feel claustrophobic. For the first time I saw a school not organized around the overwhelming need to keep students occupied and closely monitored every minute. In this school, students followed a college schedule, meaning a student might have science from 9-10:30 on Mondays, Wednesdays, and Fridays. Then history from 1-3 on Tuesdays and Thursdays. When students were not in class, they were hanging out in the large, spacious hallways or classrooms, where they could work or simply connect with their friends and teachers. Lo and behold, teachers were then not otherwise always occupied teaching or taking what time they could to prepare for class. Because it was a college schedule and teachers were not teaching all of the time. They too were free to hangout in the hallways and their classrooms and spend a great deal of their time talking with students, either about class or simply hangout and talk about ... whatever. About their lives, current events, interests. Really, just get to know the students and build relationships with them.

With this simple change in the use of time and space, the school felt entirely different. But this general feeling of focused interest and exploration and personal relationships between teachers and students was also greatly supported by the way the teachers taught. These were really good teachers, meaning the focus was not on just covering content in the usual boring, fact- or memory-focused ways. Rather, they were creative in how they engaged students. They paid a lot of attention to how kids were engaging in the content, how they were and could be interested in it, and creating means of engagement that would intrinsically push them to think about the topics of class. Mark Perry taught US history through jazz (think, similar to Ken Burns' documentary of US History through the lens of baseball). And I remember students taking chemistry through the lens of women's contribution to science.

Advisories felt real and useful.[2] Kids were hanging out with one another and the teacher. Topics of interest to the group were discussed. Birthdays were celebrated. And advisors kept in constant touch with each of their advisees to be sure they were engaged in the school, following their plans for learning, and making the most of their opportunities to learn what was of interest to them to learn.

This school, in the words of many of the students (I know because I interviewed them) was a lifesaver. In one case, a young woman told me she had been standing on the edge of a bridge having experienced a great deal of peer admonishment and bullying at her home high school and had realized standing on that bridge that this school shouldn't be the reason for her death. So having heard of Nova, she decided to give it a try. And with that, she thrived as Nova was a far more inclusive, supportive, and caring community than the large school she had been in. Teachers and students embraced who she was rather than bullied or made fun of her.

The other school I worked at was created for "those kids" who were continuously misbehaving. Getting into trouble. Acting out. A far cry from Nova, this other school was created specifically to get the kids misbehaving students out of the traditional high schools and somehow rehabilitate them with closer monitoring and attention, doable with smaller class sizes and a tight-fisted behavior system.

What I learned there also had a significant impact on my thinking about what is right or wrong about most schools – student-teacher relationships and a culture of care trump almost anything else. What the staff told me made complete sense to me and left me shaking my head. The "problem kids" would get shuffled to this new school, with smaller classrooms and more adult attention, and they would begin to act differently. Act out less. Participate. And once evidencing this new behavior, they would be sent back to their old school where, guess what, they would start to act out again.

At this point, the question is: is it the kids? Or the environment?

The husband of a friend of mine, a doctor, once told me about an elementary school in the foothills of Denver where 80% (EIGHTY PERCENT!) of the students were prescribed Ritalin. This was at the very beginning of when educators and the medical establishment began identifying students as having ADHD (the early 90s) because their attention wandered, or they couldn't sit still (meaning they couldn't stay in their seat). Diagnosing youth as having ADHD became an expedient way to explain students' behavior when their focus became lacking, or they began to get fidgety for sitting too long in their seats.

Of course, the question is: Is it the kids? Should we be expecting youth to sit quietly and pay attention to adults when the topic or activity is not of genuine interest to them, for hours at a time? Could it be that in this particular elementary school EIGHTY PERCENT of the students actually had ADHD? Or is there something wrong with the environment Is it something that works against their nature.

If having ADHD means that kids don't like to sit still in their seats for more than 10-15 minutes because they are not engaged in the topic or activity, and thus antsy, fidgety, and playful, then I guess they have ADHD. If this means that their minds drift off or they are not paying attention to someone lecturing at them about something they don't understand no less care about. If this means that the student would much rather be getting up, walking around, playing with toys, drawing, or talking with friends ... then I guess, inherently, ALL OF US has ADHD. Because guess what, this is our nature. This is how we were born!

We are born to explore. To run, play, and jump. To try new things. To build. To test the limits. To follow that which piques our interest and our curiosity. To communicate and engage with others. To be social. And to learn from one another. So ... why do we keep doing school the same way!

Interviewing the students at Nova blew my mind. The students were quite eloquent when speaking of how THIS school had been a lifesaver. How they had escaped large, personally isolating and debilitating school environments and landed in a place where the community and teachers cared. Where they were able to work at their own pace and pursue learning that mattered to them.

Later during this time period, I was given the opportunity to make a series of videos on great teaching throughout the city. By word of mouth, I had identified six teachers, from elementary through high school. Each was amazing in their own way, working within the confines of the structures, conditions, and cultures of the schools they worked in.

One of the teachers worked in an Expeditionary Learning school and what I found out was that she and her team designed a whole year around their students' exploration of "glass." Glass?, you say. Yes, glass.

After my work in Seattle, from which I learned a lot, I landed at Brown University, where I was fortunate to work with a small group of colleagues who were trying to help high schools all around New England (as well as New York and New Jersey) turn their large, comprehensive high schools into smaller learning communities, incentivized by the feds through small learning community grants.

I learned a lot, again, through this work. The feds, in all of their wisdom (sorry, I am saying that holding my breath), had finally picked up on some of the research that had shown that smaller schools were better at ensuring kids did not feel disconnected from school and that adults were more likely to know their students and vice versa. Instead of falling through the cracks, smaller schools were better at ensuring kids were known and supported.

Unfortunately, they didn't pay attention to the rest of the research which clearly showed that these schools needed to be *autonomous* and that the small learning community needed to be able to develop – and own really – their curriculum, pedagogical philosophy, and efforts to do right by their students. Instead, the feds stated that the school could pursue a number of small school-like practices, such as having freshman teams, advisories, and career academies.

Two things are important here and speak to some of the lessons from this primarily failed enterprise. One, the government totally whiffed on several of the extremely important characteristics, attributes, and features of small schools that made a big difference in the lives of youth. You need a small group of educators completely committed to supporting the well-being and success of all their students with the complete freedom to act and respond as they see best for them relationally and pedagogically.   Without this opportunity for "ownership," teachers were still cogs in a larger system of expectations and mandates that were still not theirs.

Impassioned and passionate work comes when you own the work. There is nothing like being a part of a team that is *empowered* to think, design, create, problem-solve, and act according to your beliefs, values, and intent to do right. While not every small school is or was inherently successful, the greater percentage of small schools were, with a number of small schools starting up that were ultimately successful and "cool" (my term) because a smaller group of individuals were given the opportunity to imagine a new school model and new school practices that stretched beyond what we had known before.

Deborah Meier's Central Park East, for example, was held up as a beacon for such possibilities in NYC back then. Their focus was on student work. Interdisciplinary projects and learning. Teachers planning together. And close attention to students.

The results were an anomaly in comparison to other schools in the neighborhood with the same students. Far more students were passing the state standardized tests for proficiency, graduating, and going to college. Of course, when Deborah left, things began to shift a bit and the same results were not as apparent even though there was a commitment to maintaining the practices. Which begs another question ... how important is the leader?

Ten years ago, I reviewed the work of a number of schools in Massachusetts that had previously been among some of the lowest performing academically and who, within a very short time period (3 years), with some funding, made some fairly dramatic gains – meaning a much higher percentage of their students were passing the MCAS (Massachusetts' state assessment) than before.

A good number of schools throughout the state had also received the same monies with the same expectations for a dramatic increase in their performance. While some made gains, most improved very little and a number failed to improve at all.

My colleague, Brett Lane, who I had worked with at Brown University, had been hired by the Massachusetts Department of Elementary and Secondary Education to assist them in the design, development, and assessment of their statewide turnaround efforts – something expected by the federal Department of Education at the time.   Under Arne Duncan, appointed by Obama, hundreds of millions of dollars that were typically given to districts and schools serving students in low-income communities were now to be used only by the 5% lowest performing schools in each state. There were other mandates associated with the kinds of efforts these schools were to take, along with the money, but each state had to develop their own framework and guidance for school improvement.

Four years later, the result of this effort is readily acknowledged as mixed, at best. Mostly because (1) schools and districts did not know how to use such funds to significantly turn their schools around, and (2) the state did not provide any guidance or assistance in how to do so.

The story in Massachusetts is a better one. Not all schools improved, but a great many did. Some significantly. It was those schools that my colleague and I set out to investigate. One of the things that became clear was how the principal took charge and empowered the community to take shared ownership of the effort. In most cases, it was the new principal that came in, raised teacher and student expectations, held the bar high, and let go of those who were (1) not willing to put in the effort or (2) perhaps worse, didn't believe the kids could do better.

Each of these leaders had a persona and clear commitment to change. This way of acting and thinking and engaging others is not learned by reading textbooks, and not everyone has both the social facility and strategic ability to think about the system and engage everyone in a new design that could do better.

This is true as well of the small schools that made significant gains not only in achievement, but graduation rates, college going rates, and other factors such as community well-being and student aspirations. Without powerful leadership, it is easy for behaviors to fall to the mean and for performance to remain stagnant. And for school communities to feel like they are just trying to survive ... not thriving.

A Nod to the Late, Great Sir Ken Robinson

If you haven't seen any of Sir Ken Robinson's videos on Ted.com, you should. You could start with his extremely popular "Changing education paradigms" animated talk, which points to the very error of our ways (http://www.ted.com/talks/ken_robinson_changing_education_paradigms). In this fairly short piece (~11 minutes), he succinctly and clearly points out the glaring error of our education system – designed as factories, pushing groups of students through various pathways for the purpose of "dropping knowledge" in their heads and ensuring that they all know the same. This doesn't account for the fact that we learn best by doing. That we like to be active. We feel far better when we are self-directed. And that we are not all wired the same. Some of us like to listen (aural). Some of us like to be physically active in our learning (kinesthetic). Some of us like to debate, design, and reflect, more than others (conceptual).

Schools are designed as they are because those in charge of the system do not know another way; they typically continue the only model they know and have experienced. You have knowledge that you want students to have and skills you want them to master so you simply have them "sponge in" this knowledge and rotely repeat the skills in this manner – because of the numbers. A teacher stands in front of the room and delivers knowledge (lecture) or by reading out of a book and then tells students what they want students to do, which is a fill in for having students develop the skills the school system wants them to attain.

What we know now is that we learn when we are learning what we want to learn. We learn best by taking in information and observing others and doing our best and replicating, creating, making, and doing with this knowledge as others do with these skills. So the assumption that everyone in the class is *intrinsically* motivated to learn and become competent at what the teacher is presenting is a significant flaw in our current design of learning in schools. The other major flaw is that students will acquire this knowledge and become competent at these skills without serious opportunities to put them into practice and learn through feedback from others and the world as they attempt to use and apply this knowledge and engage in these competencies.

In short, let us assume that the best way to learn is through apprenticeship. That is, an apprentice working side-by-side with a mentor who is quite good at what they do and given the opportunity to observe the mentor at work and to do what they do with the artful guidance of the mentor. "Don't hold it like that, hold it like this." "When you cut, cut it like this." "When you put the flame up too high, you see, the butter burns."

I'm not sure how one could argue against this point. I certainly would not want to give anyone a textbook on how to drive, have them take a multiple-choice test, and then based on these results, say the student is finished learning how to drive, and then send them on their way to drive. I – like you, I assume – would be a little wary that this person could actually drive.

So, what do we do? We have a period where we have the student watch what we are doing. I would say more than even that, we explicitly verbalize what we are doing – and not just what we are doing but what we are thinking. After that, we take our student (daughter or son) to an empty parking lot, to give it a go ... but slowly. We tell them what to do. Put two hands on the wheel and step on the gas ... slowly.

We then tell them how to brake (not abruptly). How to turn left and right. How to look both ways at a stop. How to look in the rearview mirror. Eventually, we gather enough courage to take them out on the open road (side street first, eventually to more trafficked thoroughfares, and finally the highway). Parallel parking becomes a feat. Then with practice and clear feedback as they turn the wheels and back in, we have arrived at some level of confidence that they can do it on their own.

We all do this and remember what it was like – those of us with kids and drew the short end of the straw, or with our significant other realized we would be the ones that could, to some degree, survive the experience.

But this looks nothing like school.

Let us count the ways ...
 - individual attention
 - individual instruction
 - individual feedback
 - constant feedback
 - ongoing support
 - practice in a safe environment
 - gradual skill development – go and stop first, then turn, then out into the "real" world
 - clear commentary on not only what to DO but what to be looking for and how to be thinking

We don't do this in school typically. Yes, there are some teachers who do this as best they can given the circumstances (20-30 students in a class), stuck in a classroom, in a short period of time. And some are clever in how they do so given the constraints. They ramp up skill sets and provide feedback as they teach, but in most cases the work is not authentic – it doesn't have any real *meaning* for the kids and is not performed in *real-world* contexts. In such cases, the activity and thinking is a far cry from learning that actually takes root in the student, which then is still a far cry from knowing how to act and apply their knowledge and skills in the real world. Which then makes everything a moot point, really. No?

So back to Sir Ken Robinson. First, his commentary is about the assumptions we make about how we learn. Second, it is about the assumptions we have about what is of value to learn. Do we need to learn about all of the wars in history? Do we need to memorize all of the US Presidents? Is the quadratic equation really that important? Of course, we hear it again and again from the students: Why do I need to learn this?

These are the two questions we need to unpack going forward:

What does learning of value really look like?

and,

What is of real value to learn?

– 2 –

The Tragedy of our Current System of Education

I have taught several classes in our Doctor of Education program, three of which are near and dear to me. One was called "The System of Education." Another, "Education Entrepreneurship." And the third, "The Power of Experiential Learning."

The System of Education class came about as a result of the following experience. Early on in my time at Northeastern, I was teaching a class on the Ethics of Leadership. As is often the case, I don't really know exactly what I am going to do when I walk into a class. I do begin to form some initial ideas a few days beforehand without getting too specific or holding on to any particular idea for too long. I'll jot some ideas down, just to be sure I have something in mind as the class draws closer. But for the most part, what I decide to do doesn't really happen until I begin to walk to the class. As I walk I begin to turnover in my mind some possibilities related to the class, and then I get a feeling for where my interest or energy is as I get closer. What would be fun? Interesting? Engaging?

On this particular evening, the entire system of education was on my mind. Why do we do what we do? And why is it happening everywhere? Why, when I walk into schools, can I for the most part expect to see the same thing? When I walk into high schools, why do I expect to be walking down 12-foot-wide hallways decorated on each side with rows of lockers and doors every 40 feet with a singular window where I can peer in and, again for the most part, see rows of desks and chairs with the students facing up front. A teacher rambling on about something or drawing something on the board and approximately a third to almost all of the students – dependent on the community – diligently writing notes. Sometimes they are in small groups talking with one another. If it's a lab, they are working in pairs on some exercise. But for the most part, I am seeing the same thing. Again and again and again.

So true. Why is it that learning looks almost the same across all of these schools across all of these communities? Particularly when we know this version of learning really doesn't translate to learning of value. When I use the word "broken," I have no problem or issue using that word. The system is broken. And for those who wish to argue the point, I don't have to go far to provide evidence of how broken the system is.

First, in most of our inner-city schools, close to – if not fully – half of those entering 9th grade are dropping out before graduation. For whatever reason, boredom, anger, or simply not seeing the purpose of school or tired of being derided or told they are not worthy or good enough, they drop out. When they do, their opportunity for pursuing gainful employment around work that they wand if not love to do has been greatly diminished. In 2021, the median income of a 25–34-year-old male without a high school degree is ~$32,500. If you are a woman, worse, ~$29,200, which means half are making less than this.[3] To say the least, the opportunity to be gainfully and happily employed becomes significantly diminished. And when your employment opportunity is grossly limited to menial and debilitating work, no wonder that some youth – particularly those who just dropped out and with little or no work – turn to other opportunities for having money. If one doesn't have to work for someone else and the opportunity for making a lot more money is available to you, why not? Why not traffic in drugs? Why not steal? Why not rob from others? Just because I decided to drop out of school – because I hated it – why should I have to suffer with less and why should everyone else have so much more than me? The result: "High school dropouts are 3.5 times more likely than high school graduates to be arrested in their lifetime."[4] And perhaps a bit dated, but the New York Times in 2009 reported that about "one in every 10 young male high school dropouts is in jail or juvenile detention, compared with one in 35 young male high school graduates." And, unfortunately, they report "the picture is even bleaker for African-Americans, with nearly one in four young black male dropouts."[5] In short, not good.

The correlation is not hard to see. If you do not have a high school degree, you are more likely to engage in illegal activity. If you do not have a high school degree, you are less able to pursue work that has personal meaning. If you do not have a high school degree, you are more likely to struggle – financially, emotionally, and relationally. The social capital you can build with further education and subsequent employment is quickly shut down for you. If you find opportunity, you are one of the lucky few. Somehow, someway, you have been able to find connections that benefit you and have luckily been placed in the position of opportunity. But those are very few. Very, very few. Far less than even 1%. For these youth, who were born with natural curiosity and interest, have, as a result of their circumstances, been funneled into conditions and circumstances where their eventual decision to leave school because school didn't work for them has left them with the struggle of a lifetime.

One of the reasons I went into education is because of my own experience of school as a youth. From 3rd grade through middle school, I was in the LA Public Schools, where in middle school I simply tried not to have my head bashed in. I was doing other kids' artwork, was pushed around in the halls, and once got clobbered on the playground for getting in someone's way, resulting in a tremendous black eye. I even remember having to hide it from the PE teacher for the next few weeks to ensure that I would not suffer the same for showing it. Retribution.

Halfway through 8th grade my family moved to Westport, CT. If you don't know Westport, let me just put it this way. Bette Davis lived down the street (literally). Paul Newman was a mile away. Martha Stewart was on the other side of town. And the kids got around on a mini-bus system made up of Mercedes-Benz buses. I remember there was a clothing store on Main Street that read: New York • Rome • Paris (and then) Westport.

Yes. Ka-ching, Ka-ching. $$$. And with that, one of the best school systems in the state, if not the country. That is most likely the reason I was accepted into Wesleyan (CT), referred to as one of the three little Ivy schools. And most likely because of that, why I got a leg up into Harvard, where I received my master's and Doctorate.

When I tell this story to others, I usually add: Well, yes, I'm smart. But there are a lot of smart people in the world. Just because my family moved to Westport, I probably got into Wesleyan. Then because I went to Wesleyan, more likely got into Harvard. Then from there, greater opportunity.

Now, is that right? Is that how it should be? Can one buy themselves into an educational track that opens doors while others can't make that choice because they can't move? By simply moving into a more affluent community? Well ... yes.

How Could we move from our Current Tragedy to Possibilities?

There are several arenas of work that need to be addressed if we are to move from a system of tragedy toward a system of possibility.

First, is a newfound understanding of what learning is – not the rote, ineffectual learning we have in many if not most schools today but the meaningful and actionable learning we need.

Second, is a rethinking of what learning is of value to support agency and opportunity for all. Moving from memorizing formulas and fact that have no real bearing on the development of our identity, our capacity to pursue the lives we wish to live, or the empathy to contribute to the lives of others and the world.

Third is an understanding that we have designed a system that has shackled our imagination. If we were to wipe the slate clean and start from scratch, imagining what we should want most for the youth of our world and their capacity to give back, would we create the institutions we have now. I would hope not.

Fourth, is an acknowledgment that we have not broken free of ways of thinking, acting, and perceiving that compels each of us and our society to assist and support everyone to thrive.

And finally, fifth, an awakening that it is our political and social will that could eradicate the systems and structures that have continued to perpetuate education in our country as we now know it and create a new ecosystem of opportunity for all.

As pointed out earlier in the book, our view of learning and the learning we press for in schools is so archaic and disempowering that it is a crime. From the way we teach reading (see *The Science of Reading Movement* by Paul Thomas) to the focus on content over deeper learning (see, for example, *In Search of Deeper Learning* by Jal Mehta and Sarah Fine; *Deeper Learning* by Monica Martinez and Dennis McGrath; and *Creative Schools* by Ken Robinson and Lou Aronica). We are perpetuating a model of education that actually does more harm than good.

Plenty of youth end up adopting views of learning and views of themselves as learners that turns them off from our current systems of learning. Being subjected to rote memorization and the acquisition of skills disconnected from intrinsic purpose and authentic contexts leads to students spending hours upon hours, days upon days, weeks to weeks, and years to years of wasted time where youth could have been engaged in the kinds of intellectual work that would benefit them.

If you were forced to spend hours learning content you didn't give a damn about, where your natural interests and natural inclination to activity was hijacked for 6-7 hours a day, day-after-day, and the modality of learning was memorizing and undertaking tasks dictated by others, you would most likely go crazy. Or as happens with many students, simply become apathetic, and go through the motions. Children do develop mechanisms to "get by" in these experiences. But this is compliance; it isn't real "learning."

There is the rub. It is actually hard to say what is worse – that youth are forced into these daily experiences or the fact that what they are learning is often immaterial.

Well, let's just say that both are bad.

For us to move forward, those who are designing learning systems of real value will need to be grounded in an enlightened understanding of what real learning is as well as reconsider what learning is of great value.

If those re-visioning a new ecosystem of education are to do a good job of it, it will require those designing the system to have a deep and comprehensive understanding of learning and the multiple ways that youth can learn. It will require those who are supporting the development of such systems (educators, policy actors, and politicians) to have a deeper understanding of how communities can be designed to support youth in their development. And when I say systems, I mean systems that actively support the ongoing development of a system that proactively incentivizes and supports educational opportunities and outcomes for all.

Let's agree that our current social and political systems perpetuate the illusion of meritocracy and that we need to move to social, political, economic, and educative systems that support prosperity and well-being for all

One of the more significant challenges we have in our society today is the very American ideology that everyone should be able to pick themselves up by their bootstraps. This ideology perpetuates the perspective that your inability to do well is related solely by your own ability to gain greater opportunity. Worse, you deserve no better. If you are not able to get after it and grab the American dream, it's your own damn fault – meaning you either haven't tried hard enough or are simply lazy, or just don't have the skill or intellect to make something good of yourself.   This is easy for many Americans to say, particularly if they have a leg up in life.

This has been argued and well-supported elsewhere, far better than I do here. For example, in Daniel Markovits' excellent book, *The Meritocracy Trap*, Daniel clearly pinpoints with laser-like erudition that there are many who are significantly challenged from opportunities dictated by such collateral circumstances as the schools they attend (low-performing inner city or rural schools for example), family ecosystems of intellectual, social, and aspirational support, and social community models of support. Volumes of data clearly evidence this fact.

I don't have to look far to see the falsehood of meritocracy in its full glory.

I was born in Pasadena and lived the first part of my life in the San Gabriel Valley. Rosemead to be exact. My grandfather moved the family there during the dustbowl days and bought some land in the middle of nowhere to raise some chickens. He eventually built two small homes out in the back to rent out. Which for some time included my brother and me and my mother, who was widowed at the age of 19 with me and my brother on the way.

My mother in the mid '60s, being the age she was (mid-20s), decided to move us to where there was more action and potential relationships mirroring the social life a young woman in the mid '60s might want – Venice, CA. Not the Venice of today (very wealthy with lots of celebrities) but the Venice of the day with drug busts, the Doors, Muscle Beach, and a lot of reefer in the air. I observed much of this from the top of our beachfront apartment – and became a young, blond, long-haired son of a hippie. Riding my stingray bike up and down the boardwalk, selling tie-dyed t-shirts, and body surfing from time-to-time.

I'm not sure what would have happened to me if we had stayed in Venice. Detailed elsewhere, in 7th grade I simply tried to survive, doing other people's artwork and getting shaken down for cash. I had my head knocked in at one point; big bruise on my cheek for weeks – which I had to hide from the gym teacher in case he should ask where I got it (I got it on the playground trying to play basketball when a classmate decided to punch me out). Other than that, I did my best to keep a low profile (you would be bullied for showing off in class) and keep an ear out every day for who might jump who after school (blacks on whites, others on the surfers, etc.), in case you wanted to jump the fence before things went down. Cherry-top cruisers circling the campus was a sign that the forecast was real.

One day there was blood in the hall and word was some of the high school students jumped in to beat up a fellow middle school student.

Now picture this. We move to Westport, CT. Yes, as mentioned before, Bette Davis down the street. Paul Newman only a mile away. And Martha Stewart the other side of town. Mercedes Benz minibuses got the kids around town.

Moving to Westport, in a calm and safe environment, I quickly excelled in school and was surprised how quickly I could do the work – and not have my head knocked in for sharing what I knew.

From there, Wesleyan. A year later, Harvard, where I received my master's and then Doctorate.

All because ... we moved.

My mother graduated valedictorian at Rosemead High (a sleepy, semi-rural community just 11 miles east of LA at the time), having by that time been married for 3 years as a result of eloping with my father at the age of 15. (She got married in Alabama to my father because that was the only state she could get married in at that age, at the time.)

After my father died my mother (she was only 19) did go on to take classes at the local college – Cal State LA. "Why there?" I asked. She said it was the only college she knew. She added, for her there was no East Coast. She had never heard of any of the elite schools such as Harvard, Brown, or Yale. All of which were on my radar at Staples HS (in Westport CT) because those were the schools you were expected to apply to – at Staples.

This is just one story. My story. As a young white male landing in a high socio-economic community where expectations were to graduate and pursue the top schools in the country, this is not the typical story. It's a very privileged story. And it is reserved for a very small few in America.

I have worked in some rather challenging contexts, much more typical – Hartford CT, Waterbury CT, Yonkers NY, Fall River MA, Newark NJ, and many, many other contexts where I saw day-to-day kids going through the motion, most detached from the purpose of schooling, and simply riding the school system escalator because they were told to do so with only a vague promise of where that would take them, supposedly somewhere better ... but without any real idea of where. College may have been mentioned. But that in itself is a vague land. Where? Why? And for who? And how many?

Once when working in the high school in North Portland, Oregon, no more than 8 miles from downtown (I could see it in the distance), I asked teachers how often the kids went into the city. They told me that many of the kids had never been. (Say what?). How could youth so close never experience the city?

Later, being the idealist educator I was at the time, I started to ask about students' aspirations. I was told that if a kid in that community were to tell their father they had aspirations to go elsewhere and find different work and a better life, he might be hit hard with the father saying, "Who are you to think better than me."

The reality is that Blacks and Hispanics who are born into the lower 20% of U.S. family income are 90% likely to remain in that percentile.[6] Whereas a White born into the lower 20% of family income is 70% likely to rise above that percentile.

I also know that youth whose home language is not English struggle mightily in school, at least most schools. True also for kids who are readily fidgety and acting out because they are exposed to daily trauma. These youth are perceived as unable to focus, pay attention, and worse, not given reason to engage in learning as their real concern is safety, fear, and care.

This self-appointed mantle of being better and having the right to privileges better than others (Blacks, Hispanics, immigrants, etc.) is causing so much injustice and harm throughout our communities (and not just learning communities), it is hard not to turn our attention away from this brutal reality. The events of the last three years, and still an ugly reality, hangs in the balance for many. And it will take years of work to repair, if at all. But if we can impact our education ecosystem to raise the moral consciousness of our rising generations, perhaps there can be inroads to how we embrace one another and begin to create systems and take actions that are more in keeping with a humane society.

Meritocracy is a sham, and unfortunately our own beliefs and systems of meritocracy has done gross harm to many in our society. Not taking into account the circumstances many are born into, including their education, family, and social context, perpetuates the belief that one's future is solely dependent on the individual, and does not take into account the ecosystem influencing and contributing to the development of that individual.

Hence ...

We need to redesign our ecosystems so that they continually incentivize and support entrepreneurial activity that continuously evolves toward greater opportunity, possibility, and prosperity for all – including our education system.

We must recognize that much of the challenges we face today is a direct result of our current education ecosystem. We must recognize that it is the result of white industry magnates and political leaders at the turn of the century who laid the groundwork for the purpose and practices of our current system, supported by an adopted paradigm of learning that in no way represents how learning of value really happens. Of course, I am not the only one to say this. The books, articles, blogs, and videos in the Resources section of this book quite bluntly and candidly provide evidence of this fact as well.

Let's revisit, quickly, the structures, policies, mindsets, practices, and use of resources that continue to perpetuate schooling as we now know it. At least in most places. A sort of Top 3 list Letterman style, take or leave. Argue as you wish.

The Top 3 Constraints

1. *Schools are run by districts which are overseen by school committees that are limited by their perspective and imagination to support active and radical innovation.*

   Well, there's a mouthful.

   Currently, districts (large and small) are directed by their local school board voted in by their community. It is the responsibility of the school board then to hire a superintendent and institutionalize policy that directs the expectations and work of the district. Unfortunately, this means innovation in the system is highly dependent on the values and vision of its members, which is primarily grounded in school board members' own experiences of school. I am all for local representation, but this means the possibilities of education in a community can be grossly hamstrung by the vision, knowledge, and willingness of its school board members and their superintendent to support if not proactively press for new designs of school.

   Pushing the envelope can prove incredibly challenging, particularly if parents and other interested community members are anxious about new, untraditional models of school. Many become anxious when others do things differently from what they are used to and know.

Superintendents themselves are hamstrung by the expectations and mandates of state policies that inhibit the kinds of innovation that could prove more valuable for youth. For example, the accumulation of credits (think, HS graduation expectations) above and beyond the focus on skills and competencies (more on this later). The focus on disconnected disciplinary knowledge (e.g., Algebra II, biology, and US History) above and beyond one's ability to learn and act in the world.

These are just some of the limiting factors, expectations, and policies that significantly limit the growth of learning environments that could far better serve our youth and our communities.

2. The Inanity of Coverage, Content, and Seat time

It all starts here. Most current state expectations hold ransom to the possibilities of learning that is potentially more meaningful and of greater real value to youth. The works of Yong Zhao, Tony Wagner, Ted Dintersmith, and Ken Robinson, among many others makes this all too clear.[7] The expectation to cover content presses most into habits of teaching in alignment with the "banking model" of learning, something Paulo Friere [8] pointed out years ago as extremely problematic. Once teachers are expected to "cover" content-heavy curriculum they fall into the trap of orchestrating learning that leans into the memorization of curriculum, sharply veering away from the more constructivist pedagogies associated with deeper learning. Inert knowledge does not hold a flame to actionable knowledge. What good is it to know something but not be able to use that knowledge? We know from a deep body of research that more constructivist pedagogies have greater lasting impact.[9]

Seat time, a sister to this inane expectation, measures learning *not* by competency but rather hours spent sitting in a class – literally. Imagine being fully competent in a domain (take your pick) and failing a class because you had 12 absences. No matter if you can do the work. Think well in that area. Evidence your competency in that domain. The you have it. It's like saying to Serena Williams, we will not recognize you as a good tennis player unless you are on a tennis court from 1-1:40 Monday-Friday from September through June. I mean, really? Is that the measure of learning? How much time you sit in a seat or listen to someone yammer on about a topic or if you write 3 papers, take 6 tests, and do 18 pieces of homework?

Thankfully, some states (not many) and some districts (again, not many) are moving in the direction of competency-based learning, and assessment. But these are very few and far between. We will not have gotten very far if we continue to measure learning by how much time a student is in class and NOT by what they know and are able to do.

Inane and insane, really. The insanity of it all is the result of the challenge schools, school systems, and the leaders and educators in them have in figuring out how to support authentic student learning. This includes learning that takes place at a student's own pace, and the use of performances that evidence student learning above and beyond traditional assessments, including assessing what one can do outside a classroom and not just in school.

This is one of the many cutting edges of schooling today, how to assess and accredit someone based on their capacity to think and act in the real-world. Not a traditional measure such as a test.

3. A system that is not designed to readily catalyze and support the development of educational models that serve all learners

We now know what learning looks like when it is focused on students' ability to problem-solve, communicate well, critically think, and create. Yet our system of education reinforces other knowledge and skills that do not directly relate to these outcomes. The laser-like focus on passing reading, writing, and math tests, and the requirement to catalog credits based on classes of disconnected and unconnected content from its purposeful use in the world presses all district and school leaders to attend to these aims whiffing at the development of youth that could far better serve them and our world.

How often have you heard students say, "Why am I learning this?" For that matter, how often did *you* say that about school.

I am not saying that we don't want youth to learn some very core ideas and skills such as how systems work – for example, ecosystems, basic human anatomy, political and civic architectures, and some fundamental understanding of history, culture, and society. But over time we have decided to cram so many ancillary pieces of information deemed "important" to know, such as meiosis, mitosis, and what ribosomes do, the number of particles in a mole, and what war was fought when and why, that it all has become quite inane.

If we are teaching anything, either content or skills, it is done in such a meaningless and ineffective way that we are simply wasting our students' time. Because the learning is not grounded in students' genuine interests or designed through experiences that result in actual learning, students are simply going through the motions of regurgitating what is expected, without any real understanding of its value and utility. Schools are doing this *to* students when we could be using our creativity assisting and supporting students in the development of their sense of agency, knowledge, skills, and competency that has actual, personal utility. In addition, this could build their capacity to give back to our communities and the world.

Is there Another Way to "Do School"?

The challenge is for us all to "imagine new possibilities" in how we support learning and learning that matters. This is the work that many educators I know are deeply involved in.   (Fellow revolutionaries, I call them.)

We have been doing school the same for so many years that it has become etched in our brains. *This* is school. So it is almost impossible for us to imagine how it could be any different. Divided by grades. Divided by rooms. Divided by content. Separate from activity in the real world.

For example, when I say high school, for the most part, everyone sees exactly the same thing. Or close to it. A large cement 1-3 story tall building with long locker-lined hallways, with classroom after classroom of 25-35 students, primarily housed by a single teacher whose job is to teach the content of that class. Perhaps in some classrooms there aren't rows of desks, but chairs and desks nonetheless. All in circumscribed boxes.

They may be an interactive Smart Board. Students each may have their own Chromebook. Teachers may be using a variety of new cloud-based tools for sharing information (Google Slides) and new means for students to showcase their work (Flipgrid), etc. But for the most part, the curriculum is teacher-directed, and the pedagogy doesn't come close to being authentic, context-situated, and student driven.[10]

In the schools I love, students are deciding what they want to learn and in many cases designing how they want to learn it. This does not mean that the educators in these schools are altogether agnostic to what they think is important for their students to learn, or how they can learn it. But they have figured out how to be facilitators of learning, inserting their thoughts and gently nudging their students when they feel it is best for the learner. Informed by both what they know of the learner and what they have identified will benefit that student going forward.

What students in these communities are learning isn't a complete free for all. Most of the educators in these communities have deliberately identified specific competencies, skills, and dispositions they want their students to learn, in some cases, helping them to be directors of their own learning. In addition, central to the work of these communities is helping youth to identify their interests and pursue their passions, design their own learning, and develop their sense of agency and possibility.

But to do this well, these schools operate differently from what we now think of school: classrooms, teachers, the coverage of content, students as receivers of knowledge, compliance over creative activity.

After asking everyone what they "see" when I say "high school," I then share with them what many agency-oriented schools look like. At Iowa BIG, for example, there are neither classes nor classrooms. Instead, the school is completely designed around students doing real-world projects in the community. At One Stone, students are solving real world problems using design thinking. At Olympic High School, youth take advantage of over 700 industry partnerships and learn through internships, ending up pursuing careers, work, and post-secondary education they wish to pursue. Then I tell them about the multitude of CAPS programs throughout the US which do the same.

At Iowa BIG and One Stone, there are no long hallways and rows of lockers and kids funneling from class to class dictated by a bell, learning focused on disconnected content resembling a monopoly game (English, Social Studies, Science, and Math). Take biology, chemistry, US History, Algebra, and physics or don't pass "Go.". In this game of school, a lot of kids are wondering how they can get the "get out of Jail" card. In these far more progressive schools, students are learning content and skills in service of projects or activities they are purposefully engaged in.

Reimagining school in this fashion can be very hard for many educators who have been chest-deep in doing school as they have. It is hard to let go of ways of doing things that one has grown accustomed to. Unshackling oneself from this familiar set of habits and routines can be very difficult for some, as they have worked hard to develop and then master the practices inherently comprising school as we have known it and know it. It might also be very hard to embrace the idea that maybe what we have been doing has not in reality been what we should have been doing all along. That's a hard pill to swallow. [11]

For many, even considering school in this very new way – not only in structure and practices but espoused ideals and purposes – is kind of like looking at the old woman/young woman image.

Just like this image, saying to someone "think of doing school differently," it is hard for them to let go of the old view, physical structures where youth move from content areas and activities in keeping with school as we have known it. When one says, no, consider this new design, it calls into question so many of the assumptions one has had for years. It creates an initial feeling of instability and raises a variety of questions that were grounded in the old paradigm, such as: If we don't teach in this way, will they learn? If I don't give a test, how will I know they have learned? If they don't take all of these classes, will they be able to go to college?

It is hard for most of us to give up what we have known and lived for years. It is doubly hard to just off-handedly relinquish the paradigm in which one has lived – like the sun going around the world. Most of us gain comfort in the routines we have mastered for years. Becoming a newbie once again in pursuit of a new paradigm of teaching, learning, and schooling can feel unsettling, and difficult, and leave one wondering if they can make the transition.

Not easy. Not easy at all.

What could be done to Turn this Around?

There are two answers to this question. The first, is to cross one's fingers and hope that some political leader comes into power with the social, ideological, and intellectual prowess to galvanize a new era in our politics, bringing everyone together with a shared vision and interest in moving our education ecosystem forward, in keeping with the ideals I have put forth in this book. Perhaps not the exact means by which we get there, but that there is a real understanding that we cannot keep doing school as we have and that there are far better ways to engage our youth that assists them to be smart, agentic, and wanting to contribute back to our world.

Apart from this there are actions each one of us can take in pursuit of these ideals. It first takes bringing these ideals to others' attention. Then sharing how these ideals can be realistically pursued through the multiple examples even showcased in this book. Then we need to be very, very good and very clear on the need to pursue these new ideals for the greater outcomes of our youth, communities, and society.

Beyond the hope for some grand political movement galvanized by a charismatic leader who can bridge the usual polarization of parties, there are specific actions you can take, no matter your place and position in your community and our education ecosystem, to potentially make a dent in this effort.

First things First ... Get in the Know

I teach education entrepreneurship in our Doctor of Education program at Northeastern University, and in that class there are typically dozens of educators that have been in education for at least 5, 10, if not 20 or more years.

Funny thing is when they come to class most are wondering why they are taking a class on entrepreneurship because they say they didn't go into education to make money. Right? But I tell them that this entrepreneurship class is not about making money. This class is about *social* entrepreneurship. Less so business entrepreneurship. (Not that making money is bad; if you can make some money doing good, that is great too!) This is about you making the difference you wish to make in the world. Manifesting an idea that benefits others – through a program, an event, or a product, etc. But the focus is not about making money. Again, it's about how to make the difference in the world you wish to make.

The next thing I try to do is to give everyone a number of clear examples of what I mean by sharing dozens of examples of educators and others going out of their way to make something very different to serve others – above and beyond how they may have been served before.

In doing this, I share a multitude of innovations and entrepreneurial enterprises that I have catalogued and come to know over time to help press others' imagination of what is possible.

So ... this is the best thing that you could do for yourself: Get in the KNOW!

Personally, it has taken me quite a while to get in the know. But I have gratefully been afforded this opportunity given my work in education. Beyond that, I feel compelled and embrace it as my responsibility to be in the know – about all of these efforts. Educators making a difference and sharing these examples of new possibilities in learning and schooling.

Most educators work hard to address issues with some minor improvements to education as we now know it. Not that these improvements are bad.   Anything that improves student engagement, deepens students' learning, and adds to students' agency and possibility is good. However, most educators, given the constraints and limitations of their context and prescribed structures, are rarely going headfirst into the consideration of more significant shifts that could serve youth better. This leads most educators to making only minor adjustments that do not pursue the drastic overhaul of schooling we need.

Let me point to a few examples from the past in the following table. This is the difference between some minor structural shifts to more significant structural redesigns that result in new practices.

CLASSIC EXAMPLES FROM THE PAST

OLD TECHNOLOGY	NEW TECHNOLOGY
Horse & Buggy Can get around, semi-comfortable, multiple people Hard to upkeep, smelly, slow	**Car** Semi-efficient, easy to store and fuel, almost anyone (over 18) can get around fairly easily
Landline Good to be able to communicate with anyone around the world, accessible in your home, can use in some places with payphone	**Cell phone** Available on your person, typically immediate access to you and access to others that have it on them at any time, NOW provides far more tools and access to information as a Smart Phone
Typewriter Can type your own papers, etc., easy for others to read	**Word Processor** Can edit in real time, print when ready

Then there is the explosion of alternative and readily accessible services by way of the internet and mobile devices, such as those I shared in the table on the next page.

It might be a bit of a leap, but what I am attempting to illustrate is the way current expectations, funding streams, policy, and mental models of how we should "do school" profoundly limits or at least funnels attention to practices that are not in the best interest of our youth today.

Think of the innovations presented in the next table. Who would have thought that an app or desktop platform made accessible by way of the internet would have greatly expanded personal options such as these. And greatly expanded services and extended access to resources such as these.

GOOD EXAMPLES FROM THE PRESENT

OLD SERVICE	NEW SERVICE
Hotels Can reserve a room. Get food. Some amenities like a pool, free breakfast, restaurant and bar.	**AirBnB** The feeling of a house, apartment, or room, with kitchen, multiple rooms, more space. MORE CHOICES.
Movie Theater & TV Can see the most recent TV in a large venue with big screen, get popcorn, candy, and soda. On TV can see movies and series as scheduled.	**Streaming platforms such as Netflix, Amazon Prime, Hulu** Can watch movies and series on demand in the comfort of your home. No driving, pinned to schedules.
Taxis & Limos Call to access or access at high volume location such as the airport, hotels, and busy city streets.	**Uber & Lyft** Can access through your mobile device, in many cases reducing wait time and increasing comfort level in driver-owned vehicles.
Pursuing funds through personal friends or loan institutions Can seek out donations from friends, family, or others or seek out a personal loan	**Crowdfunding platforms such as GoFundMe** Can request donations to support projects or personal needs from anyone access the platform, greatly increasing access to potential funding.

I argue these have been made possible because one or more individuals have been able to construct a platform that provides such options and serves as a conduit for such services and resources. What one can create is not limited by a public ecosystem that dictates the outcomes or the services. For example, prior to these platforms you could only view a movie in a movie theater or a TV series at a prescribed day and time. Or you would have to call the local taxi company to travel but would be limited to their fleet of cars (think Yellow Cab). Or you could only stay in the local hotels which, in reality, were pretty much all the same in terms of their offerings –

a bed, a closet, a bathroom, a TV. Not the affordances of a home or apartment.

The public school system is in many ways like that. You have to take these classes in these grades and learn these topics and accumulate these credits and pass this test. Hence, the "employees" of this system– the classroom educators, school and district leaders, and other staff – all must work to serve those ends, as that is their responsibility in this system. Moreover, their mental model of how to achieve these ends are pretty much dictated by the socially accepted practices of the conventional school model, grounded in decades of practices, driving our schools to operate as they do.

But there are a few who have been able to "push the envelope," so to speak, with variations of "school" that are much more in keeping with a new understanding of what is of value for youth moving forward in their lives. They have thought "out of the box" and proposed new aims of learning that benefit youth far better than what they are gaining in traditional school today. But this takes imagination and the ability to build a new platform (a school, program, or learning community) that operates differently, and truth be told, inherently have many of the same attributes as the innovations presented before. ACCESS to learning (both within and beyond the classroom). Providing personal choice. Allowing learning to happen anytime and anywhere. Putting options in the hands of the learner. Readily giving access to resources.

You get the picture. Just as these platforms afforded the end user with many new options, so too should school.

In this book, I will share how some educators across the country have pursued these new designs, centered around access to learning, personal choice, greater learning both within and outside the classroom, and options in the learner's hands. Each of these leaps, analogous to the innovations I have presented in the two tables, were the result of reimagining solutions to problems and/or imagining a new offering that would serve others far better. In these reimaginings, the "imagineers" (borrowing the term from Disney) gave themselves the permission to "think outside of the box," and consider a new design for meeting others' needs. Essentially designing an entirely new structure, system, and set of practices.

Once you get this point, that the imagineers of these new learning environments are designing brand new systems, structures, and practices that far better serve youth, then it is time to get to know these examples and sharpen your particular ability to inspire and engage others in the need for and possibilities of new designs.

Connect with Others (and Join the Revolution)

It is very important to not only get in the know and become familiar with these new models of schooling and the outcomes they are affording youth, but to *connect* with others who are pushing the envelope and actually running these new designs. It is important so that you are aware of these new designs, one, to inspire you, and two, for you to share with others. Three, so that when you need help you can go to comrades (as I like to say) for inspiration, example, and support. Going it alone when attempting to push for a new design of school can be hard. Tapping into and finding inspiration, energy, and solace with other educators and stakeholders who are aligned with your ideals can go a long way in giving you the confidence you need. And these new connections can potentially serve you in your own endeavors.

Hence, find those who are doing the work you would love to engender. Let them know you are inspired by their efforts. Then ask how you too could pursue the difference you want to make where you wish to make that difference.

I am personally emboldened and re-energized by knowing those who are doing this work and find myself re-invigorated each time we connect. We are mutually fortified by our shared interests, ideals, and aspirations. And we assist each other in how to make inroads to changing what teaching, learning, and schooling looks like today.

A Pattern Language

Many years ago, a friend shared with me a book which soon became one of my favorites: *A Pattern Language*. In the 70s, Christopher Alexander and a group of architects at the University of California, Berkeley decided to create a nested set of principles for global, regional, and local design. Down to the design of cities, towns, homes, doorways, gardens, and rooms.

These design principles were meant to guide and engender healthy communities and spaces for positive living.

One of my favorite design principles presented in the book had to do with the importance of "creating small spaces for youngsters to play in" – because, as you know, they love small spaces. There are many others that have to do with window spaces, common spaces, portals for light, etc. But the one that stood out to me, given my interest in schooling, is the one about our current design of high school.

Here's what they wrote –so true today as it was way back in 1977:

Problem
In a society which emphasizes teaching, children, students, and adults become passive and unable to think or act for themselves. Creative, active individuals can only grow up in a society which emphasizes learning instead of teaching.

Solution
Instead of the lock-step of compulsory schooling in a fixed place, work in piecemeal ways to decentralize the process of learning and enrich it through contact with many places and people all over the city: workshops, teachers at home or walking through the city, professionals willing to take on these young as helpers, older children teaching younger children, museums, youth groups traveling, scholarly seminars, industrial workshops, old people, and so on. Conceive of all these situations as forming the backbone of the learning process; survey all these situations, describe them, and publish them as the city's "curriculum"; then let students, children, their families and neighborhoods weave together for themselves the situations that comprise their "school" paying as they go with standard vouchers, raised by community tax. Build new educational facilities in a way which extends and enriches this network.

This critique included describing high schools as "adolescent holding pens," at a time when adolescents are beginning to explore their own identity and find their place in the world. A time when they are beginning to think about who they are, how they fit in, and how they want to fit into the world.

Right now the world of work is a mystery – at least for most. Mom and/or Dad go off to work – doing who-knows-what. Youth probably know very little about what their parents (or other guardians) actually do. But youth do recognize that some make more money than others, depending on what they do. They are getting a feel for the fact that some positions are more highly regarded than others, and they may be hearing how education is a route to attaining such "positions." Their own experience of work may be relegated to an after-school or summer job, but this work is most likely confined to such jobs as bussing in a restaurant, working in retail, or being a camp counselor, for example. Rarely is the experience inclusive of the kinds of work that supports a sustainable livelihood: such as managing, producing, engineering, creating, problem-solving, and designing. So how do our youth come to know what these different possibilities of work look like? What does it *really* look and feel like to be a lawyer or an architect, for example? A doctor? A business owner? An engineer? An entrepreneur?

Later in the book, Christopher Alexander and his colleagues make this recommendation in relationship to teenage society:

Problem
Teenage is the time of passage between childhood and adulthood. In traditional societies, this passage is accompanied by rites which suit the psychological demands of the transition. But in modern society the "high school" fails entirely to provide this passage.

Solution
Replace the "high school" with an institution which is actually a model of adult society, in which the students take on most of the responsibility for learning and social life, with clearly defined roles and forms of discipline. Provide adult guidance, both for the learning, and the social structure of the society; but keep them as far as feasible, in the hands of the students.

Remember, this was written in 1977. Why is it that 45 years later we have not embraced this wisdom? What is holding us back? Is it that we don't agree? Have the same values? Or simply *do not know how to organize ourselves to put this value and ideal into practice?* Or is it that the system *as it is now structured* does not allow for this ideal to be *put into action*?

Finally, the architects made this simple but significant statement, under the category *Master and Apprentices*:

Problem
The fundamental learning situation is one in which a person learns by helping someone who really knows what he is doing.

Solution
Arrange the work in every workgroup, industry, and office, in such a way that work and learning go forward hand in hand. Treat every piece of work as an opportunity for learning. To this end, organize work around a tradition of masters and apprentices: and support

> this form of social organization with a division of the workspace into spatial clusters - one for each master and his apprentices - where they can work and meet together.

Finally, 45 years later, there is a renewed interest in how education could and should be assisting students to learn about their potential futures. Explore potential interests. And pursue interests that may become their passion.

Today we are beginning to see the erosion of the walls between "academic" study and real-world pursuits, with many philanthropies, education organizations, and industry partners beginning to support such endeavors, recognizing the need to break down the walls and barriers between school learning and real-world work.[12] Schools are helping youth to see what the "real world" looks like and what work they might want to pursue through internships, community-embedded projects, and self-propelled endeavors. And through these opportunities students are interacting with the world and with mentors, learning the skills and developing the competencies that could assist them in pursuing the work they wish to pursue and the ways they might wish to give back to the world.

The Young Boxer

While working at Hartford Public HS, like in most high schools I worked in, I worked hard to find a way that the teachers and administrators could come to know their kids. What do I mean, to know them? I mean to know who they are. Their histories. Their current living circumstances. Their interests and aspirations. To know them well enough to appreciate who they are and why they act and think as they do. To know them well enough to connect them to their interests and passions and connect them to others with those same interests and passions. To know them well enough so that you can better support and serve them as youth growing up. To know them well enough ... so that they would care.

I am a big fan of stories. I think if we engaged one another in more storytelling, we would appreciate and understand one another better. Right now, we "dig in our heels" so much that we misunderstand one another. Pronouncements and assumptions are made without our recognizing them as such, and we dig into our singular viewpoints without opening ourselves up to how others see, and why. I guess I am saying that we cannot understand one another without knowing one another and our stories the: stories that have shaped us.

Once I was working with a veteran history teacher at Hartford Public HS on one of the more recent expectations of teachers in the school – something taking hold across many schools at the time: "Do Nows." A common problem in many schools (as they see it) is kids moving from class to class and what happens when students first get to class. Some would come early, some a bit later, some just on time, and some late. In this time period, all sorts of things could happen. Kids would start kibitzing about one thing or another, unloading their book bags, sometimes even jostling around (hovering at one another's desks), and the problem – as perceived by teachers and the school – was the reality that kids would get locked into these interactions and then it would take yet another 2-4 minutes to get everyone back focused on class.

As I was prone to do, I always tried to find a way to connect with a teacher and provide them with an idea that would both assist them and move my own agenda forward (if you could call it that). To that end, I started a conversation with one veteran teacher just prior to a class and asked him what he thought of the "Do Now" expectation and asked him what he did. He told me something fantastic, I thought. He said he asked students to simply write him anything they wanted, for example, something that had happened to them the day before or that morning, or that would be happening later in the day or week, or something that was concerning them. In short, he gave each student an opportunity to tell him a little about themselves. He then proceeded to tell me what he had learned about them.

One story struck me and has since stuck with me. As the students settled into their seats and began writing, the teacher secretly pointed to a young, slight Hispanic girl who barely looked 15 to me. Small in stature, petite. Very young. But what this teacher told me completely blew me away – and really hit home the importance of knowing our youth.

The teacher told me that she had written she was very worried about the night's event. Having glanced at this note he felt compelled to ask what was happening. She shared, "I am a professional boxer and I have a fight tonight. It's how I make money to help raise my son." She had been very tired lately, training late at night, also taking care of her 1-year-old baby. Training for her boxing match, going to school, and taking care of her son was taking its toll.

Of course, inside, my heart sank. As I looked at her writing away at her desk, backpack on the floor, coat still on, I quickly jumped to images of her at home, trying to take care of a baby and then off to the gym to prepare for a fight. Then my imagination turned to her in the fight. What did that look like? What did that feel like?

Then I had to ask, why was she fighting? So that she could win money to help take care of her son, her 1-year-old son.

Of course, my mind went to wondering about how she made sense of school and its importance. Learning math, history, and chemistry. How did she make sense of all that she was trying to do day-to-day, in particular the life she had in school, moving from classroom-to-classroom, desk-to-desk, listening to teachers, taking notes, taking tests, and doing "do nows." Then the reality of trying to raise a son at such a young age, boxing to bring in a little cash.

How was this work, in school, connecting to her reality? How was she making sense of what she was being asked to do in school connect to her future? No less, how could it contribute to her having a better life now?

The importance of knowing the youth we work with is critical. Again and again, I have worked with teachers and administrators who did not know who their students were. I remember working in a semi-rural, suburban high school outside of Portland OR, where, in a team meeting set up weekly for teachers to discuss their students, the teachers began to complain about a kid who was not coming to class, or when she did, often had her head on the table or was sleeping. She had by this time missed three days of school, and the teachers were once again complaining. Complaining about her. Eventually, another staff member in the school arrived, and what she told the team once again reminded me how important it is for us to KNOW our students.

It turns out that her home was fractured. Her mother was using drugs. Her father was abusive. She had been trying to take care of her younger brother. And just the other night, prior to her not coming to school, her mother overdosed and was sent to the hospital with the father nowhere to be seen.

The teachers were stunned. Fell silent. Then they wondered how they could not have known that this all was going on in this young woman's life. As all of this was going on in her life, they were expecting her to sit up, pay attention in class, and do her homework. But when should we first acknowledge the reality of our students' lives, to be able to meet them better no matter where they are, and support them in their upbringing, their experience, and their potential future?

Always. The answer is ... always.

– 3 –
Imagining New Possibilities

Funny thing is ... it doesn't have to be this way.

By sheer determination, grit, and an unfathomable disposition to move forward and do better for youth, some have grabbed ahold of the entrepreneurial spirit and created another way.

When I think of these individuals, Dennis Littky and Elliot Washor – who started the Met (short for the Metropolitan School), the first Big Picture School in Providence RI – come to mind. As does Rob Riordan and Larry Rosenstock, who co-founded High Tech High in San Diego. Trace Pickering and Shawn Cornally, who co-founded Iowa BIG in Cedar Rapids IA. And Jon Ketler and colleagues, who started the Tacoma School of the Arts, then SAMI, and then IDEA. Simon Hauger and Matthew Riggan who started the Workshop School in Philadelphia. Then Superintendent Trigg and Mike Slagle who started the first CAPS program in Blue Valley, just outside KC. And on and on.

There are many (although not enough) stories of individuals across the country who have pushed their dream for a new kind of education forward with a model of school that runs sideways to the conventional model of schooling. They saw a need, had an idea, and were able to galvanize the resources and support to manifest their idea in a place where their idea could take hold.

It is important to know these stories because they give us some insight as to how such places could take root elsewhere. What does it take? How can it happen?

Let's take a peek at just a few of these stories and see what we can take from them.

Rob Riordan & Larry Rosenstock: Why can't we do it Here?

Rob Riordan and Larry Rosenstock were both teachers at Cambridge Rindge and Latin way back in the '80s, each working in their own corner of the building. Actually, Larry was teaching carpentry in the technical program on the ground floor, while Rob was teaching English in a progressive school-within-a-school on the fifth floor. Did their paths cross often? No. As is common in large schools like Cambridge Rindge and Latin, teachers' paths often do not cross, or rarely do, and if they do it's in the lunchroom or in passing. These schools are so crammed in terms of schedules, rarely is there opportunity to engage in true intellectual discourse about teaching and learning and the possibilities of doing things differently. The development of new ideas and practices.

After seven years in the same building, Larry and Rob finally met in a faculty committee, where they found that they shared similar interests – an interest in craft-making and doing. They both felt that students' learning could be far more engaging and meaningful if students were actually able to use their heads and hands to construct things. Invent something. Larry did a lot of this in his shop. His students were crafting things. Rob did a lot of this with his young writers too – crafting things.

One thing led to another and they began to wonder if with greater freedom of time with students, they could engage students in far more meaningful, and intellectual, work. Trying to create, make, and do in 42-minute chunks is difficult. But having students collaborate, think, design, and build things together could and would lead to learning that sticks. In doing this, students would also learn how to create, invent, and pursue projects. Be engaged in cross-disciplinary inquiry. Pursue learning in pursuit of excellence. Assisting to them to get better at their craft.

In the early 90s, Rob moved to the technical program, where he joined Larry and others to engage students in projects and internships in the community. When Larry later became acting principal of the whole high school, he proposed to restructure the program to integrate hands and minds in the curriculum. That proposal met with heavy opposition from faculty and parents, as well as the former principal upon his return. The effort was defeated, and the rest, as we like to say, is history. Larry and Rob left the school in 1996 to head up a Federal project called the New Urban High School in cities across the country, including San Diego, where in 2000 they had the opportunity to open the kind of school they had been dreaming of.

Twenty-two years later High Tech High is now a network of 16 elementary, middle, and high schools world renowned for their pedagogy, with several books, articles, and even a movie about what they do. What they do with kids across the city. Because there is a story, an incredible story of how Larry and Rob were able to plant the seed in a context in San Diego where their idea could take root and grow over time.[13]

About High Tech High

High Tech High started as a single charter high school in 2000 but now comprises a network of 16 schools (five elementary, five middle, and six high schools) across the San Diego area. Its focus is the development of their students' critical thinking, problem-solving, and creativity through highly creative interdisciplinary, project-based learning grounded in real-world applications requiring collaboration, independent thinking, and hands-on experience.

With this as a goal, they make great use of a variety of technologies and resources including a variety of digital platforms, multimedia, and software for research, presentations, and project execution.

The school works hard to foster community and collaboration amongst all stakeholders and have students take ownership of their learning, exploring their interests, developing their talents, and pursuing potential passions. At the high school level, they do this through a variety of elective courses, student interest-based projects, internships, and connections with community partners. At the elementary and middle school level, this exploration is supported through student-directed inquiry, passion projects, and again engagement with the community.

Examples of the above are:

- Elementary students investigating the issue of endangered species with local scientists leading to a study of the Pacific Pocket Mouse in the local area followed by a fund-raising and education campaign in support of conservation efforts for the mouse.
- Elementary students exploring their Liberty Station neighborhood which included interviewing community members, documenting their visit to several locations, and then writing articles about their interviewees and the neighborhood, resulting in a published magazine about the community.
- Middle school students investigating the reasons for wildfires (at this time, rampant in CA) and the vulnerability to fire destruction in the Chaparral Ecosystem where they lived. Along with reading a novel where carbon rationing is employed by the government, students investigated the relationship between global warming and increased wildfires along with several other topics related to

wildfire management and the role of government and community efforts to mitigate carbon emissions.

- High School students undertaking the development, funding, and production of a documentary on the causes of gun violence, impact of gun violence, and prevention of gun violence. They interviewed numerous victims of gun violence on trips to Los Angeles, Chicago, San Antonio, and Newtown CT, pursued a Kickstarter campaign to fund their effort, and gained valuable film production skills from a local media company, and eventually showed their film at a local movie theater.

The Tacoma Schools

Jon Ketler was an art teacher in one of the largest comprehensive high schools in Tacoma. He liked art. He liked teaching art. But he always wondered why he was teaching art disconnected from those doing art. Particularly in Tacoma, which was home to a number of artists as well as art institutions. Such as the Chihuly Glass Museum, Chihuly being a world-renowned artist in glassblowing who ran an internationally respected glassblowing community in the northwest, born in Tacoma. Other artists also were abundant throughout the city. Sculptors, painters, glassblowers, dancers, and musicians, along with a number of other art institutions such as the Tacoma Art Museum, the Lemay Car Museum, and the Broadway Center for the Performing Arts, to name just a few.

Jon thought to himself, why not have the kids work side-by-side with these artists, in their studios, or in the places of art, rather than set off, aside, in a building far from their work. Far from the expertise and mentoring they could offer his students.

Spurred by this idea and his many connections throughout the city, Jon set about sharing his idea with artists and organizations he knew and began to design a way that students could indeed work directly with these artists, in their studios and participating art institutions throughout the city. So that students could see firsthand what "making art" looked like, and in many cases serve as apprentices or collaborators on installations and artist's efforts.

Several years later, Jon and his colleagues wondered whether they could start a similar school but grounded in STEM (Science, Technology, Engineering, and Math). Turns out that Tacoma is home to the largest city park in WA state abutting the Puget Sound, with its plentiful waterways full of marine life, including salmon, sea lions, and Orca whales. The city park, totaling 760 acres jettisons out into

The SOTA, SAMI, and IDEA Schools in Tacoma WA

School of the Arts. Established in 2001, SOTA provides numerous opportunities for students to pursue training in the visual arts, music, dance, theater, and media arts by working alongside with professional artists and producing their own art work. Mentoring, workshops, and master classes along with ongoing critique and reflection deepens their students' learning.

Alongside their formal training in the arts, SOTA works to have their students see the connections between their study in academics and in the arts and "their lives now and their lives as they enter the larger global community."

The Science and Math Institute. SAMI focuses on STEM education through real-world, project-based learning making use of a multitude of resources and partners in the area, such as the Puget Sound, the 700+ acre park it resides in, and the Zoo next door. An array of electives, field work, internships, and activities with numerous community partners support students' exploration of science, math, and their personal interests in STEM.

The School of Industrial Design, Engineering, and the Arts. IDEA students take on and work side by side with mentors representing a variety of varying industries in the community, including many that co-reside in the same space as the high school. These experiences include internships, apprenticeships, working with partners in "design-and-build" studies, and real-world projects where "content" learning is gained through meaningful application in such areas as robotics, bike frame building, green energy, music production, digital drawing and painting, along with core content classes in science, math, and the humanities.

The Tacoma Schools-wide Internship Program. Juniors and Seniors throughout Tacoma can apply for an internship opportunity in the city through a large network of community partners, where they undertake training in a number of professional skills, explore their interests and potential professional pursuits, and eventually engage in a 90-hour internship supported by a internship coach, culminating in a student's development of a professional portfolio showcasing their skills and accomplishments in the internship.[14]

the sound, is also home to mule deer, red foxes, squirrels, and raccoons, in the midst of a very old forest. For Jon and his colleagues, housing a STEM school in this city park surrounded by the Puget sound just made a lot of sense, as the students could then collaborate with various institutions to do original research in the Sound, apprentice at the Zoo, and make use of the grounds.

Jon, as he had done before, began to work with potential partners, contributors, and the Tacoma Schools to start the school next to the marine science center in several mobile classrooms. Not much to look at, but the students and educators were then housed in the middle of this natural habitat where they could engage directly in science projects making use of the environment.

Several years later, and with the help of a bond, the eleven portables were replaced by the building of an award-winning LEED learning center next to the zoo, with large, spacious, sun-filled rooms placed smack-dab amidst the trees, where students could intern and work.

Three years later, Jon and his colleagues created IDEA, a school for Industrial Design, Engineering, and the Arts, in an old elementary school in the center of a residential neighborhood. While not situated in downtown Tacoma in the midst of a vibrant art community like SOTA, or in the midst of a state park next to the zoo like SAMI, Jon and his team found a way to transform the traditional unused facility so that it could serve students well. What did they do? They gave space to interested for-profits and non-profits that would be willing to work with their students affording them the valuable experience of working, again, side-by-side with those running their businesses and working in the field.

These three schools now serve a fifth of Tacoma's high school students. And now Jon and his team manage the internship program available to all high school students in Tacoma, wherein students are able to explore their interests through real-world work sponsored by a mentor in a for-profit, non-profit, or educational organization in the community.

This is no small thing, as it has led to several students experiencing first-hand (figuratively and literally) what it means to work in their identified area of interest, in alignment with their potential vocational interest, gaining practical skills, exposure to the field, and connections to others in the community working in the field.

How often are students graduating from high school still clueless about what they might want to do moving forward, apart from possibly pursuing college. But to what end? Can internships give students a better feel for what work looks like in their area of interest? Do they have an opportunity to build the practical skills that could give them a leg-up in pursuing their interest in the world?

Rarely in the typical high school. Hence, the power of internships, particularly when grounded in their specific area of interest, supported by a mentor in the field as well as at the school.

A Snapshot of Internships in the Tacoma Schools

Melissa Moffett has been running the internship program in the Tacoma schools for several years now and has refined their means of engaging all of their juniors and interested students in a meaningful effort with community partners directly grounded in their students' interests.

After a semester of interest exploration and a call for potential internship opportunities with their community partners, Melissa matches students with the opportunities she feels will be most advantageous for their students and partners. The results, as is wanting in most schools, can be extraordinary and impactful, as illustrated in these three short stories of impact.

The Aspiring Chef. Noah was interested in becoming a chef in a high-end restaurant – a "Michelin" restaurant. Given this, it made sense that he would intern at a high-end restaurant, and through a connection with a staff was able to gain an internship at a high-end Argentinian restaurant in town, Sato. During his internship, he had the opportunity to work in various areas of the restaurant and learn different aspects of the culinary field, making different dishes and using various cooking techniques. It just so happens that as part of his internship experience, he was able to be part of the restaurant's dessert-making competition, and he won, which greatly impressed the restaurant supervisors and staff. And as a result of his commitment to the work and his finesse in the kitchen, he eventually was hired. And to this day, after graduation, continues to work at the restaurant as he continues to build his skill as a chef.

The Audio-Visual Talent. Cole gained his internship differently, as he approached Melissa and said "a friend of a friend works at the Glass Museum and could use some help with their audio-visual work." In the end, he took interest in operating their cameras for live streaming events and enjoyed the real-world opportunity to apply himself (he didn't like school much) and was further encouraged to dedicate himself to the job as a result of his knack for excelling at the work and the positive feedback he received from the staff. Not unlike Noah, Cole was hired upon completion of his internship and continued to gain skills working in the audiovisual department as a result of his internship. Interesting, given he had shown no similar interest in getting better at school, as there was no real personally meaningful payoff for him as was true – both literally and figuratively – at the nationally recognized Glass Museum.

The New Energy Auditor. Mariana is most interested in agriculture, as well as computer science and design. But when a new company offered the opportunity for a student to engage in an energy audit of the school, she jumped on the opportunity with the training and support of the company and ran the school's energy audit over Spring break. Turns out, not unlike Noel and then Cole, Mariana excelled in her work, demonstrating strong analytical skills and attention to detail, which the company greatly appreciated, providing the school with soem valuable insights and actionable recommendations for reducing their energy usage and subsequent energy expenditure. Not unlike both Noel and Cole, her work also resulted in yet more work, as the company subsequently asked Mariana to train other students to do the energy analysis as well, which afforded her the opportunity to take a leadership and mentoring role with them. So while the effort did not directly tie in with her original interest, she gained a valuable opportunity to analyze systems and train others.

So, what did these students gain through their internships?

Practical Experience and Skill Building: The students gained practical, hands-on experience and skills in real-world contexts.

Career Exploration: They were able to get a good feel for what the work entailed, including the challenges and rewards of working in an industry.

Networking and Connections: The students built relationships, gained mentors, and established connections with professionals in their chosen field of interest, which in some cases led to future work and valuable industry connections.

Personal Growth and Confidence: The internship experience contributed to both their personal and professional growth, gaining confidence of their ability to successfully engage in real-world, professional work.

Iowa BIG

In June 2008, Cedar Rapids was hit by a flood like never before, putting it under 8 feet of water and causing close to $1 billion of damage, with many buildings destroyed, uninhabitable, and no longer useful.

As the city turned to its resurrection and rebuilding, the citizenry, government, and industry turned to thinking about how it could rebuild itself not into what it once was but rather reimagine what it wanted to become, including reimagining its education system.

Chuck Peters, the CEO of the local newspaper the Gazette, who was well established and led the Board at the Chamber of Commerce had influence with several civic, industry, and education leaders throughout the city and beyond, took it upon himself to contribute to this reimagining. It was also during this time that Iowa's Governor had created an "Education Blueprint" for the state. Having known Trace Pickering for many years Chuck asked Trace for his thoughts on the Blueprint. Trace returned with a 40-page response essentially saying while well intentioned, it would not move the needle nor substantially improve public education in the state. In response, Chuck asked Trace to become his company's Education Community Builder to see how they could change the conversation in their community from reform-based ideas to truly transformational ones. Trace left his leadership position at the local Area Education Agency (Iowa's version of an ESA) to join Chuck.

As Chuck's community builder, with a focus on reimagining education, Trace went about talking with leaders and community members throughout the city talking about school and how it could be different., which led to him connecting with Shawn Cornally, a math teacher in a school system close by, who himself had been wondering whether schooling could be different. Even writing about it often in his blog which, at that time, had nearly 500,000 visitors.

One thing led to another, and Shawn and Trace ended up joining forces, co-hosting several community conversations and working to help the community to see new possibilities for schooling.

After several attempts with lukewarm results, Trace and Shawn were brainstorming ideas when Shawn said that they should run a "Billy Madison" project, wherein they would invite community members to go back to school for a day to witness firsthand what school was like. One thing led to another and in the end they had over 60 community members spend a day in one of several area high schools as a student. Coming to school, getting a schedule, and going to class throughout the day, one after another, just like everyone else.[15]

Shortly after, Trace and Shawn brought the community back together, to debrief what they had observed and had experienced. What came forth was striking. They were bored, moving from class to class, subject to subject, and struggled with some of the work. In short, they were left wondering about the value of most activities students were asked to do and much of the content of their classes.

About Iowa BIG

Instead of classes and classrooms and students shuffling from one class to the next, Iowa BIG facilitators reach out to the community (for-profits, non-profits, government agencies, and religious institutions) and ask: Is there a project you need done that you can't get to. And if they say "yes," they ask if they wouldn't mind if a team of students could work on that project. The projects get filled into a "project pool," where there may be as many as 100-200 projects, and students look in the project pool to find if there are any projects that catch their interest and that they might like to work on.

Students work on these "real world" projects, communicating with the partner and getting assistance as they might need over time from their facilitator. But these are not your typical "school" projects. These are very real and sometimes messy and often challenging projects, with a client at the other end.

Iowa BIG calls these projects "INBOUND" projects because they come from outside the school. But dependent on the interest of a student and/or fellow students, youth might also see a need or with to pursue an outcome that emanates from them – something they want to do, in which case they call that an "OUTBOUND" project, because it emanates from within the school OUT to the world.

The students get very real hands-on, minds-on experience undertaking a project that could have a very real, significant outcome. And in embarking on these projects, students learn how to communicate, collaborate, solve problems, and design solutions while at the same time learning about the world and how it operates and how they can make a difference contributing to the world.

As for accumulating credits (those that are required by the district and the state to graduate), students acquire those by evidencing attainment of the stands *through* their projects. For example, they can receive communication credit for presentations to others and written products that are an outcome of their project. Or social studies credit for investigating and then attending to a local or global issue.

It is in this way that students are gaining real world skills and competencies as well as achieving the more traditional expectations of the district and state.

But while the Billy Madison project was a hit in that respect, awakening the concern of all those who had participated, how it was to inform schools and the school system to do anything different was still unclear. Given the experience, now what? What could and should be done?

After several other community gatherings and continual discussion of what could be done, Trace and Shawn had reached a point where they simply said, maybe we just need to create something, no matter how small. And with that, they began to plan for the opening of a summer program for youth grounded in the ideas they had for bringing the community's desires to life and, engaging youth in real-world projects offered by local partners.

To simply just do this, and get it going, Trace and Shawn were going to open their new, small venture as a private summer program, with an eye on whether they could run such a program as a school during the year.

Using the leverage of the media company over this time to publish the results as each group of adults went through the experience of going back to high school and then imagining what might be possible. Unbeknownst to Shawn, Trace, and Chuck, Mary Meisterling, the chair of the school board in Cedar Rapids at the time, had been keeping up with the project and had learned from Chuck that Trace and Shawn were going to try to start something in response.

Mary was intrigued and saw the opportunity to leverage this work to transform school. So, she called Trace and Shawn and told them, "I want to see you tomorrow to talk about your project." Unsure of what to expect and a bit frightened as Mary was a very influential leader in the community, they anxiously waited for the meeting time to arrive.

Upon arriving at the chosen meeting place, a local coffee shop, she proceeded to tell Trace and Shawn, "Listen. I hear you two are going to start a private school to advance the ideas from your project. I don't want you starting a private school. I want that school *in* our district. I don't want you to start that school outside of our district." As serendipity often plays a role, the District's Associate Superintendent resigned to become a Superintendent in another district and the Cedar Rapids Superintendent, Dr. Dave Benson, asked Trace to join his team in that capacity to move innovation and Iowa BIG forward in the district.

Again, the rest is history. They started with twelve students (you do not always have to start big), which then grew to forty, then 100, then eventually 250.

An Iowa BIG Inbound Project

Making the Homeless Visible – In the fall of 2020, the Willis Dady Homeless Services non-profit in Cedar Rapids pitched an issue in need of a solution to the students at Iowa BIG: How could we help our homeless citizens gain more confidence and feel more connected to and embraced by our community? A team of students were interested in pursuing this challenge and immediately went to work brainstorming, ideating, and working with Willis Dady on designing solutions. A place to start was interviewing the homeless to find out more about who they were and how they became homeless. As they conducted these interviews, they learned so much more than they anticipated.

The stories themselves were quite compelling; the students learned that many of these people became homeless as the result of the confluence of a few extenuating circumstances, such as losing a job, losing their house or apartment, and facing health issues. In short, it didn't take much for some to become homeless–often it was simply because of their circumstances, and no fault of their own.

One young woman was pursuing photography and decided to photograph the homeless, to put a face to a name and a story. As they(she?) began to photograph their (her?) subjects, many of them began to share the few things they still carried with them, including mementos they kept in their pockets.

Eventually, the local library, where many of the homeless spent their time, gave the students the 3rd floor where the students could create a gallery of artifacts. The display included personal stories of the homeless on large poster boards, information and statistics about the homeless population, and an interactive simulation where visitors could experience the potential events that could lead to one becoming homeless. All of this increased knowledge and empathy for the homeless population in Cedar Rapids.

Did the students learn anything? You betcha! Besides learning the potential events that could lead to one's homelessness, they experienced empathy, the art of written storytelling, research on homelessness, how to interview, how to partner with local entities to pursue a project and event, and how to market, as well as the sociology and psychology of homelessness. Long term impact? Many of the students went on to college studies and work in the arena of doing good and contributing to communities.

An Iowa BIG Outbound Project

The Splinters Project at Iowa BIG – On August 10, 2020, Iowa was hit by one of the most destructive storms residents had ever seen: A derecho with 140 mph winds. Buildings were destroyed, powerlines knocked down, and trees uprooted everywhere, including half of those in the Cedar Rapids area.

Seeing the trees uprooted and many simply being shredded for disposal, Leah, a senior at Iowa BIG at the time, had an idea: Instead of just splintering the wood for disposal, why not have some of it brought to a public space where local chainsaw artists could make art with it, and then auction off the artwork to raise monies for the artists and plant new trees? Her advisor's response? That is a GREAT idea! And with that, that's what Leah and her fellow students did.

First, Leah contacted and then pitched the idea to the Mayor, who also replied: "That's a great idea!," adding, "How can I help?" Eventually, the mayor and Leah agreed that the public woodworking and showcasing of art could be conducted in the City Square Park. Then Leah and her fellow students had to find, reach out to, and pitch the idea to the artists, who also loved the idea. Then Leah had to work with the public works department to collect the specific types of wood the artists wanted, file a hold harmless agreement with the city to guard them from liability, develop the auction site, and then organize the week-long event.

A remarkable endeavor, no matter how you look at it. The result: $25,000 raised, $13,000 for the artists and $12,000 for the Trees Forever Foundation.

What did Leah learn? In the words of her facilitators: She learned that she is a great leader and organizer, that her ideas matter, that she can reach out to people she doesn't know and ask for help, that she can work with government officials, and that she can adapt to "whatever." In her own words, she learned that she can do anything if she puts her mind to it. She also learned that she loves marketing – reaching out to people, pitching ideas, and making things happen – which she is now pursuing in college.

Leah told me that she entered Iowa BIG because she doesn't like to sit still while learning. She likes to be active, make things happen, and engage with others. For her, Iowa BIG was the school that transformed how she thinks about herself – as someone who can make a difference in the world.

Now Iowa BIG is considered a leader in engaging youth in real-world projects embedded in their communities, and many others look to them for how to do so.

The CAPS Program

The Blue Valley School District in Overland Park, KS, a mid-to-upper income suburb of Kansas City, 10 years ago didn't have any reason to concern itself with creating any new programming or ways to improve its status within or outside of the community. Its state test scores were amongst the best in the state, along with graduation rates, and placements to top-end universities. Yet, when children of the school board came home regularly complaining about their lack of preparation post-college in the world of work, those school board members began to ask if there was anything the school district could do to ensure that the district's graduates would be far better prepared to pursue their professional aspirations. At the time, the School Board was made up of a number of corporate leaders and executives widely connected with other industry leaders not only in the Kansas City area but beyond as well. These board members, along with a number of their counterparts, recognized that the youth they were hiring were lacking the skill sets they wished they had. Simple ones like coming to work on time, dressing appropriately, communicating well, working effectively in teams, and problem solving. In many cases, the board members themselves began to identify areas of interests and how they could support youth in developing these skills.

As they began to think about this problem, they began to wonder if there was a way the school district could make an impact in this area. Was there a way that high school students, for example, could gain these skills but also explore their potential professional interests while in high school.

It helped that the current superintendent was also concerned about the drop off in senior engagement in school, with most seniors having accumulated all the credits they needed and done with their applications to college. He had been wondering how the school system could offer them something of value that would also sustain their engagement.

With the board feeling they might be on to something and the superintendent always on the lookout to find ways to increase student engagement and performance, members of the school board and district sought out potential programs across the country and visited them, thinking they could adopt something of value that would suit their needs.

Having done their due diligence, visiting several different career and vocational programs across the country, none of them really spoke to what they directly wanted, and so turned to thinking about how they could design their own program from the ground up. With that, they tasked the superintendent to think big, and to create a proposal that could really move the needle on these needs.

In the end, after some community engagement, conversations with potential industry partners, and assessing how they could create a program within the district and get it off the ground, they ended up offering a few courses in the areas of business, health, and the sciences in partnership with a few of the local industry partners, and 100 students decided to try the program out. Then 200 the next year, and more the next. Leading to the need to have a building which could house all of the teachers and students and put them together in a profession-based learning hub in the district, which led to the building of the first CAPS in Blue Valley.

Founding Principal Chad Ralston and Director Donna Deeds were able to organize the offerings and support the co-design and co-creation of various strands, as well as ground the work in some guiding principles that made a lot of sense to them, their partners, and district leaders.

Over five years, the CAPS program in Blue Valley grew into the following strands and substrands of student learning:

- molecular medicine & bioengineering
- environmental science
- bioscience
- entrepreneurship
- veterinary medicine
- food science
- teacher preparation
- medicine and healthcare
- law
- business, technology, and media

Subsequently, word got out and dozens of other districts began to visit BVCAPS to see what they were doing and ask if they also wanted to pursue what they were doing. With such interest, the district, with leadership from a new Director and Associate Director, set out to support these other endeavors and create a network of CAPS programs from which the community network could learn and grow from the support of one another. In this way, one CAPS program quickly grew into 12, then 24, then 50, until today with 100+ affiliates, now reaching into other countries as well (Canada, Kuwait, and Kenya specifically). The CAPS program, once district-owned, has become a non-profit with the explicit goal of assisting and supporting the start-up of new CAPS programs, as well as the ongoing development and learning from across the network of CAPS programs.

Now recognized as a leader in profession-based learning, many refer to it as a standout in the possibilities of how school can truly assist and support students to explore and pursue their interests and gain the skills needed to be successful going forward.

The stories of the growing alumni body are proof of how such a program can make a significant difference in the lives of others.

(More about them can be seen here: yourcapsnetwork.org. And further inspiration can be garnered here through their ongoing podcast: capsnetwork.buzzsprout.com)

The CAPS Experience

In a CAPS program, students engage in a variety of classes that are codesigned with industry partners, once again providing a variety of real world experiences and projects.

Ultimately, the focus of any CAPS program across the 100+ is to provide students with exposure to a wide variety of professions through hands-on, real-world experience, profession-based skill development, and authentic projects supported by faculty, industry experts, and mentors.

Here are a few examples across three of the profession-based strands at the Blue Valley CAPS to get a quick and dirty idea of what students are experiencing in across all of the CAPS programs.

Bioscience. Students enrolling in the Bioscience strand of the Blue Valley CAPS program are supported in identifying an area of research they would like to explore. They are subsequently connected with a researcher that can mentor them in assisting a professional researcher or gain support in pursuing their own original "real world" research in the field. For example, Neeha came into the program wanting to investigate liver disease, so Eric Kessler, a faculty member in the CAPS program, connected her with a researcher at the KU Medical Center that subsequently engaged and assisted her in her own lab work at the medical school. What was she doing? As she put it, "I'm researching different signaling pathways in the context of liver fibrosis and seeing how these different types of receptors and proteins might have an impact on the progression of liver fibrosis." Similarly, another student at the Blue Valley CAPS building was able to do her own research with the support of external mentors, using "the CRISPR cas nine system ... to make antibiotic resistant cells not resistant to antibiotics anymore." Upon which she emphatically added, "It was a fun time!" In this way, Eric is helping students to identify what they might want to explore, connecting them with the mentors that they can either work with or be mentored by, and ultimately assisting and supporting them to be self-directed in their "real-world" investigations. The result: students discovering what it is like to do real lab work and in many cases pursuing science in college and beyond.

Entrepreneurship. Students end up taking Mike Farmer's entrepreneurship class because they initially think it's about starting a business and making money. But little do they know that the class is about them exploring a potential solution to a problem grounded in their particular interest and curiosity and connecting them with others that can help bring their ideas to fruition. And in many cases, launching them into the world. For example, as Mike talked with one student about potential "solutions" she could pursue, they came upon the idea of a "rental app" for prom dresses and shoes. As Mike tells the story, this particular young woman was bemoaning the prom season with the heavy price of finding a dress, buying it, then simply shelving it. But what if she could take past prom dresses, dry clean them, then make them available on an app for those who didn't necessarily want to pay for or could not afford hundreds of dollars to buy a single-use prom dress. Why not look at all your options and simply rent one. Funny, as Mike tells the story, as when they were talking a young man who was planning a camping trip just happened to be sitting next to them thought, what a great idea for camping equipment too. Why not an app for renting camping gear too! From there Mike leads each student through ways to explore the potential of their idea, assists them in developing a prototype, and then, when possible, actually launching the idea, product, or solution into the market. But what are they really learning? Problem-finding, solution creation, market analysis, marketing, collaboration, presentation skills, and the value of ideation.

Veterinary Medicine. About 30 students take Kelley Tuel's class because they have an interest in animals. Little do they know that there is a myriad of ways to get involved in animal care, not just as a veterinarian but as a researcher, animal husbandry (horses, cows, pigs, etc.), nutrition, reproduction, animal behavior, etc. In her class, the students work on a farm, care for the animals, even inseminating cows, and after the class each student takes a deep dive into a particular disease or condition with her colleague Joe Whalen at the helm. What they learn goes far beyond just knowing about something, but experiencing it, and then gaining a great sense of accomplishment plunging into the deep exploration of animal care that interests them the most. One student, for example, explored how impact of secondhand smoke on dogs. (She shared that her father was a heavy smoker and they had lost 3 dogs to cancer). Another student explored kissing spine syndrome (which her horse had). Another student explored the impact of calcium on heart disease (something relevant to her family).

In a nutshell ... hundreds of these personal pursuits are being undertaken across the 100+ CAPS programs in a variety of ways, most beneficially undertaking real-world projects and internships with community clients and mentors, giving students the opportunity to explore their interests through "real world" endeavors with the support of a mentor, which leads to their better understanding of what the work of the profession really feels like. And, not unlike the internships in Tacoma, potentially gain the skills and connections to pursue employment post high school and/or a greater understanding of the studies they could pursue that would lead them to the work they desire.

In Sum

New possibilities *are* possible! But they tend to grow just here and there, and through an unusual set of connections and relationships instigated by a specific need that has been spotlighted. But it is important to note that these occurrences, these new schools and eventually networks, can sprout up and eventually gain traction and eventually grow as a result of careful development of a network.

These four examples show just how varied the start-up of these endeavors can be, and I have given you a taste of how these schools are different from most and the traditional, given what students are doing in these schools.

Each of these cases demonstrate how important it is to have certain individuals instigate, and eventually catalyze, support, and nurture these endeavors. Serendipity is typically the norm in the coming together of these individuals, forces, and resources in response to an identified need. Typically, two or more people have been moved to address a need and have rallied the focus, resources, and relationships to manifest a response that is atypical from the norm. In some ways, the identified need has become so well-articulated and through various channels has become instrumental in rallying resources, relationships, and the need for a response. But it definitely takes both the clear articulation of the need to drive the work, and those few individuals who can rally the relationships and resources to manifest a response.

There are dozens of other stories like this, some of which I will discuss in more detail in the next chapter. But it is important to recognize how these few instances came about so that we may be able to discern ways we can mobilize similar efforts across the country, creating and growing new and atypical endeavors that serve youth and their families far better than we do now. Not school as we have known it, but an educational enterprise that far better supports the development of our youth that results in agency and opportunity for them.

We will continue to think about these conditions and the ways such endeavors can be started, take root, and grow in other communities as we continue to unpack this problem of the status-quo and how it limits innovation in schooling. And we will continue to look at what conditions could propel innovation in communities. Then we will take a hard look at how policy and funding systems could incentivize, support, and scale innovations that better assist and support the development of agency and possibility for all of our youth.

– 4 –
And if we Don't?

Youth Wasting Away

So I have been around the block. And joke sometimes that I know as much as I do because I am 150 years old.

Clearly, I am not 150 years old, but I have been around the block, visiting schools pushing the envelope, doing things differently, as well as in schools struggling to survive – meaning they are awash in pressure and the pursuit of activity to move the needle on their state ELA and math scores.

The environment of these schools is challenging, and I will speak to that next. But here I want to speak to the malaise and challenge of most schools that have become hyper-focused on raising their students' math and ELA proficiency, many of which tend to be in lower socioeconomic urban areas, as well as those schools who are in low-to-middle income working class communities where many students are simply getting by, and then those schools even in middle-to-upper income communities where a few might be excelling in honors or AP courses but where many others are simply complying with expectations and a few simply drifting through school.

The point here is that many, far too many youth have figured out how to do school on their terms. In some cases, it's just to hunker down to do the work. In some other cases, it is to excel at the work put in front of them. But for far too many kids, they are just going through the motions, doing as little as they can to get by. And in other cases, moving through classes day-to-day as mandated but passing the time away and making do interacting with their peers for a little fun and some engagement. But the learning is really not there. If anything, they are going through the motions, but only as much as they must to get by.

For many, school is something you just have to get through, and depending on your relationship to the teachers and the climate and culture of the school, one is just shuffling from class-to-class.

As I stand in line at the grocery store, or purchase my meal at a fast-food joint, or watch the car salesmen in the dealership, or interact with the service department, or think about those who drive our school buses, I sometimes wonder: Was this their aspiration? Or did they just fall into this job or line of work by chance and by need? In what ways did school support or fail them in their pursuit of work? In what way did school fail to support them to identify what they could potentially do, what they might like to do, and in supporting the development of their talent to pursue meaningful and gainful goals?

I think many of us go through the day interacting with many others with the unquestioned assumption that this is the work this person was meant to do. That the work they do is equal to the skill this person has. A salesman, but not an engineer. A fast-food worker, but not an entrepreneur. A grocery store clerk, but not a doctor.

Of course, many other factors play a hand in the outcomes of individual lives. Family values, guidance, and direction. Social context. Personal make-up. But then I am reminded by the statement that so many of the educators who I have worked with who have gone out of their way to offer the kids they work with the opportunity to engage in work they care about and support them in ways where they can excel: With the opportunity to excel, they will. They will surprise you.

I was recently in a school where in class a student was thumbing through YouTube videos and another was online playing Fortnite. Three other girls were joking around about who knows what while half-heartedly completing an anatomy poster. Correction, while one student completed the poster and the others simply engaged in the chatter. A handful of others were on their screen completing a science challenge. Nowhere did I see a student fully immersed in pursuing an activity that had deep, personal meaning for them. Nowhere did I see a student engaged in an activity that was pushing them to develop a skill and pursue a talent that could directly impact the trajectory of their life.

It is in this way that I see many if not most schools wasting away the potential talent and potential trajectory of their students' lives.

The activities are good enough to engage them in what the state expects them to be engaged in. But the activities often do not directly connect to the student in a way that will lift them up to pursue audacious goals and glorious possibilities.

It is in this way that I feel schools fail youth. And I don't want to put the blame entirely on the educators working with these youth. They are doing, as they perceive, what is expected of them, with the supports and resources afforded them.   They, not unlike the students, are as much a victim of the expectations and historically adopted practices as the students. They are doing what is expected of them with the support and guidance of the leadership surrounding them. And that leadership is following suit a well given the expectations of the state and community.

It will take someone to be courageous and engage others in the question: Is this what we want? Is this what we want for our youth? And is this what we want for ourselves? And it will take leadership to invite the question and support the consideration and the conversation. And then it will take leadership to create the collective effort to re-imagine what the school and district community really wants to do for the youth in their community.

But for now, I see us wasting the potential of our youth to excel an excel in ways they want to excel, and to lay the groundwork for their future that has meaning and value to the student.

The Crush on Educators: I Love Lucy

So why do we have what we have? It's the crush of expectation and the crush of the ways we have always done school.

Having worked in dozens of schools and with hundreds of educators, I know the crush on educators – to cover standards, "do" curriculum, and raise their students' ELA and math test scores, to the point where ongoing assessment is rampant and some schools have created a heavily articulated system of remediation.   And intervention. The assessments tell us where the student falls short. The assessment tells us the shortcomings and deficit of the individual.   But rarely is it focused on their interest and their capacity to pursue those interests.

There is a classic clip from I Love Lucy where Edith and Lucy end up working in a chocolate factory. They are dressed in a uniform with a funny looking, patted down chef's hat standing at a conveyor belt with a supervisor in front of a conveyor belt. The supervisor strongly tells them that it is their job to wrap each individual chocolate as it comes down the conveyor belt in a tiny tissue and then pass it along down the conveyor belt. As she says loudly exclaims,

> "The candy will pass by on this conveyor belt and continue into the next room where the girls will pack it. Now your job is to take each piece of candy and wrap it in one of these papers and then put it back on the belt."

She then adds, to reinforce the task: "You understand?"

Lucy and Ethel together timidly respond: "Yes sir? Yes ma'am." The supervisor then states that this is their last chance, as they have already been moved along for poor performance in other departments, that this is their last chance. If just one chocolate makes it past them without being wrapped, they will be fired, upon which the supervisor then yells to the machinist on the other end of the conveyor belt: "Let her ROLLLLLL."

Slowly the tiny chocolates emerge from the end of the conveyor belt one-by-one and Lucy and Ethel wrap each and then deposit them back onto the conveyor belt. Lucy says, "This is easy." But after 10 seconds the chocolates begin to come a little faster, and before you know it, Lucy begins to shove some down her mouth and then down her blouse and Ethel follows suit. As the chocolates start coming faster and faster, their mouths are full and they can't keep up with the pace of the chocolates coming down the conveyor belt. The audience is laughing hysterically as the chocolates begin to pile up in front of them as well and they begin to shove them down their blouses as well. Eventually, Lucy says to Ethel:

> "Listen, I think we are fighting a losing game."

Soon, after much of the comical nature of the situation unfolds with Lucy and Ethel doing the best they can to keep up with the increasing pace of the chocolates, Lucy hears the supervisor coming and with the conveyor belt now stopped, Lucy and Ethel quickly take off their hats and begin to shove all of the remaining chocolates in front of them into their hats, down their blouses, and into their mouths and then the hats back onto their heads.

With their mouths stuffed and looking away from the supervisor so that she cannot see the evidence of their trickery, the supervisor looks at the empty conveyor belt and yells, "Fine, you are doing splendidly." Then yells to the machinist out back,

"SPEED IT UP OTTO!"

Upon which both Lucy and Ethel's eyes go big and the chocolates once again come racing down the conveyor belt faster than before!

If you want to see for yourself, here is the clip

https://www.youtube.com/watch?v=NkQ58I53mjk

So why do I share this? What is the point of my sharing this clip in the context of today's schools and schooling?

With the advent of NCLB and the push to publicly and legislatively evaluate schools based on states' standardized math and ELA test scores, many schools re-oriented themselves to increasing those scores. This does not necessarily mean that they forgot their focus on the well-being of their students or teaching and learning that was engaging and meaningful for students. But indeed many districts, particularly those with schools deemed "under-performing," began to turn up the heat and put pressure on their principals who in turn put pressure on staff to dial-up the means by which they could raise their students' test scores. While there are ways to do this that are resonant with more progressive teaching and learning modalities, a great number of schools turned to packaged interventions (online and in-person) that zero in on raising their achievement data, even when the platform is like drill and kill.

The result of all this activity was a doubling down on reading, writing and math skills in many cases disconnected from meaningful, student-centered application, in some cases orchestrating face-to-face and online skills-based interventions.

In addition, with the advent of the Common Core in 2010, there was renewed focus on teaching to the standards, and to this day, particularly in identified underperforming schools, district and school leaders employ systems to ensure that teachers zero in on the standards. Unfortunately, in many cases teachers turn to teaching practices that foreground the direct delivery of standards above and beyond student engagement in meaningful activity.

Are students' skills and standards not valuable?   I'm not disparaging the need to assist and support students' skills, or an agreement on what is important for students to learn. But when this focus includes an inordinate amount of testing and the focus on skills and standards apart from their meaningful and relevant application, a focus on students' experience and the support around other educational goals can become second to the focus on raising test scores. Then students end up asking – as I heard just last week in a school – why am I learning about the Roman empire and not about the history of Africa. (You can guess who this student might be.)

What is happening is that teachers are being asked to "cover" a bunch of content and a host of standards per expectations by the district. And when in doubt, districts are purchasing curriculum, or creating it themselves, to ensure that teachers are covering the content. A real "I love Lucy" scenario.

The kids are coming down the conveyor belt. It's your job to wrap them up and get them down the conveyor belt wrapped and on to the next step of the process. And the kids keep coming through, more and more, a class at a time, and the supervisor is checking-in on them (and sometimes then even not). Unfortunately, when set up in this factory style sequence, moving them down the conveyor built, wrapping them with content treating them as one chocolate the same as the next, not taking into account that every student has different interests and can be engaged in different ways, things go awry, and the teachers suffer for it, as the chocolates keep on coming and the system doesn't work. But they are held accountable for that.

As Lucy said, "Listen, I think we are fighting a losing game."

And the ones missing out in the end are the youth. The focus on standards and skills disconnected from authentic student interest and meaningful engagement results in students complying with the tasks asked of them. And in some cases, when pressed so hard and disrespectfully engaged, might even act out. Which many do. And then they too are lost to a losing battle that eventually leads to dissatisfaction, compliance, and going through the minimal motions necessary.

Yes, this is not true of every student. There are great teachers who given the opportunity are creating great environments in their classrooms and engaging their kids in creative and beneficial activities. But this is not true in every classroom. And because of this, we need to take a long hard look at how the system is designed for greatness for all. And not just a few.

Talent Unrealized

When the above plays out, we fail to support youth in the development of skills and competencies of real value in the world, missing an opportunity to support youth in how they could productively contribute back to our local communities, our country, and the world.

The creativity and skills of an individual relies on the development of these skills in the context of their direct application in the world.[16] While our predispositions and interests to learn and engage in such activities plays a role, if one is never given the opportunity to be fully immersed in such activities, the potential of that person to develop valuable skills and talents will go untapped,

The simplest example, perhaps, is the young athlete. Without genuine interest and subsequent support to engage in a sport of their choosing, one cannot fully develop the skills and know-how of that sport. There may be incredible untapped talent in each youth, but without the opportunity to develop that talent fueled by interest, along with the expert mentoring and tutelage of coaches, that potential talent will go to waste.

This idea is transferable to almost any discipline, not just sports, such as engineering, writing, coding, web design, etc. Or being a scientist, geneticist, data analyst, architect, or entrepreneur, for that matter. The difference is that the particular skills and talents of an individual in some disciplines may not be as overtly visible as the skills in other disciplines, such as sports. Rather, specific skills and talent in some disciplines can be hidden from explicit view, for example, as the engineer, writer, and entrepreneur is thinking. One cannot overtly "see" how one is thinking. However, at some point one's skill and competency in a field can ultimately be discerned and seen by way of the products of their thinking and subsequent actions. It is in this way we can assess the skill and talent of others, through the visible actions they take and products they create, including if needed their explanations of how they arrived at the work they produced.

Because of this, learners need explicit coaching in the development of their skills and competencies in any discipline, not just in how to act but also how to think.

Unfortunately, most disciplinary activity (intellectual, physical, and social) in traditional schooling is only shared as knowledge rather than actual know-how. Most information in schools is transmitted as to "what" to do and less so "how" to do it. Moreover, how to do it in the "real world." There isn't enough opportunity to apply and use potentially useful domain-specific knowledge and skills in rich, real, and purposeful contexts. It is in this arena that the new schools excel – situating students in authentic contexts with purposeful action for meaningful outcomes.

Countless stories exist of individuals who discovered their passion and entered a particular field through personal and professional connections or happenstance, sometimes planned, but more often by circumstance. Traditional schools rarely foster, let alone directly provide students with the opportunity to pursue experiences and connections that can lead to the development and pursuit of their talent in the world. Instead, youth are funneled through a requisite series of boxed knowledge (such as biology and chemistry, geometry and algebra, US History, and English Literature) that supposedly builds a foundation for them to potentially pursue various professions and be civically informed. But then youth themselves ask: Why do I have to learn this? The problem is that the way we teach in most traditional schools ultimately leads to vacuous knowledge, relegated to memory, rarely coupled with "how" to meaningfully use that knowledge in the "real world." Hence, the potential talent of our youth goes untapped.

The Learning that Matters

We know from observation that when anyone is given the opportunity to engage in learning driven by intrinsic motivation, they are far more likely to learn. We see this with youth playing any of the multiple games on PlayStation, such as Fortnite or Madden, or fishing, or building and making things.

These are simple examples. However, the examples tend to fade as children move through adolescence and into adulthood because their contexts shift, and youth are no longer supported to play and create in the same way, making and doing in the world, except for those few, like Cole Summers, who bought his farm at the age of nine and is continually trying to to make it work,[17] or Claire Fraise, the daughter of my good friend Cath Fraise, who decided to homeschool her daughter, to give her the freedom to do what she wanted. With this newfound time and opportunity to pursue what she wanted, Claire started a non-profit to assist animal rescue dogs, wrote her first book, then second, and now later into adulthood, her third.

It is one thing to learn the discipline-specific knowledge, skills, and know-how of a specific field (such as architecture, medicine, engineering, or business), and another to learn the skills identified as important across fields, the 21st-century skills, as they call them, such as creativity, problem-solving, communication, and critical thinking, to name just a few.[18] More recently, educators and others have begun to dive into what they refer to as "the durable skills," those skills that employers are looking for their employees to have above and beyond the domain-specific knowledge and skills in their field. These are the more specific skills falling under the umbrella of the previously identified 21st-century skills, such as public speaking, entrepreneurship, persistence, and teamwork. (See durableskills.org to learn more about these.)

1. **Leadership:** Directing efforts and delivering results

2. **Character:** Personal and professional conduct

3. **Collaboration:** Teamwork and connection

4. **Communication:** Information exchange and management

5. **Creativity:** New ideas and novel solutions

6. **Critical Thinking:** Informed ideas and effective solutions

7. **Metacognition:** Self-understanding and personal management

8. **Mindfulness:** Interpersonal and self-awareness

9. **Growth Mindset:** Improvement and aspiration

10. **Fortitude:** Constitution and inspiration

The problem is that schools tend to teach many skills, whether they are field specific, 21st century, or the latest durable skills, as knowledge (that is, knowing what they are) rather than as "know-how" (that is, being able to employ them), and in particular, how to employ them in meaningful, authentic, situated contexts.

Imagine millions of youth sitting in desks day after day, being asked to solve make-believe problems with little intrinsic interest to them, played out with little connection to authentic, real-world contexts. What we are doing is asking these youth to waste their time being compliant by learning "what" the skills are rather than giving them the opportunity to build their talent using these skills in meaningful ways. Undertaking such tasks set forth by a teacher disconnected from any meaningful application results in very little learning, and thus any learning that really matters. Think learning how to play basketball or how to drive a car without actually having a ball in hand and playing the game or sitting in the driver's seat and actually driving a car. That's what learning the "what" rather than the "how to" looks like and feels like. No fun in that. And no mastery or talent actually gained.[19]

So how can we better support the development of our youth's untapped potential in ways that are truly value to them, and in the ways that they can create, make, and do in the world?

Industry bemoans the fact that they cannot hire the employees they need because our education system (K12 and higher ed.) doesn't really support our youth's ability to think and act in ways desired by industry – to think critically, problem solve, think outside of the box, arrive at creative solutions, be self-directed, and be able to collaborate.

Think of the immense potential we are not tapping in our youth. First, we are not pursuing ways to engage our youth toward their potential talent. Second, we are not offering mentoring, coaching, and apprenticeship opportunities to help youth develop proficiency in areas of their interest and what they would like to get good at.

It is in these ways that we are doing a gross disservice to our youth, the communities they live in, and the world, as we need more talent. We need better problem-solvers. We need more creative thinkers and actors in our communities. And we need more youth interested in making a difference in the world, with the knowledge, "know-how," and skills to do so.

Prison

So I hate to say this, and I am not happy about how I put this, but would you rather spend (as a taxpayer) one trillion dollars on educating youth and adults so that they can pursue meaningful and gainful lives, while contributing back to our society, or two trillion dollars locking youth and adults in jail cells at an average cost of $50,000/year, frittering away potential talent and positive contributions to our world?

I am actually being generous with these figures. Let us consider some recent data, as presented in the figure below.[20]

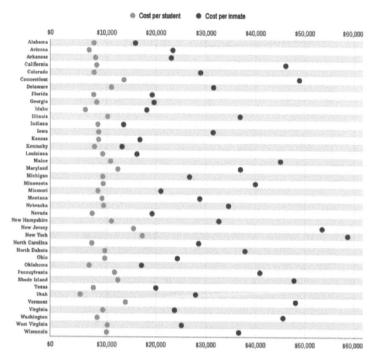

If I were a taxpayer in New York, New Jersey, or Connecticut, I would be pissed. As taxpayers, we are spending $50,000 to $60,000 per year to house someone in jail when perhaps for the amount of money we are already spending in education for our youth ($9,000 to $25,000 per student per year, depending on the state and community) we could be helping them to explore and pursue their interests and potential talents.

Let's think about this for just a minute. Let's spend $30,000 per year or more keeping our citizenry locked in prison cells not using their time or energy to contribute to society vs. spending $12,000 to $16,000 per year helping them to explore how they can pursue gainful employment and give back to our society. Wait, WHAT? You got that right! How messed up is that. Rather than being PROACTIVE, our government is being REACTIVE and wasting not only our money, but worse– our human capital.

If we care for our youth and one another, where have we failed them? That is right. How have we, as a society, failed these young men and young women? If we take responsibility for these youth,

Share of children in US from various earnings quintiles ending at the bottom as adults, by race, 2011

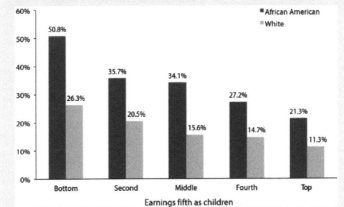

http://www.stateofworkingamerica.org/chart/swa-mobility-figure-31-
share-children-income/ Data Source: Mazumder (2011, Table 7)
http://dx.doi.org/10.2139/ssrn.1966690

Lifetime likelihood of spending time in jail or prison by demographic group, 2001

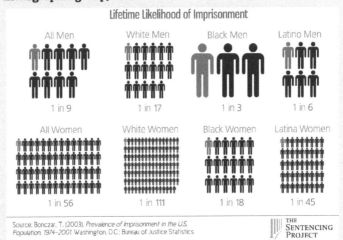

http://www.sentencingproject.org/criminal-justice-facts/
Data Source: Bonczar (2003) US Department of Justice,
http://www.bjs.gov/content/pub/pdf/piusp01.pdf

we have failed far too many. Why is it that young men in downtown Hartford feel the need (or desire) to traffic in drugs and engage in crime? In New York. Cleveland. Newark. Houston. Chicago. Oakland. Pick your spot.

It is because we have failed them. We (as a society) have not provided them with a sense of opportunity and possibility that could have possibly diverted them away from the destructive behaviors, illegal activities, and relationships that may prove harmful to their future. But let's imagine.

What if ...

- Schools were designed to give youth a sense of agency and possibility
- Schools were designed so that students could explore and pursue their genuine interests
- Schools were designed so that students could have a strong sense of self and self-confidence through the attainment of clear skills, competency, and mastery
- Schools were designed so that students could see and design a path forward in their education toward the work they would like to do and the life they would like to live

What if?

An Astute, Proactive, and Empathetic Citizenry

Finally, a topic most likely polarizing in how I will present it, depending on your political affiliation and stance toward current events and ideals.

While political, social, and ideological positions have been a wellspring of debate since the founding of the US, primarily grounded in the debate between two parties, the fissure of stances has ignited not only social, ideological, and political infighting but legislative actions that have resulted in an incredibly divisive polarization of views in the country. Unfortunately, as it seems part of human nature, crowd effects are real, and social media has only fueled crowd effects to spur and deepen particular viewpoints. In worst-case scenarios, this has led some citizens and politicians to actions that are both ideologically and physically destructive.

As I write this, the day after July 4, 2022, we bore witness yet again to a socially ostracized and mentally unstable individual who, through example, was moved to do significant harm to others by firing into a friendly crowd. Just so many days from the same in an elementary school in Texas, and just so many days from a barrage of fire in a Buffalo NY market.

While these later events are, for the most part, anomalous to the greater network effect of ideological affiliation, the network effect has clearly reared its ugly head when it comes to political affiliations driven by persona that drive destructive values and commitments.

We can see this, unfortunately, in how Trump wielded his political will to attract individuals who have felt slighted and powerless and empowered them to take antagonistic views and actions. He has also wielded his persona to lift those who wish to rise in positional stature, pursuing similarly antagonistic political action. Affiliating yourself with his ideologically-driven stances toward others and the government drove dozens to the White House and emboldened them with the assumed right to take over the capital, literally and figuratively.

The crowd effect has also garnered interest and actions on the part of individuals in the name of a collective effort to fight back against activity that surfaces systemic racism in our country. Those who feel put upon by such verbalization of the issues are fighting back emboldened by such rhetoric – whether it be denouncing the Black Lives Matter movement or LGBTQ rights.

What's worse is that such ideological stances and the vocalization of such stances for the pursuit of one's ego is being played out in our democracy, not just in social media but in those elected to power in our state and federal government.

I can't help but point a finger at our education system for failing to expand and deepen our populace's more humane stances and values towards others given this reality. I assume that we would want our education system to engender an intelligent, ethically and morally responsible citizenry, with values that embrace the well-being of all. Clearly, this has not been the case, given the overt rhetoric and actions of many of our political leaders and citizens.

We say that civic education is important, and we argue for social studies, history, and literature in the name of greater perspective and ethical understanding. Yet, the actions of many of our politicians and citizens clearly demonstrate the shortcomings of how we engage youth in the development of moral character and humane ideals. This is evident in how many of our fellow citizens think and act as a product of our education system, both K-12 and higher ed. For example, many elected officials are using social media to inflame derogatory perspectives and incite harmful actions toward specific groups in our society, seemingly ignorant of how such rhetoric can inflame and catalyze destructive views and violence toward others. Worse, they are knowingly and purposefully using social media and enacting legislation that intentionally harms our populace. Then there is the fact that a good number of our fellow citizens are supporting and voting for the very politicians who exhibit such values antagonistic to a more socially just and humane society.

Once again, this is a clear failure of our current education system. Should standardized test scores in math and ELA be determining the quality of our schools and school system? Or should we be considering the actions of our citizenry and their ability to think well and exhibit values that align with a humane society?

The Need for a New Paradigm of Schooling

Given the above, now what?

The only thing getting in the way is leadership, political leadership in particular – the kind of leadership that got us to the moon and galvanized a collective interest in the well-being of all. Is there such leadership that can "take us to the promised land?" I pray so. If leadership cannot do it, we need a wellspring of expectations clearly vocalized and demanded from who? Us. We need those who stood up for civil rights (and continue to stand up for civil rights, social justice, and opportunity for all) to do the same in education, but we need to do so with some agreement on a new vision for the purpose and practice of education. We need to go beyond just wanting to improve the way current schools work and grow new school models that give agency and opportunity for all – not singularly focused on the percentage of students passing state tests or the percentage of students graduating. Our vision needs to be far bigger than that.

For this to happen, we need to actively support the development of new and different kinds of schools, schools focused on greater aspirations than the ones they are forced to focus on now.

To say we are going to make our present schools better is like saying we are going to paint the horse and buggy red instead of black, replace rotary dials with keypads on landlines, or put more books in the library instead of putting the web in one's hand. How does that truly move our schools into the 21st century? It doesn't.

The current paradigm of schooling drives the decisions and behaviors of our educators, reinforced by the expectations, structures, policies, and practices of our state and local school ecosystem. How long can we keep repainting the horse and buggy or adding a new light or horn to it? We cannot continue to have an antiquated model of schooling doing harm and limiting what is possible when we put agency and possibility for all at the center. It is time to build a new system that gives every youth an opportunity to pursue the life they wish to live and contribute back to our communities and our humanity.

Our current schools and the school "system" that supports and perpetuates what we now know as school is like living in the days of landlines, black and white TVs, no internet, no web, and no planes. It is so antiquated that it is like we are living in the early 1900s, not the early 2000s. Why? Because our limited vision of what school could be perpetuates the status quo, and on top of that, our system works to maintain and sustain the status quo.

If schools were a private industry with consumer choice, schools as we now know them would be dead, and what we would have would be far better. But we don't. The current architecture of federal, state, and local funding and policy effectively propagates and maintains the insular design of our school systems and the conventional practices of our schools. There is no incentive to "step out of the box," to do school differently. Any success on the part of students comes by way of the particular circumstances and opportunities afforded them in their context, and for a few, the persistent drive and savvy to rise above.

I should know. I was someone who could have had a very different educational history and subsequently a very different life if my family had not moved. I was simply trying to survive in my LA public school, doing other kids' art and trying not to get my head bashed in. However, my family moved to Westport, CT, and the rest is history. Bette Davis lived down the street, Paul Newman was a mile away, and Martha Stewart was at the other end of town. All of the minibuses to get kids around town were Mercedes-Benz buses. The school system was well-funded and had a college-going culture with high expectations, good school leaders, and for the most part, good teachers.

After moving to Westport, I was able to focus on my schoolwork and did well. Given this privilege and graduating from one of the best school systems in the country, I was afforded the opportunity to go to Wesleyan (a little Ivy) and probably Harvard because of that.

I have said time and time again: I am a smart guy, but there are a lot of smart people in the world. Is it okay that just because my family moved to Westport, I was afforded the opportunities I have had?

I recognize myself as lucky. But why me? Why not others? Why shouldn't everyone have the same opportunity?

– 5 –
What is Possible

When I Turned 21

Three events in my life have had a significant impact on who I am and what I do. The first was reading *Walden*, by Thoreau. The second was my mother's 21st birthday gift to me. The third was enrolling in the Harvard Graduate School of Education.

Mind you, my mother is a bit different than most – at least as I see her. I didn't get a gift-wrapped box or cake. At the time I was going to school at Wesleyan University (one of the little Ivies), I had planned to spend the summer in LA with my mother. For my birthday, I did receive a card. But on the card my mother wrote that I would be meeting people throughout the summer who were making a living doing what they love to do. She didn't tell me who they were. Still, I thought it interesting, and pretty cool.

Little did I know that the people she had in mind were incredible. They were artists (sculptors, radio producers, writers, etc.) that had become known for their work, and had been very successful. They were outliers. They were individuals who had figured out how to pursue what they loved and make a life and a living doing that.

That they were well-known and highly regarded is beside the point. Do you have to be famous to be successful if you are able to make a living doing what you love to do? Yet here we were. I was going to be meeting all of these individuals who were making a living doing what they love to do but also highly successful and well-regarded in their fields.

So ....

I am not sure if this was my first meeting, but picture this. A young, thin, long-haired lad from the East Coast landing on the 2nd floor of a small office building in Beverly Hills to meet ... drumroll ... Ray Bradbury. Yes, Ray Bradbury. The well-known author of

Fahrenheit 451 and the Martian Chronicles amongst many other stories. I knew nothing of what to expect. Would he be stodgy? Full of himself? Formal?

It was none of those things. I remember walking into his space – a large, light-filled office with tons of stuffed animals and plastic spaceships and aircrafts, hanging from the ceiling throughout his office. At the very back, he had a big desk, from which he came from behind. It felt more like a kid's room. A 12-year-old's bedroom. A place of imagination and play. A place where stories lived.

I remember him coming from around his desk, a head full of fluffy grey hair, a corduroy sportscoat, a little unkempt I must say. He grabbed my hand with his two and said, "Let's go have lunch!"

We made our way down the stairs to the hamburger joint just below. (I imagine he had a good number of burgers there.) And we had lunch.

I don't remember much of the conversation except for this one thing, which was not lost on me and of which many others said the same: Do what you love to do! If you are not, you are wasting your time. He said not to worry about the finances, but that they would come. More important, find a way to do what you love to do.

How simple is that?

Well, for those saying, yeah, all well and good, but there are the bills to pay.

Yes, there are bills to pay, and probably mortgages, rent, car loans, etc. But what if each child and youth were exposed to this idea. What if, like my mother did for me, parents and other adults surrounding and supporting youth said, you are wonderful and you can do whatever you want to do.

Stuff your eyes with wonder, he said, live as if you'd drop dead in ten seconds. See the world. It's more fantastic than any dream made or paid for in factories.
                    - Fahrenheit 451

Living at risk is jumping off the cliff and building your wings on the way down.
                    - Ray Bradbury

I met others that summer. A sculptor. Norman Corwin, who produced the 1938 Halloween radio broadcast of the War of the

Worlds in NYC, which scared many, those tuning in just a few minutes late not knowing it was a show and not the real thing.

I remember talking to many of those my mother wrote to. Sometimes in their home. Sometimes elsewhere. But simply meeting these individuals with the intention of learning how it is they came to do what they loved to do and how they were able to make a living doing it made a big impact on me. Particularly coming after my reading of Walden, where one sentence has similarly directed me in how I make decisions as to what to do with my life. My paraphrase:

> *I went to the woods to live my life deliberately, so when it came to dying, I would not say I had not lived.*

These two experiences have had a profound impact on how I have made and how I continue to make decisions in my life, both personally and professionally. But they have also had a significant impact on how I think about the purpose of school. Which we will get into later.

The Big Picture

I fell in love with the Big Picture Schools once I learned about them.

Having been raised by a mother who said that I should follow my interests and passions, how could I not fall in love with the design of a school whose focus is just that. Rather than focus on what students should know (facts, dates, prescribed literature, and the typical conventional content thrown at students), the questions asked are: Who are you? What are you interested in? What is your passion? And what do you like to do?

When I was in Montessori school, during the first half of 3rd grade, I remember building structures with blocks (when I wanted), reading (what and when I wanted), and playing games (again, what and when I wanted).

I have a vivid memory of my staring out the window on a particularly gray and rainy day. This memory is etched in my mind. Just staring out the window, watching the rain, looking at it splash and roll down the windows and thinking: How does this work? Why does it splash? Why do the drops roll down the window as they do? This had a great impact on me, having time to just watch and think and meditate on all these questions. I enjoyed the grey wetness of the day while the others played and laughed in the background. I was not alone, and comforted that others were there, but happy to be in my own head.

I also remember arriving at this same school filled with the imagery of a dream I had had and doing my best not to let it dissipate from my memory. Finding it difficult to both remember and write it at the same time, I somehow corralled a friend to write it out as I told him the story. For some reason he was happy to do so, and my recollection is that he was using a number of different colored crayons to do so as he did.

In my dream, I was in some way conducting *The Little Engine That Could* over large cartoon hills and racing my way to raise the Golden Gate bridge before an imminent tidal wave would crash over it, destroying both it and the city. Running out of steam, I had to stop at several stations to pour jellybeans from the coaling tower and feed them into the train to keep up its speed.

The train from the book had been painted large by my mother on our bedroom wall and had clearly made its way into my imagination.

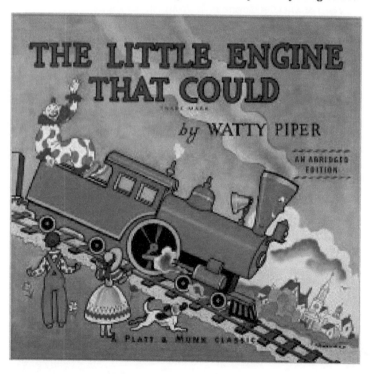

To me, this was school. Playing with blocks, playing with others, noticing things. Wondering, creating, and thinking. I remember writing a poem about rain, and racing to school to capture the story of a dream I had.

New chapter, and one of the reasons I went into education:

In the middle of that year, somehow I found myself in the local public school. It was large, and one of my strongest memories was of my trying to escape from some bully who had decided that it would be funny to race after me. The thing is, the playground monitors were simply talking and watching, which unnerved me. I don't think they had a concern for my well-being. It was large. A concrete playground with a few tetherball poles (remember those?) and swings.

The thing is, this atmosphere, this culture, was completely different from what I had grown accustomed to. I felt alone and in survival mode. I was no longer staring out the window at rain or putting my dreams down on paper.

The other very distinct memory of this place that left me completely flummoxed was the fact that I found myself sitting at a desk, in a row amongst rows, listening to someone tell me how to tell time. Now, I might not have found this altogether unsettling except for the fact that I already knew how to tell time. So as I was sitting there being told to be quiet (heaven help us if we made a sound), I became distraught, then actually angry. Here I was having to sit still and listen to someone tell me how to tell time. Something I already knew.

I could see she was struggling to get everyone else to understand what she was saying. With the little hand at 3 and the big hand at 12, she pointed and said, "See this is 3 o'clock." Then moved the hands and said, "Now see, this is three fifteen." Again and again, she said it until everyone repeated: 3 o'clock, 3 fifteen, now 3 thirty. Repeat and repeat after me.

As you can imagine (given my already angry disposition for having to sit and listen in the first place), I began to fume inside and so decided I would get back at her. Again, she repeated, 3 o'clock, 3 fifteen, 3 thirty. Then wave wave wave I did with my arm furiously as she moved the big hand to 9. Certainly, she couldn't ignore me completely. "Ok," she said. "What time is it now?" I put my arm down. Paused. Looked around the room. Then with clever determination and a slow drawl to boot (to be sure all eyes were upon me), said ... "QUARTER TO FOUR!"

I was sent to the principal's office. I had been had. She knew what I was up to, and she wasn't going to let me get away with it. I had completely screwed up her lesson and confused the heck out of everyone else. Their growing confidence of what they thought they knew had been completely knocked off, and I had proudly shown her up. I already knew how to tell time, so why make me sit here and listen to you?, I kept thinking. Moreover, I knew I could say quarter to 4 and not three forty-five. And I thought I could get back at her for wasting my time and having to sit and listen to her teach me something I already knew, by showing her up and confusing my classmates at the same time.

Funny as this story is, it continues to shine a light on how absurd our system is. A few weeks later, I was given a test. If I passed the test, they told me they would move me up to the next grade. But, unfortunately, I had missed by one question. Think of that. If I had got one more question right, they would have moved me to the next grade.

How absurd is that?

Imagining New Possibilities

Right now, our education ecosystem is not set up for disruptive innovation. Disruptive innovation is when someone (or a group) creates a product or service that is valued more than other products or services currently available ... and is *accessible*. This is the main point of Clayton Christensen's theory of disruption.[21] It is not that the product or service is better; it is that it is desired more by others (because it fulfills a specific function) *and it is also readily accessible*.

So let us turn our attention to these two specific attributes.

Schools do not sit in a space where they can readily innovate and offer an alternative educational experience to youth. Right now, schools reside within districts serving their local communities, for the most part, they offer a long-standing conventional model of schooling because, well, that's what was created in the past, and that's what others are providing elsewhere.

Rarely is there a choice. School systems are set up – historically and by design – to offer a single educational option, a neighborhood school typically in the form of how schools have been operating for decades. In rare cases, districts offer a magnet program or multiple choices of schools. NYC would be an example of this, where there are almost 2,000 schools, and families are given a choice of school. However, parents and their youth have to enter an elaborate lottery system of choosing their 1st through 12th choice of school. Of course, having a lottery system where most schools are set up to house no more than 200-600 students with a total student population of 1 million is tricky. Then there is the issue of proximity and realistic access. We would be hard-pressed to have 5-10-year-olds taking the subway an hour each way to go to a school that might benefit them better. Even so, it is not unheard of to have a high school student select and attend a high school as far as an hour away by subway because that school is offering something that is of greater value to them.

Then there is the issue of a family and youth not knowing what their options are and how those options may or may not benefit them. Additionally, even with options publicized, research shows that most families will, in the end, choose a neighborhood school over an alternative, even if that alternative may benefit their child more than their local neighborhood school.[22] Transportation and convenience are no small matters. Families, particularly with little ones, will more likely choose proximity over other things, particularly if the alternative is not perceived as much different from the school nearby.

However, most district systems, given their size, typically offer only one model of schooling (the typical school) within a specific boundary. Thus, most students across the country are attending Plainville Elementary, Local Figure Middle, and Historical Figure High School.[23]

While many of these schools may be filled with well-intentioned and caring educators, they are still offering only one form of schooling – the conventional model. The one they know and most likely were educated in themselves. Your standard elementary, middle, and high school. Hence the ongoing practice and continued replication of the conventional school model perpetuated because it has been widely adopted and familiar and readily meets the expectations of most families and communities, as that is what they have known ever since their own upbringing and schooling. However, this school model continues to perpetuate and sustain the teacher- and content-centered model of learning, which as we have known and continue to learn, does not serve our youth best.

Access. And this is where it gets difficult. Access is not a small thing. Getting into a school and then even just getting to it can be a big problem. You have heard the stories of numerous charter and magnet schools having huge waiting lists. Well, there is a reason for that. Students and families want into these schools because they are offering something unique from the conventional design, and in most cases, they have good reason to.

When schools have a distinct identity and word gets out that they are serving youth differently and in ways that parents want for their children, or students want for themselves, then why shouldn't they pursue those alternatives? The question then becomes, is it okay that some youth are cut off from such options because of a lack of space or a dearth of options? Or could there be a mechanism to ensure that every youth and family can access alternatives that speak to the needs and interests of all students and families?

This then becomes a matter of how to create and provide multiple alternatives to the conventional model of schooling that may serve families and their children far better than the singular traditional model we tend to see everywhere in and across systems.

Equity does not mean that better is available only to some. Equity means that better is available to all. So that means that in the design of our new system, we need to build in ways to ensure that (1) multiple options are available for every family and youth, and (2) when an option is desired by a family and student, the system knows how to create, support, and scale that option for anyone.

Let's play with this idea a bit. Let's consider that your only choice is to eat at McDonald's because that is the only offering in your community. And for the sake of this playful thought experiment, it is publicly funded. Not only that, but by law, your child has to eat there every day. And by design, every child is offered the same thing. McNuggets in the morning. Cheeseburgers in the afternoon. Possibly a choice of fudge or strawberry sundae at the end of the day. Nonetheless, each child is eating the same thing, whether or not they want it or if it is good for them. The model works, at least for the system, because this typically means there is only one building in the community that the system has to effectively routinize to provide the same for each student. And if they need more across neighborhoods, they can basically blueprint how those buildings run too, based on what they and others are already doing elsewhere.

This model works for local school systems because they can then build, replicate, and use this model to fulfill the litany of current traditional state expectations – credits in various subject areas and passing of the state tests. In sum, this focus has resulted in an institutionalized protocol for the design of schools that dictates not only what is taught (the curriculum) but also how it is taught (teacher-directed pedagogy), because the design makes it far more manageable to funnel kids through the system given these expectations as well as monitor the outcomes.

To continue with this playful analogy, when kids then graduate from McDonald's Elementary, they can move on to Burger King Middle. Maybe with a few more choices, but still Whoppers, fries, and soda, not far off from the cheeseburgers, fries, and drinks offered in elementary school. Again, this works for local school systems as it is manageable and, by design, directly responds to the expectations of the state. Again, passing tests and accumulating seat time in subject areas expected by the state.

In High school, things shift a bit. There are more choices, so maybe the offering is more like a buffet – a variety of electives and more well-defined subject classes. Such as calculus, environmental science, foreign language, computer science, robotics, and theater, for example. Unfortunately, some kids get to eat from one buffet while others are offered another (think those who are afforded honors and AP classes vs. "college prep"). There are more choices other than just burgers, fries, and soda (the main fare, so to speak, such as algebra, biology, English literature, and US History), with extracurriculars and clubs, perhaps, just like tacos, pasta, sandwiches, and salads.

Still, there is typically only one McDonald's Elementary in each community, or in larger communities, there may be more. But for the most part, they all operate the same, as do the Burger King Middles, all feeding into one or more larger high schools that pretty much look the same, except for the few districts who create magnet schools or programs. Unfortunately, these schools really are not that very different from one another. They serve the same curriculum, although the quality of service might vary from one school to the other.

Most of these schools are not truly grounded in students' personal interests. Vocational schools may be a bit different, as they teach students how to create, make, and do in the world (when done well). Then again, the choices in most vocational schools may be limited.[24]

For large systems that have already built huge facilities to house 2,000 or more students, offering different learning environments that focus on students interests and a variety of ways to learn might mean breaking these behemoth high schools up into a variety of different options, each with a different focus and pedagogy. The same could be said for middle and elementary schools. Does the same curriculum and pedagogy work for *all* students? Or should there be variation in keeping with the different learners in the building?

A good example of this would be NYC or Denver. Denver, in particular, has seen some success in allowing for the development of several alternative schools and schools of choice.[25] NYC, for years, has worked to support the development of new small schools after identifying and then closing a number of low-performing schools, offering those students a choice to go elsewhere.[26]

Unfortunately, despite some families and students taking advantage of choice, many students and families particularly in lower socioeconomic households do not pursue many of these new school options, choosing instead to attend their more conventional neighborhood school as it is more convenient to attend and familiar to them, even when those schools are significantly underperforming in comparison to others. There is only a very small slice of students and families who go out of their way to seek out and attend the more non-traditional schools that might serve them better. But most end up attending the schools closer to them despite the model they employ: NYC's version of McDonald's elementary, Burger King Middle, and Cafeteria High.

In short, there is still a lack of different kinds of schools to serve different kinds of learners with different interests, passions, and aspirations. If we continue to offer up the same conventional model of schooling we have been doing for years, we will continue to fail our youth and limit the possibilities of their lives. What we need to do is catalyze new and better options for youth across communities, and I mean all youth across all communities, not just those with a leg up due to circumstances. This means first incentivizing and supporting the creation and proliferation of schools that can meet the needs and aspirations of youth and then ensuring that all youth have access to if not advocacy to pursue and take advantage of these opportunities.

The question then is, how could we redesign our public school ecosystem so that (1) innovation is incentivized and supported, (2) innovative models and practices are shared to "feed the imagination" of others, and (3) creative and effective practices are scaled to provide all youth the same opportunities?

The New Model

The following proposed model of our public school ecosystem is just a rough sketch of what could happen if we wished to provide all youth with learning that expands their possibilities and increases their sense of agency.

In presenting this model, I need to make it clear that these proposals are grounded in specific examples from across the country so that no one can argue whether any of these ideas is doable. They are doable because they are already taking place somewhere.

Are all of the details completely worked out about how each idea could be moved into action, such as the incentivization of new school designs, community engagement, new school funding, and new school monitoring? No. Could the details be worked out dependent on local state, community, and district context? Yes.

Let's go!

Moving from a Charter School model of School Innovation to an Entrepreneurial Model of School Innovation

The charter school movement recently celebrated its 30th year of enactment. There are now approximately 7,700 Charter Schools across the US serving over 3.4 million students, and the debate over whether they have proven successful or not continues.[27] In short, there are some exceptional charter schools that families believe have been serving their children far better than their neighborhood school would have. But, in reality, there are also a number of charter schools that have not served youth well.

The fact is, there are good, not-so-good, and awful charter schools just as there are good, not-so-good, and awful "traditional" schools. Just because it is a charter school does not mean that it is or will become a great school. Depending on the report you read, some have claimed that you are far more likely to get a better learning community as a result of being part of a charter school as charter school communities tend to rally much more effectively around identity, core practices, shared ideals, and concern over the learning outcomes of their students. In many ways, this is a byproduct of how charter schools come to be, with a community coming together to start a new school founded in a new vision.

One of the biggest hangups, however, is the antiquated expectations charter schools are ultimately judged upon, which in many ways shackles them to the historical model of schooling we have now, identified as a significant shortcoming of our system. Zeroing in on standardized test scores in ELA and math and ultimately being held accountable to those measures can put a significant stranglehold on these schools. Whereas private schools and home school communities are afforded the freedom to decide and pursue what they believe is of the greatest value to their youth and how best to support the development of their youth, charter schools – not unlike traditional public schools – are beholden to the same policy constraints and shortsighted state-assessment mandates as other public schools.

When this set of state-mandated expectations drives the work of the school, it can easily crowd out other foci that may be far more beneficial for their youth in the long run.[28]

Certainly, there was an initial aspiration that charter schools could potentially drive innovation by (1) offering alternative models of schooling, and (2) press other schools to improve by creating a competitive ecosystem for learners.

Unfortunately, neither of these expectations played out as most charter schools developed were not truly innovative. Nor did local public schools see them as models that they could (or even wanted to) learn from. Moreover, many educators opening charter schools, particularly serving lower socio-economic urban communities, decided that they needed to double down on practices that foregrounded gains in standardized achievement scores above all else, as this is what they were being judged on.[29] Unfortunately, there are also other schools which, despite the freedom to potentially grow new practices in service of student engagement, community, and learning, did not in reality depart much from the same ills or traditions of most conventional schools. The only difference being that the community felt some ownership of their school – which is no small thing. Not, however, necessarily translating into better teaching, learning, or schooling.

In free enterprise systems, entrepreneurial activity reigns king. Anyone or any entity able to create something of value and desired by others can take root and grow, at least if those demonstrating the value through a given product or service is effectively made accessible to others.

Thinking and acting entrepreneurially means providing something of value, which is desired and subsequently pursued by others. Of course, others have made the claim that privatizing schools could lead to the kind of free-for-all development of better schools through an open marketplace of competition. But I myself do not subscribe to such an ideology as it then becomes unclear as to how such an open marketplace of schooling and learning options would indeed be made available and accessible to all – both youth and families. It is also unclear how one could regulate the various "pop-up" of options to ensure that every youth and family were served well.

Don't get me wrong. I am not against affording educators and groups of educators the opportunity to develop and then offer options to youth and families across communities. I *am* for incentivizing, supporting, and assisting the start-up of new designs through a variety of mechanisms that are in keeping with entrepreneurial intent, affording school and program developers to develop and offer their own aims for education and metrics of success – not those as typically dictated by traditional charter school mandates and expectations. **We need to allow, if not incentivize, individuals, groups, and communities to imagine new possibilities.**

The public school ecosystem is not set up to similarly incentivize innovation and entrepreneurial thinking as is our free-market for-profit, non-profit, and social systems are. In fact, most educators expect that they are entering a fixed and predictable routine: the educational factory system. Many who went into education went into it because it seemed stable, and one's work would be clear. Based on what they have experienced and how schools have historically operated, most educators go into education thinking that they will fill the same shoes. The same role. Teaching in classrooms, teaching subjects, and teaching by discipline. Students compliant. Following orders.

The same is true of school and district leaders. They have come to know school as it has been. They did not grow up in the kinds of innovative schools as showcased in this book. As an educator rising up through the ranks, one has become familiar with how school has always been done. One feels safe in expecting they will be shepherding youth and adults in the same way as they had experienced before.

These new ideals and practices will likely cause discomfort to both new and veteran educators, as these are new waters. Being asked to do, if not lead, new endeavors ever before experienced, let alone practiced, could make anyone a bit anxious, particularly if it comes after doing something the same for years.

Dozens of books and articles have been written about the "human side" of change,[30] and why humans are often resistant to it. But with the need to move forward and not hold on to the old, leaders and communities need to figure out how to support one another in trying and getting better at something new.

What we Need

Giving two or more highly creative, innovative, learner-centered educators the runway to create and pursue a new school design

As I shared earlier, most of the most amazing models of schooling were started by two or more highly creative, innovative, learner-centered educators. I'm hesitant to say this because I am wary of criticism on pointing this fact out. But if we are to learn from the past, we must look at it with eyes wide open and not hope for it to be different than it is. In reality, when you look at the best new school designs, it is the result of 2-4 individuals with a shared vision for what is possible and a determination to manifest that idea by taking advantage of a local opportunity to manifest the idea.

There are several of these examples, and I will detail now just a few:[31]

Rob Riordan & Larry Rosenstock of High Tech High (in San Diego)

Dennis Littky & Elliot Washor of the Big Picture Schools (first in Providence RI and now across the Country)

Jon Ketler & colleagues of SOTA, SAMI, and IDEA (in Tacoma WA)

Olympic High School and now Palisades High School (in Charlotte NC)

Design 39 (in San Diego)

Iowa BIG (in Cedar Rapids IA)

The Blue Valley Center for Professional Studies (in Overland Park KS, and now beyond)

Charlotte Lab School (Charlotte NC)

Note that these startups and schools of innovation are across the country!

Story 1: The Start of High Tech High. As shared earlier in the book, Larry Rosenstock and Rob Riordan's idea for a school, joining "hands and minds," was readily dismissed by the Cambridge high school faculty, school, and district leadership ("No, we don't want to do that."). It is quite amazing then that Larry, through a serendipitous series of events and people he met, was able to co-found the school with Rob in San Diego.

Following his time at Cambridge Rindge & Latin with Rob in the late 1990s, Larry become involved in the New Urban High School project, a joint initiative of the Annenberg Foundation and the Corporation for National Service to create a network of innovative urban high schools, wherein he began to sharpen his ideas for a new school, including the value of interdisciplinary project-based learning and community partnerships.

From there, through a chance meeting where Larry was describing what high school could be in San Diego, Sol Price asked Larry, "How much you make." In reply, Sol said, "You don't make enough. See me in my office on Monday."

Sol offered Larry the position of Executive Director for his charitable foundation, where he began to engage with several community organizations and interested parties on issues of affordable housing, economic and community development, and initiatives to promote social and economic mobility in underserved communities in San Diego. Through that work, Larry ended up talking with the San Diego business roundtable about how school could benefit youth for their future. Upon hearing this, they immediately turned to Larry and told him, "We want that school." Larry decided to pursue the opportunity, which allowed him to manifest all of the ideas he had been thinking about for years, partially facilitated by Irwin Jacobs, the co-founder of Qualcomm, providing $2 million dollars to the start-up of the school, the availability of a recently vacated warehouse where Larry envisioned the school could start, and the potential of bringing his dream team together. – those he had worked closely with in the past, including Rob.

The point of this story is that when you dig into the back story of how these schools started, they were started by one or more educators with a vision for a new school that clearly addressed an identified need, and then a series of opportunistic and serendipitous connections and events, sometimes purposefully pursued, that resulted in the manifestation of the school.

Such as Larry taking the position of directing Sol Price's charitable foundation the result of a chance meeting, which then led Larry to talking to members of the San Diego Business Roundtable about the idea for a school, whereupon hearing his inspiring vision, the business leaders said, "We want that school here!" (unlike the Cambridge faculty and leaders before), who had been bemoaning the state of education in their local school system. They wanted youth who were self-directed, problem solvers, good communicators – the kind that Larry was speaking to. With that, members of the roundtable supported Larry and Rob to create High Tech High. With significant funding from the co-founder of Qualcomm, they started the school which has since grown into a network of 16 elementary, middle, and charter high schools throughout the San Diego area which have gained worldwide recognition for excellence and their model of "schooling."

In so many ways, the story is both crazy and amazing. The runway for getting the school of the ground was created by virtue of a series of serendipitous events and connections, eventually landing with the business roundtable's political, social, and financial interest in supporting the start-up of the school. Without this, Larry, with Rob and others, would not have been able to create anything. But serendipity here met vision with resources and creativity with political and social support. Should we have to rely on such serendipitous events for us to have schools that serve our students well across the country? Yes, maybe serendipity has a role in some small or large way in any truly creative activity. We shouldn't have to cross our fingers for such serendipitous and opportunistic events to take place with a select few to have schools across the country that serve our youth better. There must be some ways we could redesign our public eco-system so these acts of creativity happen far more often and resources could support the start-up of these schools that serve our youth and communities far better.

Story 2: The Start of Big Picture. That story is not so different from when Dennis Littky and Elliot Washor saw the opportunity to potentially start the school of their dreams. In 1994, the Commissioner of Education in Rhode Island, bemoaning the Providence School's offerings to all students, wanted to start a vocational school. A request for proposals was sent out, and being opportunistic, Dennis and Elliot met the Governor and Commissioner (Peter McWalters) but told them both that they had an idea for a school, but it wasn't the typical vocational school they probably had in mind. Rather than being funneled into particular vocational tracks, such as culinary, automotive, or construction, students would be asked what they were interested in and then they would help the student find someone in the community doing that work and arrange for them to work with them. In addition, they would work closely with the families to create a system of support to ensure each learner's success.

Upon hearing their design, the Commissioner and Governor also said, we want that school! And with that, Dennis and Elliot were given the opportunity to create their own school. Even better, they were able to be a district unto themselves, with no direct oversight except by the Commissioner himself.

That kind of autonomy can go a long way. And the rest is history. Out of the four original schools they started in Providence (known as the original Met) has now grown into a network of over 80 Big Picture Schools across the United States, and another 100+ around the world.

Story 3. SOTA, then SAMI, then IDEA. As detailed earlier, in the early 2000s, Jon Ketler was an art teacher in one of Tacoma's comprehensive high schools doing what he loved to do, engaging kids in art. But as he thought about what he was doing and kids at the school, no less any school in Tacoma, no less most schools across the country, Jon began to think that what would be better for kids who had any interest in art was to actually work side-by-side with artists.

Jon, being Jon, had many connections with artists and art institutions and organizations around the city. Artists that had their own studios. Organizations such as the Chihuly Glass Museum (a world-renowned glass blower from Tacoma) and the Tacoma Art Museum, etc. As he thought about it, he wondered if kids, rather than working with him for 45-60 minutes per day in his classroom in the school, could in fact work with some of these artists and organizations throughout the day and get involved in creating original pieces of art under the guidance, tutelage, and mentorship of these artists.

Fast forward. A year later, SOTA (the Tacoma School of the Arts), became a reality in a building situated downtown in proximity to the artists, art institutions, and facilities students could work with and within. Of course, it was helpful that the Gates Foundation, having gotten wind of Jon's idea, decided to help by giving Jon $500,000 to get it off the ground. Still, it was Jon's idea with the support of many others in the community that galvanized the possibility of becoming a reality, and the support of the district to give him a chance to materialize his vision.

Eight years later, and with SOTA a success, Jon and his colleagues then proposed a Science and Math Institute (SAMI), which they opened with four portables in the middle of the largest city park in WA state, surrounded by the beautiful Puget Sound. Then seven years later, they started the School of Industrial Design, Engineering, and Arts (IDEA), right smack dab in the middle of a residential neighborhood where they invited city partners to cohabit, so students could make use of the partnerships for learning too.

With Jon and his colleagues' success in starting these innovative, learner-centered, project-driven and community-immersive schools, Jon was given the freedom to start and grow these new schools.

Story 4. Olympic High School. In 2005, a North Carolina judge laid down a stark and strong ruling against eight of the state's largest high schools: they had committed "academic genocide." The 45-page report detailed how these high schools, and consequently their districts, were egregiously negligent of providing their youth with an appropriate education. One of those high schools was Olympic High School, in the Southeast corner of Charlotte.

Fast forward 17 years, and Olympic High School – against a multitude of measures – is one of the best high schools in the country. And, indeed, one of my favorites.

How so?

Serving approximately 2,500 students today, each student chooses amongst 5 different career academies – Engineering & Advanced Manufacturing, Finance & Business Ownership, Health Sciences, Hospitality & Tourism and Information Technology. From the get-go, students are trained in interpersonal skills, undertake an interest inventory, and participate in a "living your best life" curriculum, borrowing from Stanford University. Beyond that, and as a result of the hard work of Mike Realon and the rest of the staff, Olympic has cultivated over 700 industry partnerships, and students are interning throughout their time at Olympic, with some juniors and seniors making as much as $15/hour in their internships.

Beyond that – and this is what makes Olympic one of my favorite schools in the US – Olympic has cultivated relationships with industry partners that become a pipeline for students' gainful employment. Gainful not only in the sense that students are able to sustain themselves financially, but also in the sense that students are choosing to pursue potential career pathways in fields of work they really enjoy. From the get-go, students are given the opportunity to explore different vocational possibilities but the industry partners are also able to invest in those who may very well end up joining them as employees.

On a recent visit, I met two graduates who had interned at Groninger while at Olympic, and subsequently were offered, and gladly accepted, apprenticeships at Groninger, providing them with a $40,000/year salary inclusive of 3 weeks' vacation, health, and dental. And if they should wish, would be paid to attend community college.

There are thousands of these stories, which are even more noteworthy when one realizes that the majority of the families of students attending Olympic are making a living below the poverty line. Hence, many of the youth graduating from Olympic are making twice what their families are making upon graduation and in many cases five times as much as their families within 10 years.

Then again, how did they get to where they are? Supported by a Gates Small Schools Grant shortly after the ruling, and then partnering with the then National Academy Foundation (now NAF) to break into 5 career academies, and then hiring Mike Realon as community partnership coordinator, the school was able to turn the corner towards what it is today.

Again, certain resources and relationships came together, in what I have called "a perfect storm,"[32] into the beginnings of what it is today. The support systems and individuals involved were given the opportunity to re-vision the school which has resulted in what it is today, accelerated in response to the courts' appraisal that the school and district were committing "academic genocide."[33]

Story 5. Iowa BIG. As shared earlier, Iowa BIG in many ways grew right out of the very unfortunate washout of Cedar Rapids (IA) in June 2008. On June 13, the city fell victim to a flood the size of which it had never seen before, with the Cedar River reaching a record of 30 feet, 18 feet above flood level. Ten square miles of the downtown and surrounding neighborhoods were flooded, with 7,749 properties severely damaged and 1,300 eventually demolished.

As the town (citizens, industry, and city leaders) took stock of the damage and began to consider how to rebuild, some began to ask if they should only be thinking of rebuilding to resurrect what they had in the past or should also begin thinking about what else they should consider for the city's future. While the city had done well in terms of the meat and grain industries of the 1900s, the world was changing and new commerce and industries were beginning to thrive elsewhere. The city, however, hadn't done a lot to proactively support and foster the growth of new 21st century work. With that, the city turned to finding ways to support new entrepreneurial activity and the support of new industries in the city. Alongside this effort, some began to ask if the city's education system couldn't also involve a significant transformation moving forward as well.

Long story short, out of this event came a sequence of conversations and relationships that resulted in the convergence of many individuals in an effort to rethink school in such a way that resulted in the start of Iowa BIG. Trace Pickering, a long-time educator and district leader had for years been questioning the status quo of schooling, always attempting to give voice to policies and practices that put students at the center. So when Chuck Peters, a prominent media, industry, and city leader, had seen the need to not only focus on the potential reimagination of the city's industry, he also asked the question of whether the same should be true of its education system. With this burning question, upon meeting Trace, and fed by Trace's written commentary on the failure of the Governor's recent pitches to improve education, Chuck asked if he would take the position of a community builder, engaging the community in rethinking education.

Fast forward, Trace serendipitously met Shawn Cornally, who, as a young classroom STEM educator, had been bemoaning the state of affairs in education through his highly popular blog. In seeing resonance in one another's concerns, the two decided to do the community building together.

They tried a number of different things-- from hosting coffees to Trace paying for dinners-- in order to bring community members together to share their perspectives on the need to reimagine education in Cedar Rapids.

Nothing really stuck however until Shawn, after one such event, simply blurted, "We need to do a Billy Madison Project." Of course, if you haven't seen Billy Madison, the reference is lost on you. But in Adam Sandler's movie, Billy Madison goes back to high school and does what he needs to do to check all the boxes to graduate. Well, upon really thinking it through, Trace and Shawn ended up inviting the community to "go back to high school" for a day to truly experience what school is like today.

To their delight, 60 community members responded, and with that, they were able to organize all 60 to attend high school for a day.

As detailed earlier, the result was transformative. When the participants came together to discuss what they observed and had experienced and juxtaposed that against what they would hope high school would be – encouraging and assisting students to do in the world we are in now and in the future – they were troubled and concerned. They saw kids going through the motions, complying with the schedule and curriculum, but not truly engaged in learning that could benefit them for their futures.

Still, the awakening did not immediately result in any significant changes and so Trace and Shawn finally decided they would just "do it," and start their own version of a school as a paid summer program, which Chuck was more than happy to support. Funny thing is, Chuck happened to know the chair of the of the local School Board and mentioned it to her, whereupon she immediately called them to her office.

As told by Shawn and Trace, they both ended up going into Mary Meisterling's office feeling as if they had been called into the Principal's office.[34] Mary shared that she had heard they were going to start a school (private, she thought), and basically said: I don't want you to start this school outside of our system. We want that school in our district. And not only did Mary want Trace and Shawn to open the school in the Cedar Rapids District for the students of Cedar Rapids, but she wanted to make it available to students in the adjoining district as well, for which she had already spoke to the chair of that school committee. In disbelief, both Trace and Shawn were at first dumbfounded (self-reported). But within 3 days they had come from *how* will we start this school to *now we have to start this school.*

That fall, 12 students enrolled and then they too became the central cheerleaders of the school.

It wasn't designed around a 7-period schedule. It was about kids in teams working together on authentic projects offered by the community (think industry partners, non-profits, govt. agencies, and religious institutions) and kids problem-solving, collaborating, and providing solutions to challenges provided by the partners. And getting credit based on their work. Not tests. Not papers. But based on their performance.

Eight years later, Iowa BIG has grown. Iowa BIG serves youth choosing to participate full or part-time from five districts. Students continue to work on real-world projects and problems. And where before Iowa BIG staff and students often had to reach out to the community for projects to be undertaken, now at the beginning of the year the community comes and pitches projects to the kids. Not science fair type projects where the outcome is a posterboard, but projects that serve community partners with real-world needs. Like redesigning a warehouse to be far more efficient. Or developing a downtown apple orchard so that families can have access to fresh fruit. Or creating and running a mini shark tank for middle school girls so that they could get the experience of being young entrepreneurs.

Iowa BIG is VERY different. Kids aren't learning sitting class after class artificially divided into science, math, English, and history. Kids are developing real-world solutions to real-world problems. And in doing so, youth are learning how to be problem-solvers, collaborators, critical thinkers, and good communicators.

Once again, we have the story of two individuals who were compelled to change the system and wanted to start a new opportunity for youth. And through a serendipitous series of events and relationships were afforded the opportunity ... to make it happen!

Story 6. Design 39. This is the story of a Superintendent who empowered a district leader with a small group of educators to "reimagine" what is possible. And to do so not just out of their heads, but to be inspired about what is possible by visiting other schools, schools pursuing their own creative models of teaching, learning, and schooling. From there, they engaged in a process of design thinking,[35] bringing select other educators in from both outside the district and within the district to build the idea.[36]

A year later, they were off the ground! Pods of 150 students work with 5-6 educators designing what they want to learn and how they

Design 39 Guiding Principles

 Design Thinking is a creative, problem-solving process which helps people design meaningful solutions.

 Inquiry helps to clarify an issue & probe deeper to understand why things work the way they do.

 Connecting Globally emphasizes the need for leadership, ethics, cultural competence, and personal responsibility in a global world.

 Growth Mindset springs from the belief that everyone can learn, grow, and become more intelligent.

 Personalization allows each learner the freedom to progress forward at their own rate, and in ways that they learn best, as they pursue their passions and prepare for their future.

 Communication & Collaboration is the cornerstone to successful working teams.

 Creativity and imagination are our most powerful tools as humans.

 Technology is leveraged to create content, communicate voice, publish work, and connect globally with people from around the world.

The Designing Design 39 Learning Experiences Framework

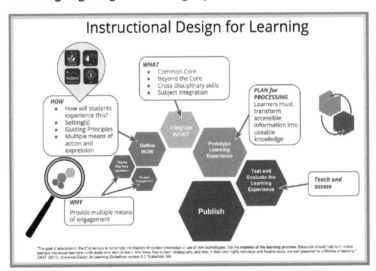

want to go about learning it. Choosing the "deep dives" of inquiry and learning they wish to engage in, students are empowered to choose what they want to learn, how they want to learn it, and all with the educators helping them to design their learning experiences.

At Design39, learner- and competency-driven learning is guided by design thinking and informed by critical thinking along with

The Design 39 Shifts: From Compliance to Innovation

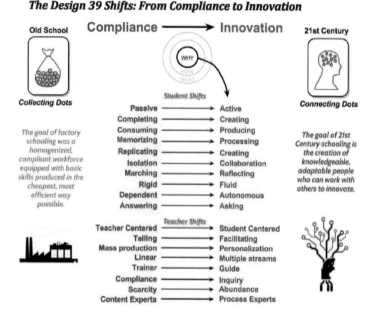

collaboration. With this focus at the heart of Design39, the school's design itself is the result of design thinking. So kids are not trapped in generic subject matter classes rotating through a 45-minute rotation of subject learning. Rather, the focus is on the projects and the structures and use of resources and time that support design thinking activities, making the school stand out as a very unusual school on the cutting edge of where most schools should be. Not singularly focused on having their students score well on their state's standardized test scores, but actively baking their aspirations of student learning into the day-to-day practices and pedagogy of the school.

To build the design, the superintendent gave the design team free reign to visit other schools across the country that would "feed their imagination," as I like to say. They visited over 40 schools (amazing, really, no?), such as The Neuva School in Hillsborough CA, The

Story 7. The CAPS Network. Way back in 2005, Superintendent Trigg in the Blue Valley School District, just outside Kansas City on the Kansas side, wanted to engage youth in more community-embedded, student-centered, engaging projects. He wasn't sure what this would look like, but he knew he didn't want kids to just go through the typical motions of school. So, he assembled a design team of eight educators and director Mike Slagle – a district administrator who had a background in civic engagement, industry partnerships, and community building – to lead the initiative.

Interestingly, when they arrived back from visiting the schools they thought would give them a vision of what they wanted to do, they informed the Superintendent that they really didn't find anything as he had imagined. They didn't find students involved in real-world projects of genuine interest to the students and connected to industry.

To test the waters, Mike pulled together a draft model of what the program could look like and hired a focus group organization to ask parents whether they would want such a program for their kids. Upon reviewing the report, the focus group organization detailed that the parents really didn't like the idea. So, Mike reported this to the Superintendent, who then accepted the outcome and directed Mike to prepare it to give to the School Committee – the bad news.

So Mike took the report back to his office, feeling extremely disappointed, not just in what the report had said but in letting Tom and his vision down. A funny thing happened, however. As it is with such stories, Mike began to review the questions asked by the focus group partner one more time and then begin to question whether they were the right questions. As he considered them, he started to think they were not the right questions. That in fact the focus group facilitators really hadn't shared the true vision, and so were not able to harness the community's response.

So a half hour later, Mike returned to Tom's office and reported: I don't think we asked the right questions. He broached the idea of hiring a new group to run the sessions with a new set of questions more in keeping with the vision.

Lo and behold: the response to the second set of focus groups was overwhelmingly positive. And, with that, Tom presented to the board a vision for creating a new facility where students would gain the kinds of skills that could lead them to their professional success. Upon hearing the news, the Board directed Tom not to wait to start the program until after completion of the building in a year– but to get it up and running next fall. Turns out, many of the school board members had children who had graduated from the Blue Valley schools and were lacking the skills needed to pursue employment out of college. So they loved the idea of a profession-based learning program.

The rest is history. Because the building was not open yet, students ended up having to engage in their profession-based work on location, in the buildings of their partners. Which in hindsight turned about to be a great accident, because then the students were able to learn from within and see day-to-day firsthand the work they were studying.

When word got out, more and more students wanted to partake of the program. And from there the CAPS program was up and running.

Story 8. The Charlotte Lab School. The Charlotte Lab School was co-founded by Mary Moss and Vikki-Rose Turner in 2015 primarily motivated by Mary's desire for her 5-year-old daughter to have a different experience in school than the one she was having (a lot of rote memorization and worksheets). It turns out, not only was Mary highly motivated to pursue a new possibility for her daughter, she also had a wealth of experience helping to start innovative schools, such as New York City's iSchool,[37] which received a great deal of local and national attention when it opened in 2008, as it was uniquely focused on real-world, collaborative, project-based learning.

Following her move to Charlotte, Mary became a principal coach in the Charlotte-Mecklenburg School District (one of largest in the US, with approximately 147,000 students), wanting to see if she could have an impact in local education through this position. During this time, she developed a relationship with Vikki Tunick, who was also doing some exceptional work as a curriculum coordinator in a neighboring school district, while also working to get her principal's license. After a year of doing some work together, Vikki off handedly asked, "Hey, do you know of any schools that might be interested in hiring me as an Assistant Principal?" That's when it hit Mary. (Serendipity strikes again!)

This was when Mary was bemoaning the experience her daughter was having in school, leaving her to wonder if she could open her own school. But while Mary had a lot of experience in designing, starting, and running high schools, she did not have the same experience with elementary schools. But, guess what – Vikki did. And Vikki was someone she had grown to trust and align herself with as a result of a shared belief in good instruction and affinity to real-world, interdisciplinary learning.

Voila! Here was opportunity again. So Mary asked: "What do you think about starting a school?"

Now there are several ways one can go about starting your own school *outside* the local public system. One, you can start your own private school. But in this case, families have to pay for it, which Is not necessarily doable by all families. Two, you can create a non-profit and run a school, with the potential of some philanthropic funding (but hard to get and sustain). Or three, you can start a charter school (which can also be done as a non-profit) but with the advantage of receiving state monies per-pupil. However, starting a charter school requires a great deal of work. Each state has its own process, but similar to other states, in North Carolina you have to provide evidence of a need for the school, pursue a facility, create a board, develop a curricular and instructional plan, etc.   Then depending on if you are a state charter school or district charter school, you must present your application to either the state charter school board or sponsoring district and defend the application.

Not that all of this activity isn't necessary to start a school. But this means that if a parent wants to send their son or daughter to another school because the local school is not serving their child well, they either have to move (which is actually the way many families, with means, do take advantage of school choice) or are beholden to the offering provided by the district whether or not they feel it is serving their child well. Or if you have the wherewithal (energy, time, and commitment), pursue starting a charter school. That is if you want to tap public monies to serve your child and other families in the community.

Then there is the issue of caps on charters. Each state allows for only a certain number of charter schools (hence the term, the number is "capped"), and it just so happens that the year Mary and Vikki were considering starting their school, the state had just increased their cap, meaning now they could pursue opening their their own school.

The point of this story is to show what it takes to pursue an alternative to what your local district provides you.   It means moving, if the district doesn't offer any alternatives. Or it means sending your kid to a private school. Or it means opening your own charter school, not something the average parent either has the time or expertise to do.

Fast forward from its inception as an elementary school in 2015, the Charlotte Lab School has grown into a K-12 vibrant, progressive beacon for what school could be. Mary and Vikki's vision took hold, and others, like Ricky Singh and Shane Capps, decided to jump on and contribute to its design, growing from a K-5 school, to middle school, to its second year as a high school.

The focus of the school is interdisciplinary, project-based learning, with attention to critical thinking, collaboration, social justice, communication, innovation and community. They do this through "quests," a short or long-term pursuit of a real-world project with a driving question addressing a community need. Through these projects teachers integrate lessons related to the typical disciplines (science, math, ELA, and social studies), but knowledge and know-how in these disciplines comes through meaningful and purposeful activity within the Quest.

Taking Stock of Where we are At

The schools highlighted above and the stories of their start-up gives us a glimpse at what is possible. Indeed, there are hundreds of stories of such innovations – big and small – across the country. There are just not enough – at least at scale.

Every time I take a Lyft to or from the airport, nine out of ten times the Lyft driver asks, "So what do you do?" Eventually we talk about how I am doing what I can to help others see that we don't have to do school as we have been doing it. Then I ask about their high school experience. And this is typically where things go south. To date, I have heard dozens of stories, not only about the drivers' experiences, but their siblings' and cousins' too.

In a nutshell, they don't feel that the school served them well, except as a place to see their friends and maybe do sports. Then when I share with them some of the schools I know, where kids are exploring their interests, doing things in the "real world," doing internships and apprenticeships, they are amazed that such places exist. Each ends up asking: "Why wasn't my school like that?"

Indeed.

As many of my colleagues have pointed out, it's not true that all schools operate as factories. Or have kids doing rote work and menial worksheets. In education, there are thousands of public elementary, middle, and high schools doing some exceptional work, working diligently with a commitment to all of their students employing some of the more recent strategies and practices to support student learning.

Yes, school has changed a lot from the past (see picture below), with more active, learner-centered practices from the past. There is more attention to student-activity, Q&A, classroom discussions, student projects and collaboration. Many younger grade classrooms have a classroom meeting space on a rug or carpet at the front of the room for morning check-ins and small group instruction. Desks are arranged in small groups. More posters and motivational sayings and pictures of scientists, writers, and contributors to our society representative of our diverse population are more evident, as are workspaces, writing centers, and learning spaces.

You see this less so in the later elementary grades, and less so in middle and high school. Yet the spaces and schedules of middle and high schools do tend to dictate how the school operates – with kids moving from one classroom to another with a single (perhaps two) teachers teaching in a discipline – the usual: science, math literacy and social studies. The spaces for kids to "do their work" and engage in their learning are not as conducive to collaboration with flexible meeting spaces and meeting rooms as they could be. Of course, as youth get older, we should be facilitating their learning out in the world and not within the confines of the brick-and-mortar buildings we have constructed. Instead, we should be building their skills to engage in their own learning – take learning into their own hands and be self-directed in their efforts. Ultimately, they should be the ones to design and pursue their own learning based on personal interests and goals as they launch into the world.

So as much as we can applaud those educators, schools, and school systems doing what they can to redesign the teaching and learning that goes on in their classrooms and schools, it must be noted that many of these pursuits are still not practiced across all schools. And we still have a long way to go.

The examples above give us a glimpse of what is possible. The educators starting the schools portrayed above saw a need to do school differently and then found a way to do so. The purpose of this book is to show how far we still have to go. Even though we have made some headway, the possibilities are growing as more and more educators (teachers, school leaders, district leaders, non-profits, for-profits, community members, potential industry partners, and parents) create new tools, platforms, and opportunities for learning. The question is whether the design, funding, and policy environment of our current public school ecosystem can shift fast enough to keep up with the array of new possibilities. Which is the second purpose of this book, to clearly show in what ways our current public school ecosystem is constraining the pursuit of new possibilities and offer ways funding and policies could be implemented to far better incentivize and support the flourishing of new possibilities for all youth across the country.

This is not to say that there are not ways that the federal government, state agencies, and local communities have not created some mechanisms to support innovation and the scaling of innovative practices (some of which are referenced in the next chapter). But in reality these mechanisms (funding, policies, and district press) are not effectively incentivizing and supporting the pursuit and adoption of new possibilities fast enough. So for the greater majority of youth, families, and educators, schools as we have known them to continue to unfold as they have for decades, and by all the traditional means I have pointed out before (such as siloed learning, credits and graduation based on seat time, and learning that is not grounded in student interests, the development of competencies or real world utility).

Indeed, there are an ever-growing array of alternative learning opportunities for youth across the country. Some in our public school systems and beyond that a great many that are growing but require parents to pay for. Which is another thorn and again points to the limitations of our current funding and policy system supporting learning for youth and options for families. In short, if these other alternatives are serving youth better and are desired by families, why is it that they should have to pay for these alternatives instead of being able to access them through the public school system.

As a good friend of mine says, "It's not always that teachers don't want to pursue new ways of teaching and learning, but it is the infrastructure of schools along with school leadership and the expectations of the district that get in the way." And as another one of my principal friends says, "We could rock what we do along the lines you prescribe, but the state is doubling down on its expectations of state mandated curriculum that is getting in the way."

And there you have it. So ... in sum, there are other possibilities. We don't need to do school as it always has been done, or close to it. There are others out there in the world who have reimagined what is possible, and beyond that, have been able to take their imagining into reality. We can learn from them, not only in ways to do school differently (including the purpose of learning and how we can learn) but *how* to get these schools and other learning opportunities for all youth off the ground.

Easy? No. Worth it? Yes!

It took all kinds of persistence and connections and imagination and entrepreneurial fire to get these places up and running. Again, easy? No. Worth it? Yes!

In the next set of chapters, we will focus on what could be done and by whom to make new, learner-centered, future-focused schools a reality.

– 6 –
How it Could Happen

Insights Gained about How Innovation could be Catalyzed and Scaled

Let Innovators ... Innovate. The first thing that becomes apparent to me as I listen to and reflect on all of these stories of innovation is the central importance of empowering a small group of educators passionate about a vision to manifest that vision. And support them in realizing the vision.

Who these individuals are plays no small part. These educators were and are mavericks. They don't wish to abide by the status quo. Or continue to play under the rules that limit the possibilities of giving their youth agency and possibility. From Dennis Littky and Elliot Washor, to Jon Ketler and partners, Trace Pickering and Shawn Cornally, and Larry Rosenstock and Rob Riordan. In every case, each educator had been thinking for a long time about what could be rather than simply accepting what was. And their consternation with the current system spurred them to reimagine the possibilities and propose new designs.

However, while each of these educators may have had glorious ideas of what could be, the ideas would have remained mere ideas without an opportunity to plant the seed of these ideas in a garden of possibility made possible by others who could manage the social and political context and financial support needed to grow the idea. It is the offering of a place to grow the idea, with the social, political, and economic support of others, that creates the space for these ideas to take seed and grow.

The San Diego Business Roundtable and Qualcomm co-founder Irwin Jacobs offered Larry and his colleagues the financial support to put the idea onto paper and submit it as a charter school application made the difference in San Diego. But it was also the social backing of the Roundtable that laid the groundwork for its start. So too of Iowa BIG, where and when Chuck Peters, the owner of the local newspaper, gave Trace and Shawn the runway to put their ideas into action, followed immediately by the chairs of two local school boards telling them both that they wanted the school to be a part of their districts – not separate. So too of Jon Ketler, who gained the support of the district to start his new school (SOTA) with the financial and ideological backing of the Gates Foundation, making all the difference.

Again and again, through each of these stories, we see highly innovative educators being given the opportunity to make their dreams a reality as a result of a seemingly lucky confluence of social, political, and economic support.

Gratefully, these educators have been able to plant and grow their idea in a context which was supported by district leadership (e.g., the Tacoma Schools and Design 39) or external partners that supported them to grow as a Charter School (e.g., High Tech High) or, as is the case of Iowa BIG, school board leadership. More often than not however, new ideas are not as readily accepted or supported in the context of districts concerned with creating options or new models that may make them vulnerable to criticism. It is in these cases where individuals (whether they be educators, parents, or others) need to pursue their innovations *outside* the local public ecosystem. In the case of charter schools, this then requires jumping through a number of state-mandated hoops for authorization, or if pursued within a district, often is met with a great deal opposition as well, even when a state mandates they must be supportive of such an application.

Examples of the challenges to starting a charter school are rampant across communities. The start-up of the City Neighbors School in Baltimore is just such an example. When Bobbi Macdonald and friends decided to pursue their charter school – now well-recognized for its learner-centered, progressive practices – the district (district leadership and the school committee) made it extremely difficult to get their school off the ground, citing such issues as attaining a building, staffing, curriculum and instruction, when in reality they just didn't want an alternative learning environment to made available within their system for fear of how their stakeholders may view that opportunity against the options they were providing in their own schools. This despite the fact that state law directed all districts to effectively support the growth of charters in their districts.

On the other hand, some districts have been more proactive in supporting the start-up and proliferation of charter schools, such as the Denver Public Schools which has embraced growing a "portfolio" of educational options in the district, and the Minneapolis and Indianapolis Public Schools, whose focus has been serving their youth with multiple options a well as growing new practices.

Having said this, just because it is a charter school does not mean it will be an exemplary, learner-centered school effectively supporting the development of their students. In which case, districts (and the state) should be pursuing mechanisms to ensure that those starting the schools are founding the school with a vision and capacity to lead the school towards aims that benefit their students, their families, and the community.

Nonetheless, I argue it would be far more desirable to unleash the creativity of educators and other stakeholders to create and when successful grow their school models, learning opportunities, tools, and platforms throughout their district if not beyond it.

The CAPS network is an excellent example of this wherein the district actively supported the development of the CAPS program within the school system (the Blue Valley Public Schools) and, with much success and interest on the part of other systems across the country, developed their own non-profit to assist and support the development of such programs across the country, which now number of 100 affiliates and 3 continents.

Unfortunately, there are also many educators and other stakeholders who have an idea in mind for starting a school, a program, a platform, or an array of tools that support student learning they recognize will be difficult to start within the public school ecosystem so have created their own endeavor privately, such as the Acton Schools, Prenda microschools, or Thrively platform.

This is the dilemma: If as a society we are keen in investing in education for all, why are we creating systems where some educators and then the families of youth have to use their own mone to afford the education they believe, and want, their youth to have?

Support Communities of Innovation. Once seeds of innovation take root, leaders from within and the people and systems from outside the system need to find a way to continue supporting these communities, in such a way that they can grow. Upon having a fresh start and getting underway, no matter how small – Iowa BIG started with 12 students, SOTA with 20, and the original CAPS program in Blue Valley 100 – the schools and programs grew through word of mouth, and the "cheerleading" of its founding students.

Still, growth is hard. Starting with four portables near the Point Defiance trailer parking lot, the Science and Math Institute in

Tacoma eventually grew and eventually was able to open its own award-winning eco-friendly learning facility right next to the Point Defiance Zoo and Aquarium as a result of a passing bond in 2015. Iowa BIG went from 12 students to over 250. And the CAPS program in 2009 from 100 to its current enrollment of over 900, in a building also built for the diverse ways students can learn within it. Large meeting spaces, lots of workshop space, many areas for students to study and learn on their own.

Starting in 2015, more and more districts came to see what was going on at CAPS, drawn by a reputation quickly growing. Kids were engaged. Gaining the skills that would benefit them in college and work. Harnessing their interests and passions. Learning with cool faculty and gaining guidance through real-world work and internships.

As a result of the plethora of school visits, more and more districts wanted support in growing their own CAPS program. With an intrinsic desire to support anyone and everyone that wanted to grow their own version of CAPS, CAPS leadership decided to begin formally organizing much of their work and resources in support of what they called affiliates. Not like a "my way or the highway mentality." But in gladly sharing their practices and eventually three playbooks that any district could adopt. Moreover, they recognized that the power of their effort would be even that much more powerful if the network was harnessed and any individual or group needing assistance could get it.

From there, the CAPS Network has grown. To over 100 affiliates today. A monthly gathering of CAPS leaders from across the country to problem-solve around any needs. Three playbooks. And their "Summer Huddle," a gathering of CAPS affiliates across the country, where they share strategies and practices, and think about next steps.

Pursue new Aims of Education.   Another fundamental consideration when pursuing a new design for teaching, learning, and schooling is the reassessment of the purpose of education. Right now, everyone continues to pursue those aims arrived at decades ago, despite our further understanding of what it takes to be successful today. Reading, writing, and arithmetic have ruled the day for decades (the 3Rs). Then individuals thought everyone needed to know our history. And then civics. And then at first rudimentary science which later spilled into the current three areas typically taught in high school: biology, physics, and chemistry. Then for the erudite, a foreign language should be thrown into the mix. And math was then chopped into the four subjects it is today:

algebra, geometry, algebra 2 (at a minimum). Calculus if you were so academically inclined.

Take note how silly this is, this bifurcation of knowledge and skills into these siloed domains of knowledge that have very little real connection to students' future. Yes, we want everyone to be able to read and write. To know basic math. It certainly is helpful to have some foundational understanding of certain science topics: ecosystems and human systems; molecules and matter. And social studies and civics: some history and the fundamentals of government, our government, and human rights.

Most of the good stuff, however, gets lost in schools as information to be memorized, regurgitated, and used for the sake of getting by. Passing the class. Graduating from school.

While Dewey may have coined the need for "critical thinking" way back in 1910 and some have pursued since, the teaching of critical thinking didn't really take a strong hold in public education until the mid-1980s, ramping up quite a bit in the 90s. This foregrounded a continued questioning of what the aim of education should be, and this led to what many referresd to as the 21st century skills – such as collaboration, communication, problem-solving, critical thinking, and creativity. But for the most part these were referenced but rarely truly attended to in regular schooling. It was good talk. But in reality given loose reference and a minor nod to what was actually being taught. The practice of school did little to truly dig into and assist students in the development of these skills.

Enter stage right those schools that decided to go all in, from scratch, not only on the how of school but the what of school. Take One Stone's "Bold Learning Objectives," for example:

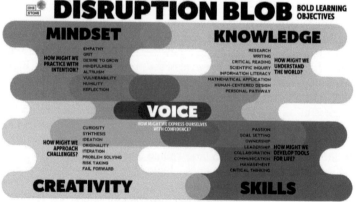

Note how Mindset and Creativity are positioned up front. Knowledge and Skills are also a big part of their Aim of Schooling. But Knowledge is not dissected down into extreme details that result in a student doing the best they can to memorize the information. Rather, they are performance-based. Not simply content but know-how. How to do research. Critically read. Use math. Critically assess information. Write well.

Note too how the skills are efficacy-oriented. How to pursue a passion. Set goals. Lead. Communicate. And then collaborate, communicate, and critically think.

The difference here is that the schools are in fact designed around their students gaining these mindsets and skills. The activities students are engaged in support the development of these skills and not the encyclopedic information typically relayed day-to-day in our schools.

Take, for example, the competencies of Building 21, [38] the brainchild of Laura Shibula and Chip Linehan coming out of the Harvard Educator Leadership program. They wanted to reimagine what school could be for the youth in Philly, and through their inquiry and numerous conversations with colleagues and others, arrived at their five core areas of competency.

Note that it is inclusive of Habits of Success, Wayfinding, and Personal Development, and once again not dissected into the domains of knowledge that lack direct utility unless you pursued certain careers (e.g., the sciences).

The CAPS program too, above and beyond their focus on profession-based learning (such as in the biosciences, entrepreneurship, education, or veterinary medicine, to name just a few) also took a stand on identifying some BOLD aims for learning in their program.

Below are five key guiding principles that unite, define, and guide the caps experience:

Profession-based Learning

Instructors develop real-world, project-based learning strategies through collaborations with business and community partners. These interactions enhance the learning experience, preparing students for college and career.

Responsiveness

CAPS supports high-skill, high-demand careers through ongoing innovation in curriculum development, programs and services based on local business and community needs.

Self-Discovery and Exploration

Students realize their strengths and passions by exploring and experiencing potential professions. This allows them to make informed decisions about their future, while learning to exhibit leadership.

Professional Skills Development

Unique experiences allow students to cultivate transformative professional skills such as understanding expectations, time management and other essential business values. These skills are critical to providing students a competitive advantage in their post-secondary education and professional careers.

Entrepreneurial Mindset

Instructors create an environment where creative thinking and problem solving is encouraged. An innovative culture is key to fostering entrepreneurial learning and design thinking.

Certainly, we can understand the interest in foregrounding professional skills development and profession-based learning. But Self-Discovery and Exploration, and Entrepreneurial Mindset goes above and beyond the specific knowledge and skills of profession-based learning.

This speaks to the need to reconsider the Aims of Education when rethinking, reconsidering, and redesigning or designing a new educational program. To break free of what has been handed down for decades. To expand one's thinking about what is truly of value for youth as they become young adults. And to redesign your school not in what it DOES but also what it VALUES – in terms of knowledge, skills, mindsets, and perspectives – that can more truly assist youth as they go forward.

Create New Metrics of Success. This is so important as many will use standard metrics to argue whether a school is, or is not, successful. And, unfortunately, one of the reasons we are in the mess we are in today is the result of the bipartisan decision to use standardized reading and math scores to measure the quality of schools.

The intention was to find a quick and dirty way to identify schools that were not educating youth well. And there are certainly many schools not doing that.

Unfortunately, the eager politicians and hopeful educators crafting the policy did not have the foresight to see the unfortunate consequences of the policy as designed. Supposedly, if a school was identified as underperforming, they would receive additional monies that could be used for additional tutoring and services for youth, and light a fire under the school to do better. Well, in most cases, this did not happen. The tutoring didn't help, and the schools did not know how to improve themselves.

What the policy did do is concern schools and their districts with the test scores of their students and in many cases responded in such a hyper-focused way that it really did more harm than good for students and their schools. Schools turned to double-dosing reading and math instruction, bought computer-based remediation programs, and in many ways simply sucked the life out of the potential joy of school.

The pressure to perform well on state tests for fear of being called out as underperforming basically refocused schools to the remediation of students, teachers, and principals at the expense of time and energy that could have been used toward creating enthusiastic and joyous communities of learning.

Unfortunately, this is one of the great hindrances to moving forward over the last 20 years. Billions of dollars and billions of hours and millions of adults spending their mental energy on raising the test scores on student reading, math, and a few other domains rather than focusing on the kinds of competencies and dispositions presented above. The ability to think well. Problem-solve. Create. Pursue interests. Find creative ways to engage youth in real-world problems and contexts. No less ... just focus on what fun, engaging, and enlivened classrooms could look and sound like.

This created an unnecessary and thwarting headwind to the direction we should be heading. Even the charter school movement, which was supposed to be a space where innovation and creativity could showcase possibilities and serve as potential models of excellence, has been significantly undermined by the narrow expectations of standardized testing.

It's a tragedy, really. Not only in how it has strangled the energy and attention educators could have given to these higher ideals, but also in how it has stalled the wider edification of these greater possibilities across educators, communities, and worse, parents and our youth.

An Inventory of Good Practices

So what could we have been working toward? And what have those who have pursued bigger and greater ideals created?

Here is where we are now.

> **An Inventory of Good Practices**
> **Learner-Centered**
> **Project-based**
> **Self-directed**
> **Competency-based**
> **Community-embedded**
> **Agency-oriented**

Learner-centered. First and foremost, central to any of this work should be the focus on the learner. Right now, our systems are focused on other things. The standards, the tests, keeping order in the building, ensuring that every kid is coming out with the required credits mandated by the state. In reality, our systems are NOT designed around each learner, except to identify the way in which he or she is deficient and how to remedy that.

Being learner-centered is not new.   Maria Montessori foregrounded this movement which paid particular attention to how youth could engage in their own learning through interaction with their environment, hands-on experiences, and interaction with their peers, resulting in the 15,000+ Montessori schools around the world today.[39]

In Reggio Emilia (Italy), Loris Malaguzzi started the first Reggio school when, in the midst of WWII, parents fought for their children to have school during a governmental closure of all public schools.[40] Despite the closures, the parents still wanted their children to have a place to connect and to learn. And the rest is history, as they say.

Endeavors such as these with the creative imagination of thoughtful educators has resulted over time into thousands of learner-centered schools and dozens of models of schooling paying attention to the learner, serving their needs and interests, and supporting their development as youth.

Some have worried that being learner-centered means being hands-off, with little direction or guidance by others. But this is far from the truth. Indeed, it puts the educator in a position of noticing and observing, taking note of the proclivities, interests, motivations, and abilities of the learner. But it then places the educator in a position of artfully providing and deftly assisting the student in their pursuit of the kinds of knowledge and skills, competencies, and dispositions, through various learning activities that support learning.

Finally, each of these communities is highly sensitive to WHO the learner is. Meaning, who is this person? What are they interested in? How do they learn best? How do they like to learn? What are their aspirations, and how do we afford them the learning experiences that will benefit them best? Even better, how do we help them design their own learning?

This is clearly borne out in the motto of the Big Picture Schools – "One Student at a Time." As well as the other schools mentioned in this book, for example, such as CAPS schools, Tacoma Schools, Highline Schools, and One Stone. It is manifested in how they work with each student in support of each student's individual interest – finding internships, working with community members, or engaging in a project that contributes to the local community (see Iowa BIG). The work, however, is always grounded in what the learner is interested in, wants to do, and what they want to be able to do.

This often entails helping each student to develop their own portfolio of learning. Presenting their learning to fellow students, staff, and parents. As well as having each student focus on their history and potential future. In the Big Picture Schools, for example, each student writes their own autobiography, as a means to reflect on their experiences and what has shaped who they are, if not gain some insight of who they want to become and how. At One Stone, students continually reflect on what experiences they want to have, to what end, and how it has or has not assisted their development of the Bold Learning Objectives (presented earlier).

All of these schools have their own way of being learner-centered. But it starts with caring who each child is and then assisting them to be reflective of what they are learning and how.

Project-based. This is the one practice that most likely all teachers and many parents have heard about over and over again. Having a meaningful, engaging project with some authentic outcome can make all the difference in focusing and motivating a student's learning. When there is a meaningful product or performance with an authentic purpose to the student, the framing goes a long way to creating purpose in the activities and subsequently students' learning Furthermore, an authentic project can ground students' acquisition of knowledge and skills in a context that assists them in being able to employ that knowledge and related skills in the world, atypical of the kind of learning that is the result of activities more in keeping with the banking model of teaching. For example, when students are given the opportunity to create a product or performance that has a real-world purpose, such as a presentation to a panel of community members, they are more likely to engage in the learning process and retain the knowledge and skills gained. Conversely, when students' role in the learning activity is to memorize content for the sake of passing a test or simply fulfilling a typical class assignment, little learning sticks and little learning that is actionable in real-world contexts takes place.

I don't need to go into much detail here as there are several other sources and resources that astutely and poignantly show how projects can drive learning. Moreover, what characteristics of project-based learning need to be in place for learning to happen. See, for example, the Buck Institute's Gold Standard for projects (www.pblworks.org/what-is-pbl/gold-standard-project-design) and the numerous examples evidenced at such schools as:

High Tech High (see https://changingthesubject.org)

One Stone (see https://onestone.org/about)

Iowa BIG (see https://iowabig.org/about-iowa-big)

EL Education (see https://eleducation.org/resources/ differentiated-projects-and-products-in-el-schools), and

Da Vinci Schools (see https://www.gettingsmart.com/2017/ 04/10/personalization-projects-deeper-learning-at-da-vinci) amongst many others.

When you look across the schools I have mentioned so far, you can bet that much of the learning revolves around students' engagement in projects. And the more authentic and meaningful to the student, the better.

Note that what I mean here by projects extends far beyond the simple search for information to throw in a paper or on a posterboard. When you look at the projects the students in these schools are engaged in, they are typically community-driven and purpose-driven. This ranges from the students at Iowa BIG working with the City of Cedar Rapids to build and run a downtown apple orchard so that families could easily access free fruit, to students in Little Rock doing an in-depth audit of how the school system was using electricity, and then proposing the installation of solar panels that would save the school system $33,000-$60,000.

Again and again, pick your school: authentic, real-world, student-centered projects drive learning in these schools.[41]

Self-directed. In most cases, these projects (at least eventually) are self-directed. Yes, there can be a lot of guidance and support and scaffolding with students early on as they build up their skills to undertake the projects under themselves. But a big focus for the educators in these schools is to scaffold their students' skills and capacities to undertake projects on their own. Or in most cases, in teams, fostering their students' ability to collaborate, communicate, problem-solve and pursue solutions together.

If there is one thing employers have been saying for a while now and continues to be something high on their list of desired competencies, it is that their employees can be self-directed, problem solve, collaborate, and communicate.[42] Being able to be self-directed is high on this list. And the ability to manage one's time and undertake projects in their work and organizations also ranks very high. What better to set youth up for success than by engaging them in the development of these skills from a young age. And not the "science fair" sort of projects, but projects where students are taking on a real need and challenge in a community and finding a solution for that community.

Competency-based. Something a bit lost in the shuffle for many (not all), is a focus on competency- or mastery-based learning. There are various ways to think about competency-based learning. Some very shortsighted, and others much more nuanced, rich, and complex.

The first argument for competency-based learning lies in the criticism of learning being time-bound, with the factory model version of schooling winning out in this area. "We will spend 2 weeks studying meiosis and mitosis. Then a week studying genetics." Everyone is expected to take the learning journey at the same speed, with content doled out by the instructor or textbook in a slow dribble to the class. In reality, given the resources and possible options in learning as one learns best, different learners could and should learn at different speeds. There is no reason that the entire class should be tied down to a generic pace that may be too fast for some and too slow for others.

Beyond this, how educators are assessing "competency" varies greatly. Multiple-choice tests are a terrible way to measure mastery, as they typically measure what students know – in terms of facts or knowledge – but are terrible in assessing the capacity to think or act or perform in a domain. We certainly would not use a multiple-choice test or essay to assess one's ability to play the piano. In short, there is no other way to assess one's ability or "competency" to play the piano than ... drumroll ... to play the piano.

Yet here we are assessing students' skills and competencies and the ability to effectively use knowledge in ways that are not actual demonstrations of being able to think, act, problem solve or create in that domain. Which doesn't make sense. Yet, because of our focus on memorizing information and the de-contextualized application of skills, we have stripped learning from purpose and context.[43]

Competency-based learning puts the development of learners' competency front and center and forces a shift to the purposeful use of knowledge and skills in authentic contexts. We would never say that someone was able to drive by simply answering a test or showing us how they drive an arcade game car.

Competency-based learning can force a shift in one's paradigm of teaching and learning as well. From the accumulation of knowledge to the capacity to think and act in contexts that have authentic meaning. When an educator embraces competency-based teaching and learning, then it forces one, as an educator, to ask what *is* the competency I want my students to attain. And then simplifies what it means to teach: create the circumstances where students can develop those skills, apply the relevant knowledge, and do so in a rich context of authentic performance. I am not saying it is easy. But the end game becomes clearer. What can one do in the world? It is then up to the educator to scaffold and support the development of those skills and the relevant and effective application of knowledge in the world through modeling, guidance, coaching and practice.

Community-embedded. One of the things that has become much more popular, and rightly so, is a focus on community-embedded learning. As I wrote earlier, some have criticized high schools for keeping kids out of real-world activity and isolating them from what it means to be doing good in the world, let alone how they can pursue their interests in the world, no less pursue work in the world. If anything, youth need to know about their communities, how they run, what their needs are, and what they have to offer.

Some schools do this in a highly substantive and meaningful way. One Stone, for example, presses students to explore their interests "in the real world," taking on projects in their community. Students in Project Good, for instance, go out of their way to identify needs in their community and reach out to organizations to see how they can contribute to others given the need. During COVID, for example, many youth in the Boise area came to the local Boys and Girls club for social activity and tutoring, which helped youth work in the new online environments created by schools. Through ideating a response with the Boys and Girls Club, students from One Stone served as tutors for many of the youth, building relationships and helping them to focus on their learning in the new virtual world.

Another team of students collaborated with CATCH, a rehousing non-profit who works with families experiencing homelessness. Upon reviewing the possible needs of CATCH and the families they served, the One Stone students recognized that many of the spaces CATCH had found for families were not decorated or furnished in keeping with what might make their kids happy. So the team went to work, talking with their children who were moving into their new spaces and together designing the room they would like to have. For example, finding stuffies and toys and building a box to put them in. Painting their bedroom a desired color. And working with the woodworking team at One Stone to refurbish a used dresser, embellishing it with elaborate stencils as well.

Activities like these give youth a sense of how they can contribute to others' well-being. In the case of One Stone, they also want students to see how "design thinking" can help one find solutions that work. Empathizing with those experiencing the need, analyzing the system surrounding the need, ideating solutions, then prototyping and iterating on potential solutions. Something we need more of in this world.

Iowa BIG similarly reaches out to potential community partners (for-profit, non-profit, religious, and civic organizations) asking if there is something they need to get done but can't get to. (Many organizations have these.). These potential projects are placed in what they call the "project pool," whereupon the students look into the pool and decide what project they might like to work on. Then with the partner, they make a plan and the kids go at it. There could be as many as 100 projects in the project pool. And now at the beginning of the year organizations come to BIG to pitch projects to the kids.

These are real-world projects serving the need of real-world partners. So like One Stone, youth get a chance to get both their minds and hands dirty with authentic needs resolving genuine problems. At first, the kids at Iowa BIG take on what they call "inbound" projects, these are the projects that the partners bring to them. And eventually, many of the kids end up pursuing "outbound" projects, these are projects that the kids themselves identify as something they want to give back to the community. For example, one group of students decided to make an art installation celebrating the people of Cedar Rapids.   Another group of students, in partnership with the city, developed and grew a downtown apple orchard so that everyone could access free fruit.

There are dozens of other examples of students working with businesses and non-profits that demonstrate the possibilities of youth contributing to the world, and in very real ways.

Agency-oriented. In the most future-focused schools, educators are assisting and supporting students to explore their interests and passions, build their durable skills, and engage their students in meaningful and authentic activity to build their knowledge, skills, and competencies. In addition, they are focused on supporting students' developing sense of agency. By agency I mean one's confidence in themself and the possession of skills needed to pursue personally desired outcomes in the world. Without a sense of personal agency and the skills to effectively pursue desired ends, one can feel at a loss as to what they can do and therefore be unable to pursue their personal or professional aspirations and make an impact in the world.

In typical school, very little attention is directly paid to the development of students' sense of personal agency. Sure, some educators and schools might go out of their way so that students to feel some assurance that they can perform a task or feel good about their work, but this is not the same as having a holistic sense of your strengths, your skills, and confidence in the knowledge and actions one can take to become good at something, problem-solve, effectively engage others and use resources to pursue desired outcomes.

How do schools that explicitly focus on the development of their students' sense of personal agency do so?

- They put learning in the hands of their students, asking them what they want to learn, how they want to learn it, what difference they would like to make in the world, and then go about supporting them in the design and pursuit of that

Example Projects that support students' development of skills, competencies, and agency[44]

Building and testing 3D-printed products. For example, a prosthetic hand for a child in need or a prosthetic leg for a dog

Creating a podcast series on a topic of their choice. For example, highlighting the experiences of underrepresented voices in their community; environmental topics, including climate change, sustainability, and local ecology; a series on local social justice issues.

Doing research on a local issue and presenting the research and recommendations to local stakeholders. For example: the impact of climate change on their local environment and presenting their findings to community leaders.

Creating a documentary film on a social issue or current event. For example, a documentary exploring the civil rights movement and its impact on modern-day social justice issues.

Starting a non-profit. For example, to provide resources to local animal shelters, or to provide computers and internet access to low-income families or provide support to children who have experienced trauma and abuse.

Creating social media for a local organization. For example, to increase visibility and support for an organization's mission, or a local animal shelter, art center, food bank, or museum.

Designing and building environments. For example, designing and building an aquaponics system to grow vegetables and fish, or a playground using recycled materials, or a sustainable housing prototype featuring solar panels, rainwater harvesting, and sustainable energy.

Creating a mobile app. For example, a mobile app that helps students find healthy food options in the area, or to help people discover and explore art in their city.

Working with clients. For example, fourth-grade students partnering with a local restaurant to create a healthier kids' menu or providing print and graphics design services.

Interning in local businesses and organizations. For example, a local hospital, business, non-profit, civic or govt. agency.

Designing and building a tiny house.

Designing and building a solar- powered car.

Creating a Farm to School & Community Garden. For example, starting a community garden and hosting a "Farm to School" event.

Doing Good in the Community. For example, creating a community hub that offers a variety of services to refugees, including English classes, tutoring, counseling, and access to basic necessities like food and clothing.

Schools pursuing meaningful "Real World" Learning, Future-focused Competencies, and Learner-Agency

Big Picture Schools, Expeditionary Learning Schools, CAPS (Center for Advanced Professional Studies) Programs, the Virtual Learning Academy Charter School (New Hampshire), High Tech High schools (San Diego), the New Tech Network, the Da Vinci schools (Los Angeles), Summit Public schools, Acton Academy schools, One Stone (Boise ID), the Charlotte Lab School (Charlotte NC), Design 39 (San Diego), Odyssey STEM Academy (Lakewood CA), City of Bridges HS (Pittsburgh), Latitude HS (Oakland), Crosstown High (Nashville TN), High School for the Recording Arts (St. Paul MN), the Portfolio School (NYC), Embark Education (Denver), City Neighbors School (Baltimore), Casco Bay High School (Portland ME), the Workshop School (Philadelphia),

learning and impact. When they do that, they make sure the learner sees how *their* designs and actions have led to their learning and impact in the world.

- As discussed above, they engage their students in real-world projects where they experience the act of designing and acting in the world for impact and then reflect on the knowledge and competencies they have gained through the project, leading toward a greater sense of agency.

- As also discussed above, they have their students work with partners in the community that can mentor them, coach them, and offer them real-world feedback on how they go about pursuing their desired outcomes. This then contributes to the development of their skills and competencies and helping them to reflect upon, assess, and acknowledge the skills and competencies they have gained.

What does this look like in and across schools? There are a plethora of examples from across numerous schools across the country that exemplify what this looks like and could look like across all schools. The key is to be very deliberate in your focus. The objective is not trying to just have a student feel good about the one piece of writing they have done, or what they have scored on a test or exam, or how they answered a question in class. The idea is to engage students in meaningful projects that have authentic outcomes for actual stakeholders in their community. And being sure that they can readily see and embrace what they have been able to accomplish. Moreso, how that ability lives within them moving forward, not just in what they accomplished just now.

In Sum

Good stuff!

And there are hundreds of more schools doing the same. We just don't do enough. We don't build in authentic ways for youth to get involved and contribute to the world. And learn not only about the world, but how they can contribute to it too.

Hence ... more is needed.[45]

Now what?

To be continued ...

– 7 –

The Aspirations of a New Ecosystem

If we agree that supporting the development of our youth's sense of agency and possibility should recenter our focus in education, then let me propose seven aims of a new education ecosystem, with the intent that focusing on each of these could propel us forward as designers of our own futures and contributors to our communities, society, and the world.

The Seven Areas of Focus for a New Education Ecosystem
- Intellectual Agility
- Social Acuity
- Personal Agency
- Empathy and Social Good
- Systems Thinking
- Wayfinding
- Thinking and Acting Entrepreneurially
- Experiential Learning

Intellectual Agility

No one would argue that the ability to think and think well is not advantageous not only for our own personal pursuits but in our ability to contribute and make a positive contribution to our organizations, community, and beyond.

Unfortunately, our current schooling practices do a very poor job of cultivating our ability to think well. Often we are told how to think. And/or told to think about content and contexts that truly do not transfer across our ability to think well in real-world context with real world problems. Not unlike learning how to ride a bike, drive a car, or cook a good meal, you cannot replace learning how to think well without being put into context where you need to think well and you are able to discern how to think in ways advantageous given the circumstances, including being able to think about the desired outcomes of thinking, and action.

It has become abundantly clear as our world becomes more complex and dynamic that the ability to problem-solve, navigate change, be creative, and innovate are essential to responding to the needs of work and a quickly changing world. The ability to evaluate information, attend to multiple perspectives, and discern the essential attributes of a system to best engage with that system is essential.

Without intellectual agility, one may not be able to pursue the work they aspire to pursue, perform well in future work, or take advantage of or pursue opportunities that could benefit oneself. In turn, the lack of intellectual agility can significantly limit an effective, productive, or desired outcome in the workplace, our communities, or the decisions or actions we take.[46]

This is not a small thing. Being or not being intellectually agile can have significant implications for our personal and professional lives and social actions.

How can intellectually agility be fostered and supported? It isn't worksheets or scaled-down problem sets. A quick review of the research[47] shows that it takes:

- Encouraging active questioning and critical discourse
- Practice and coaching in critical thinking through the analysis of assumptions, information, evidence, and reasoning
- Engagement in critical thinking, problem solving, and creative activity across multiple contexts and through a wide-variety of challenges
- Explicit modeling, coaching, and mentoring in meaningful, relevant, and authentic contexts
- Fostering one's ability to engage in effective self-reflection and metacognition.
- Supporting and building up one's ability to engage in deliberate inquiry

In sum research and literature consistently emphasizes the importance of intellectual agility for individuals in navigating today's complex and dynamic world not only for their own benefit, but the benefit of our communities, and the world. Thus it is incumbent upon our public school system to ensure our youth develop their ability to think, and think well. By fostering our youth's intellectual agility, schools can empower all of their students to think critically, problem-solve effectively, and contribute positively to their personal and professional lives, as well as our communities and the wider world.[48]

Social Acuity

Common sense and research has consistently shown the importance of relationships and the ability to socially engage with others.[49] The ability to communicate well, build relationships, and tap social networks greatly contributes to one's well-being.[50] Social acuity also means knowing how to communicate well (orally, physically, in writing, etc.) and how the various modalities of communication can lead to different outcomes. It also means knowing how to build relationships that can assist and support one's desired efforts.   Finally, it means embracing the value of relationships in supporting and feeding your own sense of agency and possibility.

Social acuity also means knowing how to engage and sustain healthy relationships. It is clear how some relationships could result in the opposite – be unhealthy, caustic, and detrimental to one's well-being. Being socially adept means being able to recognize when relationships have gone awry and, if unable to be positively re-anchored, should be let go.

It is hard to argue with the value of being socially adept in our world – not just to be "successful" professionally – but to contribute to one's own well-being.

Besides aiding us in being able to build and maintain relationships, social acuity can greatly contribute to our ability to collaborate, network, adapt to a variety of cultural contexts, engage in effective conflict resolution, and lead, amongst many other valuable capacities.

Apart from these benefits, a great number of studies have also correlate social acuity with greater mental health, life satisfaction, and healthier relationships, with the ability to navigate social complexities.

Given all of this, how could we not pay attention to the development of social acuity in our youth. How?[51] A quick list:

- Model, coach, and practice through real-world, context-rich
situations, with a focus on active listening, empathy, respect,
and effective communication

- Create community where these skills and mindsets are readily modeled, promoted and reinforced
- Do so in a variety of contexts requiring the individual to learn through their ongoing experience and reflection on their social interaction and the interactions of others
- Encourage and build the capacity to think about one's choices in social interaction toward desired outcomes
- Provide effective guidance, coaching, and mentoring with feedback

A deep review of this research and the importance of social emotional supports and the development of social emotional competencies clearly points to the need for this focus on the well-being of individuals and our communities in the future.[52]

Personal Agency

Another area of development where we, as a society and in our schools, have been lacking is in assisting and supporting our youth's sense of agency and capacity to be agentic. By a sense of agency I mean "the belief that one can materialize outcomes." By agentic, I mean "the capacity to manifest outcomes." Having a sense of agency, along with one's agentic capacity, can make a significant difference in one's life. It can mean the difference between feeling that "life happens to you" vs. "I can design and pursue the life I want to live." Beyond that, it is the capacity for one to manifest desired outcomes. A lot goes into this. Manifesting certain outcomes can require a lot of "intellectual agility," as well as entrepreneurial thinking. It involves ideating on the desired outcome and the means by which it can be pursued, and then coalescing the resources and relationships to manifest the outcome.

I myself care that youth develop a strong sense of both personal identity and of agency so that they can pursue life toward their own version of "happiness." Define that as you wish: gratification, satisfaction, purpose, well-being, or other. If one continually feels that life is something that just happens to you and that happiness is entirely subject to the whims of personal circumstance, then one will feel little control or agency to pursue the life they wish for. And don't we all want our youth to feel that they have the opportunity to choose actions and perspectives to achieve desired ends? Whether that be the work they wish to pursue, the relationships they would like to have, or the life they would like to live?

Reasons why a focus on the development of personal agency in youth is so important? Children and adults are able to pursue their desired actions, outcomes, and lives and have a far greater sense of well-being and personal fulfillment when they:

- feel empowered to make personal choices that are meaningful to them, aligned with their values, and give them a sense of personal ownership and responsibility
- can actively work towards their personal goals, overcome obstacles, take initiative, and see outcomes as a result of persistence
- engage in activities that support and evidence their self-efficacy
- see gainful outcomes as a result of informed risk taking and the pursuit of new ideas and desired activity

These outcomes with a greater sense of personal agency are clearly evident in the literature, including personal well-being, life satisfaction, and capacity to pursue desired outcomes.[53] And how one can support the development of youth's sense of personal agency, in classrooms, schools, and the family can be found a great number of resources, inclusive of these practices:[54]

- creating opportunities for youth to practice autonomy, giving them voice, choice, and ownership of their decisions and actions
- creating opportunities for goal setting, action planning, meaningful goal setting, and achievement of those goals and actions
- providing role models and mentoring in personal action planning, decision making, and successful activity
- supporting personal agency activity and success through an inclusive and supportive social environment of encouragement, support, and recognition for personal agency
- model and actively support one's personal reflection on their personal agency and the outcomes of their personal agency

Unfortunately, one can see how much many of these practices are not in play in most school environments, dictating what students should do and to what end, not affording them the opportunity to both exercise and ultimately grow their own personal sense of agency.

Attending to the development of personal agency in youth is crucial for fostering their overall well-being and success in life. Personal agency empowers young people to take ownership of their actions, make intentional choices, and pursue their goals with determination and resilience. When youth have a sense of agency, they are more likely to navigate challenges, overcome obstacles, and persist in the face of setbacks. This not only contributes to their personal growth but also prepares them to be active participants in their communities and society.[55]

Empathy and Social Good

Without empathy and a belief that we should work collectively for the benefit of all, we get individuals who wish to gain power, wealth, and privilege at the expense of others. Personally, I cannot abide by this value system, and I would hope that we as fellow citizens would not advocate for a few to have greater wealth and power at the expense of the well-being of others. Yet, we see this every day in our current systems – social and educational.

I remember watching a documentary about an intentional community in the Netherlands, where each family had their own apartment but there was a common community space (indoors and outdoors) and kitchen for the families to interact and support one another in their living. It struck me when a mother commented on how much she gained from her daughter having access to that many more adults and peers day-to-day, and how grateful she was for the social connections and supports in the community. The built-in safety net was invaluable, such as when she had to work late, and she could call upon a few to look after her daughter until she came home.

Unfortunately, there are too many stories of others barely being able to make ends meet. A single mother having to work more than one job just to get by. Older siblings having to take care of their younger siblings. Families having to move from one apartment to another, not being able to make rent.

In more humane societies, health care is free, and in some cases, college and further education are as well.

It seems to me that where we are currently is a direct result of many lacking empathy and/or feeling that they have to hold tight to what they have for fear that giving any to others means they themselves would have less. Unfortunately, the paradigm of "getting ahead" and "every man for himself" has won the day in our history and etched a perspective adopted in our everyday outlook that seeps into who we vote for and to what our politicians promise, further perpetuating the policies that limit the well-being of all.

What would it take for there to be a shift in this reality? Some schools focus on the development of empathy in our youth and do it well. Not through formal lessons or reading, but by putting youth face-to-face with others who elicit and speak to the need for empathy and build youth's sensitivity to the well-being of others and their inclination to do good where good is needed.

Research has shown that individuals with a strong sense of empathy are more likely to engage in acts of kindness, compassion, and social activism, and possess a deep understanding of the interconnectedness of human experiences and the significance of collective well-being. By nurturing empathy in youth, we not only foster their personal growth and emotional intelligence but also contribute to the creation of a more caring and inclusive society.[56]

To foster empathy and social good in youth, we must create opportunities for youth to engage in meaningful interactions with diverse individuals and communities, encouraging dialogue, perspective-taking, and promoting a sense of social responsibility. By prioritizing empathy and social good, we empower young people to become agents of positive change, capable of shaping a more compassionate, inclusive, and just society where the well-being of all is valued.[57]

Systems Thinking

One of the greatest societal and personal shortcomings of the past and present is the lack of systems thinking. Most look to attaining immediate rewards through actions without taking into account the the interdependence of factors within the system they are acting in and how those actions will truly impact the system.

I am reminded of a very funny, though in many respects not so funny, story told in the New York Times shortly after the global outbreak of the Swine Flu in 2009. The President of Egypt decided that he would take an action that would save his country from the illness,[58] and make himself look smart and good in the eyes of his citizens and the rest of the world for doing so. Upon hearing about the flu – I kid you not – he directed the country to kill all of the pigs in the country. Certainly, the swift action of his decision for the benefit of his citizenry could only put him in a good light and raise his stature as a smart, strong, and caring leader.

What he didn't realize, unfortunately (and I really do not know how someone didn't inform him of this fact) was that the Swine Flu has *nothing* to do with pigs. But the circumstances in Egypt being what they were, with, a *lot* of pigs running freely in the streets, the idea of eradicating pigs to stop the spread of the Flu seemed like a good and heroic decision.

Unfortunately, the reality was, as was reported in the Times, pigs running rampant in many parts of the cities and towns in fact played a very important role in reducing the amount of waste in the streets. In short, many simply threw their garbage out into the streets and it was the pigs, in their abundance, that consumed much of it and kept the garbage at bay. Fast forward. Pigs indeed were killed in the hundreds of thousands and, you guessed it, the waste typically eaten by the pigs began to accumulate and itself became a serious health issue for many of the cities and towns in the country.

This is the result of not paying attention to the ramifications of one's actions or considering the interactions in the environment resulting from those actions. Swine Flu, bad. Let's kill all the pigs. And then ... oh! Hmmm. What happens with the accumulation of waste they typically ingest?[59] Crazy: Pigs have nothing to do with Swine Flu.

The lack of systems thinking in individuals and organizations (including governments) is rampant.[60] Taking action without a thorough analysis of the repercussions of those actions in a system can lead to outcomes that are neither desired or intended. And sometimes these actions ultimately do more harm than good as a result of how they play out in the system. The No Child Left Behind (NCLB) policy that came into being in 2002 and is the primary reason we have nationwide standardized testing in schools today would be just such a case, as argued by many.[61]

Given the value of systems thinking to be more conscientious and mindful of how one's actions ultimately impact the system, it would go a long way to helping us to make a better world.

Wayfinding

The original discipline of wayfinding was the study of how one can create markers and signage to help others get around physical spaces. Like airports. Cities. Malls. Sporting venues. Etc.

Several years ago, some educators and psychologists started to think about wayfinding in another realm: the personal, social, and professional. Instead of "how does one make their way around an airport?" or "how does one find their way through a city?", these educators, psychologists, and professional guides started to think about how people find their way (drumbeat .....) through life. Yes, what are the social markers or signs that could orient people through their personal, educational, and professional decisions, choices, and pathways. And sometimes, it is not about the signs being there, but more so about the signs you proactively seek out to make your way.[62]

Today there is an increasingly emergent focus on individuals making decisions regarding how they want to make a living and doing what they want to do, who with, and where. We can see this in the growth of individuals making a series of jumps from one institution to another, and in some cases one profession to another. Many have also moved from pursuing the typical career trajectory within one company to pursuing the gig economy, taking on one job then another, and going from one project to another, depending on their personal and professional interests and aspirations.

Of course, the unfortunate way wayfinding comes into play for most today is as follows:

As youth travel through the escalator model of schooling, moving from one grade to the next, they accumulate subject area credits as prescribed, supposedly in their best interest. However, at some point, most students just end up asking, "Why am I learning this?" and "When will I need this?" Good questions.

I am not going to argue that much of this knowledge or "know-how" isn't good to know or be able to do. But much of this knowledge or "know-how" is often taught dissociated from its purposeful use, worse, disconnected from the learner's genuine interest. When this happens, most students simply become compliant and engage in rote learning (if any) which in the end doesn't amount to much.[63] Mitosis and meiosis, a mole of gas, the quadratic equation. I myself remember being in a class on modern European history and wondering, "Is the point of this class to remember all of these dates, rulers, and wars?"

This is not to say that there isn't good teaching and good learning going on. Many teachers know how to authentically engage youth, through fun and intellectually challenging projects, Socratic discussions, and various means that tap students' authentic interest. Nonetheless, much of the typical school-prescribed knowledge, know-how, and classroom-based activities does not typically lead students to know how to use these skills or apply this knowledge in the real world. And it rarely serves to help them pursue their intrinsic interests. No less assists or supports them in imagining the domains of activity they may want to pursue in their future lives.

That's why we need wayfinding. So that students can develop the skills, tools, and mindset to pursue one's desired future. I frame this as the difference between "having life happen to you" and "designing your life."

When we think about Wayfinding, the issue we are attempting to address is that most youth come out of high school not knowing what they are interested in, much less passionate about. (Apart from the usual, like perhaps playing Fortnite, playing sports, certain music, movies, and shows, and hanging out with friends.) And then they tend to choose a college dependent on variables such as reputation, familiarity, location, size, and finances, rather than seeing college as a means to pursue their aspirations. Then they end up in college and are asked to choose a concentration, taking a stab at what might be of greatest interest to them or benefit them post-school.

Deliberately supporting youth in thinking about how they can explore their interests and eventually design their educational and vocational pathways in pursuit of their genuine interests can go a long way toward their subsequently being (1) vocationally successful and (2) happy. My good friend Mike Realon, now at Palisades HS in Charlotte, NC, often references the fact that most people end up working in a field that is not even directly related to their education,[64] and that people are much happier with their work when it is matched to their interest[65] and educational pursuits.[66]

So that begs the question, what are we doing in K-12 and beyond to sharpen a student's perspective on being an agent of their own destiny?

This harkens back to my mother's 21st birthday gift to me. She identified several individuals in LA who she felt were able to make a living doing what they love to do. And then wrote them asking, "Would you mind having a burger or a coffee with my son, and share how it is you came to do what you love to do?" Cool, no?

How many of you reading this right now are making a living doing what you love to do? And if so, how much of that was the result of deliberately pursuing your interests through the connections you made with others and the kinds of learning opportunities you put yourself in either in or outside of school?

Now there are a few schools that do deliberately focus on students' wayfinding.[67] They explicitly work with youth in helping them to consider and think about these questions and how they can pursue their interests and pursue work they want to have. And they consider this work essential in providing youth with the tools and mindsets that can assist them in being agents and directors of their own lives.

The one I am most familiar with and that I greatly admire is One Stone,[68] in Boise Idaho. For years, wayfinding has been central to their work with students, assisting and supporting each to deliberately focus on the pursuit of interests, what it is that they may be interested in and what they might like to do in the future. One Stone provides students with the opportunity to explore their interests and passions.

I remember talking with Ethan, a senior at One Stone a few years ago, and asking him how he came to choose his career path. Two years prior, he thought he wanted to pursue being a Navy SEAL and so was supported by his advisor (Chad Carlson) to try out various challenges and experiences related to the field – to try the idea on for size, so to speak. After several of these experiences, he found that it was not the path he wanted to pursue. Remotivated by the pride he took in his father being a 27-year firefighter, he then decided to pursue emergency medical training, which led him to acquiring his EMT certification and then pursue training for rescue operations with the fire rangers.

I heard many stories like this while interviewing the youth at One Stone. Based on their work and evidence of outcomes, One Stone has created a mentoring framework to assist educators in other schools to do the same, called "Living in Beta."

Living in Beta here harkens to the idea of people exploring potential designs or solutions to problems through an iterative process, taking place over time. A good design or solution is rarely arrived at the very first time one arrives at one but can become very good if revised and refined over time. Particularly as one tries the design or solution out – prototype, test, and then refine it. As is the case in life, there are things that happen along the way, relationships and resources, events and circumstances that present themselves, including those you purposefully and deliberately pursue oneself. You can make use of those events, relationships, resources, and circumstances and pivot along the way. Pivoting is important because sticking to a plan that yields undesired outcomes is a waste of time.

Ethan, at One Stone

So, for context, my current career path is working as an emergency medical technician on a couple of ambulances this summer, and then continuing my education into rope rescue, training, paramedicine, fire, whatever I think I'll do and what emergency services can get me. So I've chosen that career path I think because of my upbringing.

My father was a Boise firefighter for about 27 years, retired as battalion chief, and he has always been someone that I admire greatly and admire for his work ethic. And then the serious work that he did. Every two days, he would come home from his shift smelling like smoke and tell us stories about the calls that he went on to help others. And that was something that really motivated me.

I originally wanted to go into the military, so I started looking at some different areas I could work in related to that. Chad, my advisor said, Okay, then let's go out and let's try some things like that. So I went out and I joined the Civil Air Patrol, which is the auxiliary of the Air Force for civilians. Young men and women went out and joined them and I left that experience not liking it, and really having a huge shift in my passion and my career choice that I had had for years.

So I started looking around at some different things and someone helped me to find a wilderness first aid course taught by the National Outdoor Leadership School. I took that and I left that feeling incredibly motivated and passionate about the topic. So I immediately registered for a wilderness first responder course also taught by the National Outdoor Leadership School. Then after that, I decided I wanted to take some EMT training.

So One Stone was incredibly helpful in helping me cultivate those passions and also giving me opportunities to look into those passions. And helped me to cultivate my passions. And I figured out what I am passionate about.

The living in beta program, which you can get an overview of by going to onestone.org/livinginbeta, is designed so that a group of youth with a mentor can go through the process of pursuing their interests through identified experiences and ongoing reflection. The questions asked and exercises pursued lead to some insights as to how you can be an agent of your own life, rather than being a passive recipient of whatever life happens to give you. No small thing.

If I ask you what you want for your children, do you not say that you want them to be happy? For them to be enriched by their relationships? Enlivened by their friendships? Able to make a living doing what they love to do? And perhaps more than anything, that they have a sense of personal agency and opportunity – the focus of this book.

We could question whether it's the purview of our public school ecosystem to work with youth in such ways. But I would argue yes, this is sorely missing today, not just on behalf of each person, but our communities and society. Not tapping into the potential creativity and talent of each individual to contribute to our communities and the world is a loss. I would say ... a tremendous loss. And I for one do want everyone to be afforded to live the life they want to live. Pursue the work they wish to pursue. And contribute back to the world in ways they wish to contribute. And you?

Assisting and supporting youth to be skilled wayfinders can help, and focusing on this in the education of our youth can go a long way to assisting our youth's sense of agency and possibility not just now, but the rest of their lives.

Thinking and Acting Entrepreneurially

Several years ago, I read a book called *World Class Learners* by Yong Zhao. Yong Zhao is a prolific writer and I believe one of the most astute individuals looking at our education systems and how they operate and function today. [69] One of the primary theses presented in the book is that the most important thing we could give youth is the ability to think and act entrepreneurially. To have an entrepreneurial mindset. The notion is that if we want to get ahead in life – doing what we want to do, making what we want to make, and living the life we want to live – we need to think entrepreneurially.

For several years now I have been teaching classes on education entrepreneurship with several colleagues at Northeastern University. In a nutshell, one can frame entrepreneurship as *being able to harness resources and relationships to manifest an idea*. Pretty simple really.

So what do entrepreneurs do? They see a need in the world or they identify a process or program or product that individuals may want. Then they figure out how to create and provide that offering to others. Yong's commentary is simple: all of us, to a greater or lesser degree, make our way through life thinking entrepreneurially.

Where do I want to go? Where do I want to be? What do I want to do? How can I create an income for myself? How can I support my family? Etc. All of that actually requires thinking and acting entrepreneurially. And so in reality, living our best life, as much as we think about that and how we think about that, is hyper-dependent on the degree to which we think and act entrepreneurially.

So the idea of thinking and acting entrepreneurially is intimately connected to the rest of this book. Supporting youth's sense of agency and possibility is actually assisting and supporting the development of their skills and mindsets to think and act entrepreneurially. Being able to look around the world and identify and then access and use the various resources and relationships to make one's idea a reality is Wayfinding – seeing and pursuing markers or signals in the world pointing to an opportunity of value to you.

While wayfinding, agency, possibility, and thinking and acting entrepreneurially go hand in hand, all of these are super-boosted through systems thinking. If you can see the entire system and how the system operates, then you are in a better position to think about what *you* can do to impact the system.

Most don't realize that a big part of thinking and acting entrepreneurially is thinking about your idea, engaging others in the revision and refinement of your idea, then building and refining the idea through the development and testing of a prototype, ultimately starting at a scale that's manageable and realistic. Eventually, growing it over time.

Take Starbucks, for example, which started in Pike Street Market over 30 years ago. In short, it started as a single coffee shop. It didn't start as the global giant it is today. Dunkin Donuts similarly. It didn't start as a coffee shop on every street corner in Boston. Rather, it started as a small doughnut shop in a town just south of me, Weymouth MA. McDonald's, the same, a little hamburger place that decided to serve burgers differently, in San Bernardino CA.

Moving to educational programs, One Stone in Boise started with Joel and Teresa Poppen sitting at their kitchen table with five or six kids, asking them if they would like to engage in community service. Fourteen years later, One Stone now runs an incredible array of after school and summer programs that impact over 3,000 youth in the Treasure Valley (Boise, ID) area. And now, at the request of the youth in these programs, they host an incredible tuition-free student run high school.

Incredible schools and educational programs do not need to start off small. And indeed they rarely do. In the far greater majority of cases a few individuals had an idea and were impassioned to get it off the ground in some small but significant way. And as they figured things out and found success, the enterprise then gained traction and grew. Hence, my ongoing commentary: think BIG, start small, be strategic. You don't have to start with a large school or program. Indeed it's probably smart not to do so, so that you can iterate and pivot and revise and refine as you go, much more nimbly with fewer students and fewer educators.

So this is true of almost any endeavor, educational, for profit, non-profit, etc. But knowledge of this process and the value of incubating, prototyping, resource and relationship building, and iterating is essential in moving forward, and at the heart of thinking and acting entrepreneurially.

Experiential Learning

It would be remiss of me not to ground all of the propositions in this book through the lens of experiential learning. Since my time at Harvard in the early '90s, how people learn through experience has been on my mind. And now teaching and advising in our Doctor of Education program at Northeastern University, even moreso, where we pride ourselves in foregrounding students to be change agents through the experience of their Dissertation in Practice.[70]

In the simplest of forms, many refer to experiential learning as "learning by doing." Or hands-on. Or real-world. But these don't really detail the true nature of learning through experience. For sure, experiential learning can and in many ways should be "hands-on," but it needs to be minds on as well. For sure, one should be *doing* something, but it is this "doing" that is really important. Not just any doing, but for learning to happen, learners should care about what they do, and the doing should in many ways mirror the thinking and activity involved in real world contexts.

There is a plethora of research that clearly points to how a learner's "intrinsic" motivation (meaning they are invested and care in the activity of learning) contributes to actual learning, meaning not in one ear and out the other, or memorizing to regurgitate for another time. We can see this, as I pointed out before, in how kids learn how to play sports or video games, or for that matter how adults pursue any learning that actually matters to them. The intellectual investment in picking up the knowledge and gaining the skills and getting good at the craft or activity is qualitatively different from what one does "just to get by." Which is what most students in school do, or for that matter what many adults do in professional development that is poorly offered or that individuals don't see the need for.

In our experiential learning classes at Northeastern, we take great care to unpack what really happens when one designs for and engages in experiential learning. It's not just "doing" something but being sure that the interest and motivation of the learner is taken into account and tapped, so that it is personally meaningful and of value. Then the social context of learning is attended to: Why does the learner want to learn this skill? What motivates them to learn this skill or way of thinking and acting? What are the relationships with classmates, peers, friends, co-workers, others in the field, possible mentors, social groups, and instructors that creates a social web of support and creates a social context for wanting to pursue one's own learning activity? This is no small thing. SOCIAL context is huge.

Finally, examples, models, and practice are provided to scaffold a student's ability to engage in the activity. Starting with realistic and doable activities and ways of thinking that challenge the learner but are within reach. Note how videogames are particularly good at this, challenging the novice user so that they are engaged in being successful but not so much that they end up simply quitting because it is just too damn hard! Increasing the level of challenge as players get better and better with each subsequent increase in challenge. So we are scaffolding toward success, such as putting training wheels on a bike, or taking anyone learning how to drive a car into the empty parking lot first. Better, the coach is there guiding and providing just the right feedback along the way. (Think mom or dad running alongside the four-year-old while learning how to ride the bike; the mom, dad, or other offering what they can while the 16-year-old is driving the car.)

This is the art of learning and the art of learning through experience. Creating meaningful as well as authentic contexts and experiences tapping the learner's intrinsic interest to learn. The learning is situated in authentic contexts, you cannot replace the value of that. Learning how to drive in a video game is not the same as actually learning how to drive in the real world, and this is true of any meaningful skill or competency.

So why do I put this as the last of the aspirations for a new public school ecosystem? Because most public schools do not adequately operate with a thorough understanding of how experiential learning – or real learning, period – actually happens. They default to teaching and learning that perpetuates "surface" rather than "deep learning," learning that sticks and is used by the learner in meaningful, authentic contexts – the "real world." Writing a 5-paragraph essay for a teacher is *not* the same as working hard at crafting an opinion piece for the local paper, no less the New York Times. Or doing a science fair poster vs. engineering a solution for one's community or community partner.

This is what the "cool schools" I reference through most of this book are doing. Educators are tapping into students' intrinsic interest in doing something and subsequently learn in that doing by creating a meaningful product, providing a real-world solution, and/or pursuing a desired outcome in a context that is of value.

The educators in these schools recognize the need to pursue and support their youth's learning in these ways because that is where they see real learning happening. And in this way, it isn't just "experiential learning," but learning. This is what learning looks like when it is pursued to impact one's ability to see, think, and act in the world in new agentic ways. For real world impact. In service of youth's agency and possibilities as they might wish to pursue them.

Next ... we'll talk about how we can get from what we have now, to what each student and community deserves moving forward.

– 8 –
Building the New Ecosystem

As alluded to in several other parts of this book, I am a big fan of empowering a small group of individuals to create something unique and wonderful for their own youth, families, and community. Big, rule-bound bureaucracies and organizations scare me, for many reasons. Not to say that the worst is true of ALL large organizations. But I would say for most.

Let me highlight several strategies that could help to mobilize a plethora of possibilities for our youth and communities, and how these activities could serve you directly. If employed, these strategies could inform how bureaucracies (if we need them) could far better work toward the development and proliferation of schools that serve our youth, communities, and world better than they do now.

> **To move toward a Revolution in Education, we could do a far better job by ...**
> - Scaling innovations throughout a state
> - Making new schools
> - Building local vocational ecosystems
> - Funding and growing local innovation schools
> - Supporting new school networks
> - Scaling new schools and successful practices across the country
> - Creating more networks
> - Publicly funding and credentialing alternative educational programs
> - Engaging and then mobilizing the local ecosystem toward new designs with far better outcomes

Scale Innovations throughout your State

Of course, each state has its own particular bureaucracies, idiosyncrasies, and long-held socio-political value systems tied to their populace's views on education. I will not dissect the differences across states here, but you can intuit for yourself what some of those long-held positions and value systems might be. Nonetheless, the examples provided here can inform how a state could put energy into the proliferation of a valued school design or program in a state.

P-Tech. This is the one model I have seen really take off. Clearly, when you pull back the curtains, one can see how influential Stan Litow, then Vice President of Corporate Citizenship and Corporate Affairs at IBM, was in co-founding and subsequently growing P-Tech throughout New York and beyond. When you have an institution like IBM and someone as high up in that institution as Stan, with the connections Stan had, one can see how such connections can play a significant role in getting a new idea, such as P-Tech, up and running. Like Stan asking President Obama, who he happened to be advising at the time, if he could mention P-Tech in his State of the Union address.

Not an unimportant part of the story. Relationships, connections, affiliations, political support. In the end, the state legislature created a Request for Proposal process with funding that is, in fact, still ongoing today to fund P-Techs across the state. The RFP calls upon the local school district, a local community college, and an industry partner to put forth the design for a local P-Tech, and with that design some start-up monies to get it going.

When you look across the country, you can see the impact of such state-supported legislation and funding. There are now over 48 P-Tech programs across the state of NY as opposed to far fewer in many other states. Why? Because the state legislature has incentivized the start-up of such programs across the state with an ongoing request for proposals each year.

Similarly, when I looked at the distribution of NAF-affiliated (previously called the National Academy Foundation) Career Academies across the US, lo and behold, as of October 28, 2021, North Carolina had 49 NAF-affiliated Career Academies across 40 High Schools serving 8,801 students while South Carolina (just for comparison) had only 1 NAF-affiliated Career Academy in 1 High School serving only 217 students.

I asked myself long ago why there was such a discrepancy in the number of P-Techs in NY State and the NAF academies in North Carolina versus most other states. Well, it just so happens that in both contexts, there was a push by the state to grow career academies. And this made the difference.

States can be much more proactive in supporting such programs. As is also the case in Massachusetts where a number of regional vocational schools are supported through additional state funding beyond the typical Chapter 74 or Perkins federal funding.

VLACS – the Virtual Learning Academy Charter School of New Hampshire. The other model which I think is something every state should be replicating is the Virtual Learning Academy Charter School (VLACS) in New Hampshire. In 2007, the NH Board of Education approved the Virtual Learning Academy as a charter school, with ~700 students enrolling in January 2008. Eleven years later, in 2019 the school had received a total of 16,519 course enrollment requests. And then when COVID hit, those requests blossomed into over 31,000!

The beauty of this innovation is that, unlike in other states, any NH student is able to take classes or take advantage of any of the learning opportunities at VLACS *without any district losing money for their students' enrollment and at no cost to the student.* This is a BIG shift as in all other states the greater majority of districts and the populace get worked up about how a local charter school or charter schools is "taking away" their school funding, as is the case in most states where roughly 80% of a district's state funding for that student would go with the student. Districts and parents and others that align themselves with this mentality that new, innovative schools disadvantage existing schools is a very real impetus for districts and others to be vocal in their distaste of charters. In a lot of these cases, they state that the charter schools are taking money away from public schools, in which case I feel the need to remind them that charter schools ARE public schools. But I digress.

The point here is that this is not an issue in NH with VLACS because VLACS is entirely state funded, without any of the sending districts and schools losing any state monies from their allocation of sending students.   Districts, schools, parents and the students themselves are extremely appreciative of being able to take classes and engage in learning experiences through VLACS because VLACS is, in fact, serving a very real need. In a state like NH, many of the schools are not able to provide all of the learning opportunities that

Example Learning Opportunities for Students at VLACS

Classes

Robotics	Mobile App Development	Green Technology
Cybersecurity	Digital Music Production	Advanced Art Design
Game Design	Environmental Science	Law & Order

Example Badges

Robotics	Leadership & Service	Sustainability
Global Citizen	Digital Media & Design	Entrepreneurship
Sustainability	Virtual Reality Developer	Cybersecurity

Example Student Projects

Created a **website** for a local animal shelter to increase adoptions

Built and tested a **3D-printed prosthetic hand** for a child

Developed a **video game** to teach programming skills to students

Created a **podcast series** on a topic of their choice

Conducted **research** on the impact of climate change on their local environment and presented the findings to community leaders

Designed and launched a **community-wide recycling program**

Created a **short film** on a community topic

Internships

A student interested in **photography** interned with a professional photographer and learned about lighting, composition, and editing

A student interested in **computer science** interned with a software company and worked on a team to develop a mobile app

A student interested in **veterinary science** interned at a local animal hospital and learned about animal care, surgery, and emergency medicine

A student interested in **social justice** interned with a nonprofit organization to promote diversity and inclusion in the community

Independent Learning Projects

Developed a video game	Wrote a novel
Created an art portfolio	Started a business
Produced a short film	Developed a mobile app
Designed a tiny home	Built an electric guitar

VLACS can. Many of the rural high schools, for example, cannot offer such courses as AP biology or economics, or a lab science. But VLACS can create this opportunity because it has the resources and capacity to offer such courses virtually.

While the ability to offer such learning opportunities across the state may be worthwhile enough to warrant VLACS's existence, I myself am more impressed with the fact that VLACS doesn't just offer online courses, but they are also offering these courses based on *competency*, which is something the state has been pushing for years. So the competency-based model of assessing learning becomes a truly valued part of the VLACS experience. In addition, they have been growing their focus on experiential learning where students can gain credit for real-world projects, internships, and independent learning.   While some schools attempt to offer the same, many struggle in effectively doing so. But as a state-wide school in NH that has been intentional in trying to grow competency-based teaching and learning for years, VLACS' ability to make this a part of their educational ecosystem is the state's way of providing such an opportunity to all students across the state.

While in all other states, districts, schools, and charter schools attempt to provide such offerings for their local community, VLACS is an example of a state finding a way to provide this offering to every student in the state.

Make New Schools

This is by far the easiest and fastest way to engender new models of teaching, learning, and schooling.   While the small schools initiative funded by the Gates Foundation ended up with a mixed-bag of results (discussed elsewhere), one finding was clear: It is FAR easier to engender a new set of practices by starting a new school than it is to try and change a pre-existing school. As is the case with any pre-existing organization that operates with a loose-set of expectations, MOVING an organization to operate in a completely new way is like – using the well-known expression – trying to turn an oil tanker. It takes forever ... and a great deal of energy.

Everyone in the old "system" is used to thinking, acting, and behaving in a certain way. Changing these well-rehearsed and familiar behaviors is not always desired by everyone. Nor should we assume that educators would know how to act and think differently. Worse, people familiar with the systems they have been accustomed to and who have some security in the systems they operate, will outright fight and resist (directly and/or indirectly) to maintain their "space," their comfort zone of doing what they know how to do. This difficulty of not knowing how to think and act differently makes for a difficult process of change. Can it be done? Yes? Can it be difficult? Also yes. And in some cases, the skill set desired, if not required, in the new system is not easily acquired by those previously in the system.

Certainly, one can engage the community in initial and ongoing professional development that can support the development of these skills. But there is a transition period here. And such transitions for employees may take some time. And, to tell the truth, there may be just as significant a transition for those in the organization they are serving. In this case, the students.

Transitions, particularly significant ones, are hard for everyone. Most don't like operating in these circumstances. Familiarity with one's environment and how one can be successful in it is typically more desired than not knowing what to do.

So ... let's imagine ... what COULD this look like?

Build Local Vocational Ecosystems. Vocational schools are not new to our educational ecosystem, However, many of these schools could be "retooled" to more closely resemble what former National Principal of the Year Sheila Harrity and her colleagues created in Worcester starting in 2008. With a new building and multiple industry, community college, and college partnerships, they developed a much more rigorous academic and vocational program than the one they had. Like many vocational schools, they have an automotive center, working restaurant, beauty salon, and carpentry, electricity, and construction programs. The difference here is that each of these is state of the art. And the school (meaning its students) are contributing back to the community in some very real and significant ways. The 16-bay automotive center is servicing over 100 cars a month. The beauty salon, supported by Avon, services 100+ clients a month. The working restaurant and associated Bistro serves over 400+.diners a month.

In addition, and as a result of Dr. Harrity getting a Swedish company to donate state of the art printing equipment, half of the top floor of the school housed an active print shop wherein the school did printing for the city of Worcester as well as a number of clients in the surrounding area. And, by way of a partnership with Tufts Veterinary School, the school contains an animal clinic wherein Tufts veterinary faculty work side-by-side with both Tufts veterinary and Worcester Technical High School students, providing free medical care to low-income families with pets in the area. Besides all of this, students are helping to build Habitat for Humanity houses in the community, where they are putting to use what they have learned in the school.

In this way, Worcester Technical High School is a part of the community. Not a cement building keeping kids locked inside only to learn content they feel has no relevance to them. Rather, the students are learning content and obtaining skills that are then put to use in the real world to enhance and solidify their training.

Why aren't there more places like Worcester Tech throughout the country? In Massachusetts alone ... why isn't there one in such socio-economically depressed communities as Fall River, New Bedford, Chicopee, Springfield, Lawrence, or Boston?

Mentioned elsewhere in the book is the incredible accomplishments of Olympic HS in Charlotte NC, where students can choose across five different career academies which are supported by and connected to over 700 industry partners. In this way Olympic is affording students the opportunity to go right into gainful employment in local industry that needs skilled labor. And students are graduating into apprenticeship programs and jobs making $40,000+ a year. And if they want to continue on with their education, they are paid to do so as well.

Other systems too, such as in Danbury CT, are revisioning their vocational and professional pathway pipelines where students get hands-on experience working with local industry with an eye toward gainful employment.

Many systems are missing opportunities like these to partner with local industry and create pathways to future employment for their students. They should look to these exemplars to learn how to do so.

Get Kids engaged in Meaningful Projects in the Real World. Iowa BIG. Let's start there. I LOVE Iowa BIG. How they started is detailed earlier in the book, but students are not sitting in desks or rows and not taking a revolving cycle of science, math, history, and ELA courses. Rather, they are DOING projects in the community. At its start, the Iowa BIG team traveled across the community and visited various organizations – non-profits, for-profits, government and other civic agencies, and religious institutions – asking if there was something they needed to get done but couldn't get to it. In short, the 10th item on their to-do list that they simply couldn't get done. Per usual, there always was that one (or two) things the organization would love to get done but were simply too busy doing all the other things further up on their list. Receiving their response, the Iowa BIG folks would say, "Hey ... you mind if a group of kids took a crack at it?" Feeling that it could only benefit their organization (if something came of it) and that the task certainly could contribute to students' learning, they would say yes.

I think early on these community members might not have expected much. But with the support and guidance of the Iowa BIG facilitators, kids took on these projects and earnestly went to work on them.

One thing to keep in mind is that students choose these projects. They are not assigned. As the Iowa BIG staff collects the projects, they put them into what they call the "project pool" and when 50+ of these projects are placed in there, students can look into the pool and decide what they would like to work on. In this way, they are ensured that they have an interest in the project. And it is up to the facilitators to work with the students to ensure they are both engaged and learning in the project.

And so, when I say project, many might think, something like a good science fair project, with a poster board like presentation of activity and learning. But in reality, these projects were not like your run-of-the-mill science projects (e.g., a prototype potato peeler or volcano demonstration). Rather, these projects are genuine, real-world projects of fairly significant import. Particularly as they were presented by a community member, representing a real issue in the community where the project has some real value.

So, for example, upon approaching an architecture firm that thought it would be nice to give students the opportunity to design a $1.3 million pedestrian bridge to go over the river, little did they know they would indeed, and with great earnestness, actually present a blueprint for a design along with a sketch of engraved glass that would bridle the walkway in such a way that as you walked along you would see birds fluttering along with you. And that this design would be one of three to be presented to the city council for building.

Or the group of kids who partnered with the United Way to create a survey to identify trauma hotspots throughout the city – food insecurity, poverty, etc. Or the kids who presented a redesign of a warehouse for a company that was growing so fast its old warehouse was quickly becoming unserviceable. Or the kids who teamed up with the city to design and grow a downtown apple orchard to increase access to fresh fruit to families.

These are real projects of value to the community – whether you were a company, a non-profit, or a government agency. Kids don't have classes (although when desired, they can request a seminar on a particular subject or topic) and kids are not shuffling from classroom-to-classroom and subject-to-subject to learn the subject (typically out of context and out of books or as presented by the teacher). Rather, kids were learning what they needed to learn to do the project and in doing so were gaining knowledge and skills in real-time for a genuine purpose and because they were employing that knowledge and skills in context and for a genuine purpose were seeing its application and learning how to use that knowledge and those skills.

Kids were also exploring different kinds of work, realms of work, and learning about the issues and challenges of the world. It was real. It was in front of them. And they are engaging with and learning from people doing that work in the world.

And now, several years after the start, and after youth have gained some confidence in doing projects for others, the community now comes to pitch projects to the kids. And in many cases the kids now create their own projects they wish to contribute to the community – such as a mural representing the people of Cedar Rapids. Where the projects provided by the community are called "inbound" projects, the projects now that the students create to give back to the community are called "outbound" projects.

The beauty of this design is several-fold. One, students from across four districts in Cedar Rapids can choose to participate at Iowa BIG full or half-time, allowing students to maintain a close connection with their home school taking 2-3 classes but also taking advantage of being at Iowa BIG. Two, they are given the opportunity to be immersed in real-world projects of interest to them, learning as they go through real-world, immersive activity. And, three, they are able to see and explore what the world of work looks like, so that they can begin to explore what they might be interested in exploring further and pursuing.

This rarely happens in "typical" school. Subjects are traditionally taught typically in isolation of one another and not in the context of their genuine application. Thus, the "banking" model of education rules, while we know that learning with purpose and in the context of application results in deeper learning – learning that is not merely rote but learning that has meaning and results in application.

Above and beyond all of this, students are gaining some of the soft skills identified as of value in the real world, the ones that 21st century employers have been referencing in need over the last decade and the more well-defined array of "durable skills" identified and made note of as of late.[71]

Related to the focus of this book, contexts and programs such as Iowa BIG go a long way in assisting students to help build their sense of personal agency.   If you can design a bridge, build an apple orchard, redesign a warehouse, and do such things in the world with real impact, your sense of efficacy and your sense of what you can do – your sense of possibility – goes WAY up. And this is what our youth need. Experiences that afford them development of their sense of efficacy and their sense of how to pursue possibilities.

That's what Iowa BIG does.   And that's what a number of innovative, think outside of the box schools are doing across the country.

Fund and Grow Local Innovation Schools

Here and there, there are school districts that support the growth of new kinds of schools. These schools operate differently, serving students who thrive in different kinds of learning environments, and/or are focused on subjects that the students are truly interested in. Unfortunately, this is far too uncommon.

Not all students like to learn in the same way or are interested in the same things, or have the same aspirations, or have the same needs. But most districts offer just the one kind of school – the traditional school– for all learners, which simply does not work.

A compliance model of education, where students are told "drink this cod liver oil, it's for your own good," does not necessarily mean it tastes good or is in fact good for you. Many kids love sports, for example, such as my grandson, who loves to run, compete, and get better at things he cares to get better at. We know this because we see it all the time. When kids love to learn something and get better at it or are interested in something and want to explore it, we typically do what we can to support and feed that interest and support them in their exploration and pursuit of the endeavor. But when it comes to school, we all of a sudden decide that it's what *we* want them to learn and get better at that is most important. Why? Why don't we design schools and provide learning opportunities grounded in what they want to learn and in *how* they would like to learn it.

Yes, there are kids who love to play Fortnite or Madden, baseball or soccer, and want to get better at such things. And then there are kids who love to cook, dance, and create music. Other options we should offer include building and racing solar-powered cars, finding ways to combat climate change, making music, and doing good in the world, etc. The fact is, there should be a variety of schools that provide students with the opportunity to go deep in any interest area and explore how they could pursue those interests in the world.

These are the best schools, the "go deep" schools, the "explore the world" schools, and the "go deep into who you are and where you might want to go" schools. They exist, but again, only here and there.

Big Picture Schools have for the past 25 years been giving students the opportunity to explore their interests and potential passions by working with others in the world, grounded in an ongoing conversation about who they are and what their interests might be. Iowa BIG gives students the chance to explore what they can do by engaging in real-world projects that interest them. They get to select what they want to work on from a "project pool" of projects, and sometimes they can even create their own projects of interest that give back to the community. Do they learn anything? They learn a ton because to do any of these projects, they need to learn the content and skills necessary to complete them. Better yet, they need to problem-solve, create, make, and collaborate to complete them.

In this way, students are not passive recipients of knowledge that others think they should have but learners who actively seek out the knowledge and skills they want in order to successfully complete their project. As one Iowa BIG alum put it: "It's 'just-in-time learning' instead of 'just-in-case learning.'" Just-in-time learning has a real, actionable purpose, such as when you need to fix and solve something. Just in case learning is accumulating information and skills "just in case" you might need them in the future. But when learners actively pursue knowledge and employ skills for a real outcome, it results in learners actually learning how to use that knowledge and those skills in the world. 'Just-in-case learning' is just the opposite. Just-in-case learning is typically learned outside of a meaningful context and with little direct authentic purpose. And when anyone, not just youth, learn in this way, it rarely contributes to one's ability to effectively use the knowledge or employ the learned skills when needed in real life.

I have shared several other examples throughout this book. The CAPS programs across the country gives students the opportunity to dig into veterinary medicine, the biosciences, filmmaking, entrepreneurship, and more.

In St. Paul MN, over 25 years ago, Tony Simmons and colleagues started an independent charter school called the High School for the Recording Arts. Yes, you guessed it, a big draw for youth interested in music, hip-hop in particular. With the opportunity to actually explore their potential talents and pursue their interest in hip-hop recording, the school has now impacted the lives of thousands of youth because the school is not focused only on the creation and business of music but also coming to know the youth, creating relationships with them, and creating a culture of support and self-discovery. Twenty-seven years later, it operates in a 20,000+ square foot space home to two recording studios that the students run and create and produce their music from.

In the Highline School District, just south of Seattle and nestled against the beautiful Puget Sound, three alternative schools have grown and flourished the past several years. First, the first Big Picture School in the Northwest started there in Highline. Next, with the serendipitous joining of interests, Aviation High School was born in 2004 as an aviation- and aero-space based STEM school, where students are engaged in a variety of hands-on, project-oriented engineering activities each connected in some way to aviation and aero-space. The use of this theme made sense given that Highline is home to the Seattle Airport and Boeing field, and the many industries that support these ventures. The presence of aviation as a driving focus for the school was even more realized when the school's new home was built right next to the Museum of Flight on Boeing field, in a beautiful new 72,000 foot facility with large glass windows opening to the sky, Boeing field, and the Museum with the such legends of aircraft as the Concorde and previous Boeing airplanes. With the students taking advantage of over 200 flight-related businesses through internships and a variety of learning opportunities, they are gaining valuable skills through relevant projects and real-world work.

Finally, in this very same district, partially based on the success of Aviation HS, Maritime High School was started just over a year ago (as of this writing) and is grounded in the very real and prominent marine industry encompassing the greater Puget Sound area, including shipping, marine science, and a wide-array of marine-based professions. Started in partnership with the Port of Seattle, Northwest Maritime Center, and the Duwamish River Cleanup Coalition, and involving over 200+ partners throughout the area, any student in the surrounding area can attend by lottery, with 51% of seats reserved for those students who live within the district. Note, the high school and its focus makes a whole lot of sense when you consider that there is projected to be a wave of retirements in the area whose professional activity is connected to the rich and abundant maritime activity in the area, so this is one way a K12 system can support interest if not galvanize a passion for pursuing work in this civic, ecological, economic, and social arena.

Not far down the road, in Tacoma, reside the three unique high schools mentioned earlier in the book – The School of the Arts, the Science and Math Institute, and the more recently founded Industrial Design, Engineering, and the Arts schools of Tacoma, all grounded in student interest and partnership throughout the city.

Purdue's Polytechnic High School, a partnership between Purdue University and the City of Indianapolis and many other industry and community partners, is working similarly. With hands-on, real-world projects supported through local partnerships and mentors, the purpose is to create a highly engaging opportunity for youth to consider STEM pathways that contribute back to local industry.

These schools, from which the above are just a handful, are here and there. But as I say, "There are cool schools here and there ... but there should be cool schools everywhere."

Why is the status quo not to identify the potential interests and needs of a community or region and design schools that support students' potential interests in the areas of need, opportunity, and potential?

In Denver, Embark Education runs a middle-school learning community in the back of a coffee shop and bike repair shop that they contribute to, sometimes work at, and use as a learning hub.

In Melbourne, FL, a former police officer and his wife, who had a wide variety of school experience from around the world, tried their hand at home schooling their young son and even tried private school. Eventually, they sought out a way to connect families around a shared interest of following their children's learning and immersing themselves in the context where they lived – rich in the arts and lush in the outdoor environment – the Verdi EcoSchool.[72] Again, the focus of the school, like many of the other schools referenced before, is to pay close attention to the interest of their students and then support what they want to learn and how they want to learn by affording them agency.

Ok, yes, there are at least 100 other stories from across the country and another at least 200 from around the world similar to those above. But 100, even 200, and even 500 out of 20,000+ schools in the country does not speak to the power of redesigning schools around (1) the interests of youth, (2) their connecion to place, people, and the community, (3) their sense of agency and possibility in the world.

Right now, schools are like TV dinners. Small portions. Precooked. Lacking taste. Packaged and divided. With limited options. And possibly not very nutritious.

I am not saying the educators are not well-meaning, or kind, or doing their absolute very best. Most educators have their kids' best interest in mind. But after years of being part of the factory. Being a part of the assembly line of learning. The "I Love Lucy" assembly line of chocolate curriculum expectations,[73] cynicism, and eventually feelings of being overworked, inadequate, and at a loss as to how they can sustain their energy and well-being.[74]

If teaching has become an assembly line and schools have become factories where standardized test scores become the measure of success, we are not only killing our kids (their potential interests, talent, and creativity, no less their sense of agency and possibility), but the interests and potential of our educators.

In short, by NOT allowing for the creation and ownership of "cool schools," as I like to call them – schools with identity, a strong-sense of community purpose, educator and community buy-in, along with a focus on the current and future well-being of each kid through the pursuit of their interests, agency, and sense of possibilities – we will continue this deep plunge into apathy. Not good. Really, not good.

Support New School Networks

As Lydia Dobyns, the CEO of the New Tech Network, and Tom Vander Ark, CEO of Getting Smart and former Executive Director of Education for the Gates Foundation eloquently put it, it's "Better Together," meaning we can go much further and have more impact when we team together and network.

If we think about scaling innovations and new school models and programs, it happens far more quickly and with integrity when the effort is supported through and by a network. When Tom spent a day at the original Big Picture School in the basement of the Rhode Island Department of Education in Providence, he emerged from his time there and approached Doc Littky and Elliot Washor saying, "Here's five million dollars, I want 10 of these schools." And with that, the beginnings of the Big Picture School network came into being.

In reality, when attempting to get something new off the ground in a context that has not been prone to doing much different – such as the case of a Big Picture school where there are no classes or classrooms or a rotating schedule of classes as most high schools operate – it is very hard to "sell" a new model of school that feels very different from what those in the system know. As a district or school leader, no less an individual educator, to say something like, "We want to run a program with no classes or classrooms and we are going to focus on the passions of kids and have them do their learning in the community" just sounds CRAZY! What? What are you talking about? And when things sound so different and it raises lots of questions like, "Well how will they learn? What will they learn" and "What about college? Will they be able to go to college?" come, the school or district leader, less so even the classroom educator, is caught between a rock and a hard place. Knowing it is best for kids runs up against an insurmountable if not deliberately resistant group of parents, fellow educators, and school board members.

However, if you present an alternative school design that has been up and running and has evidenced beneficial outcomes for youth to parents, school board, and educators, then people are more likely to listen, ask questions about the program (less so directly targeting you) and you have some chance for others to consider the possibilities.

That's the first benefit of networks. They can create an opportunity to be heard and considered given it isn't your crazy idea but that the model or program is operating elsewhere (albeit differently) and with some results that might appeal to those listening to you. My friend Jeff Petty probably knows this all too well. It's one thing to get your own new school or program up and running, but getting others to see the value of the new model is another thing. Jeff, who was the founding Principal of the first Big Picture School in the Northwest, turned his attention many years after to growing Big

Picture Schools throughout the Northwest. Because many school systems have an "alternative" school for students who are disengaged and on track for dropping out but their programs continue to not work for these youth, hearing about a program that has had such success can be a godsend.

So when Jeff would approach the leaders of a school system asking if they have such a program and asking how it was working, it wasn't really that hard to sell them on the idea that a Big Picture environment might serve their students better. What would create their interest in hearing more and considering the new design? The fact that there are 50+ of these learning environments in play elsewhere serving similar students (disengaged from schooling, at risk for dropping out) who are now engaged, learning, graduating, and in many cases going on to college.

The fact that the model is working elsewhere with students similarly disconnected and having an impact can play a big role in a school system adopting the program and giving it a try. Next, the system benefits tremendously from how others in the network have developed their new learning environments. In addition, they benefit from the documented practices and successes and know-how of the other schools in the network.

Scale New Schools and Successful Practices across the Country

Besides being able to sell the idea grounded in experience and outcomes, probably the greatest benefit to building from a network is that the network comes with tried practices that have evidenced impact. In addition, you are joining a network of specialists and educators from across the system that you can draw from to build your own practices.

One of the best examples of this is the CAPS network, which prides itself as not being a "top-down" organization, expecting its affiliates to duplicate without consideration of its own context. Affiliates, rather, are invited to join the network and to take what is of use to them. Affiliates are invited to join monthly zoom meetings to share best and new practices, problem solve challenges, and share resources that have proven to be useful. In addition, the network hosts an annual "summer huddle," where affiliates share new ideas, new practices and are inspired by others in the network.

The same is true of the Big Picture Schools, New Tech Network, Summit Public Schools, EL Schools, and NAF network too, to name just a few.

In reality, as much as I am in favor of a small group of individuals starting from scratch and creating something awesome and wonderful, it isn't easy to land on just the right idea and have something up and running that has the immediate outcomes and results desired. And if it is hard to get something off the ground that is entirely different than what is being offered now in a school system, connecting to and aligning yourself with a network can be just the thing needed to gain the willingness of the local stakeholders (such as the district, school leadership, school committee, and families) behind the endeavor. For that matter, the support and guidance offered by the network can be invaluable to getting your version or iteration of the model up and running.

If we want to see an exponential growth of new schools or learning environments that have the kinds of desired impact we have been discussing in this book, then joining and being a part of and learning from and with a network can prove to be the game changer in growing such schools across communities and school systems. These networks will provide an environment for schools to learn from and with each other.

Create more Networks

Having said that, I am not saying that we should put all of our eggs only into the current networks we have. I am saying we should use networks to scale new models, particularly models that have evidenced the kind of impact we desire, and the kinds of networks that effectively assist others to grow their versions of the schools or programs the network has grown. In addition, through grants, district-supported efforts, and community-based activities, we should continue to incentivize and invest in the growth of new models that address the needs of local communities. And upon demonstration of their success, there should be efforts to incentivize and support the leaders and educators of those new models to assist and support others to consider and when desired grow that new model in their own community and system.

We want continual innovation, creation, and exploration of new models of education in communities. And once these models prove promising, we need to invest in the potential proliferation and growth of those models elsewhere through networks.

Publicly Fund and Credential Alternative Educational Programs

Probably the most well-known mechanism for using public monies to fund "alternative" learning programs is charter schools. Charter schools are set up a little differently across states, but there is typically a state charter school board or commission that can authorize a charter school – though in many cases a local school board can be an authorizer or co-authorizer as well. And in some states a university can be an authorizer of a lab school as a charter school.

But apart from this mechanism of creating a new school, I believe there should be other mechanisms in place to offer youth, their families, and the community with alternative learning programs that could benefit youth either entirely separate from, or in tandem with, one's local schools.

VLACS is one excellent model of this, and there are several other examples of the same across states. VLACS, as detailed earlier, is an independent charter school sponsored by the state of New Hampshire, affording any student the opportunity to take one or more classes offered by VLACS. The original intent of this offering was to provide any youth across the state with educational opportunities not provided by their local school system. Take AP Biology or AP History for example. Due to the size of local systems in New Hampshire, many of which are quite small, many youth did not have the option to take several specialized elective or AP courses, such as in Psychology, Biology, or History. Well, in steps VLACS, which offers a wide variety of these classes as they are able to host a class virtually, and more likely several sections of such a class, because they provide these offerings to students throughout the state.

Of course, this is not the only reason that VLACS stands out as a beneficial and valuable asset to the entire state. VLACS, over time, has been able to develop and grow a variety of different offerings for youth across the state which are not often provided by a students' local school system – such as internships, community-embedded projects, and career exploration.

Students from across the state can take advantage of these offerings *at no cost to them* and importantly, *no cost to the sending district*, unlike what happens across many other charter schools across the country. In many cases, local school boards and even parents dislike local charter schools because they feel as if these schools are taking away financial support that they desperately need. And in many cases, it is true that the money follows the student into the new charter school. But, then again, now the sending school system typically loses its allotment of funds for that student. Or in many cases 80% of the funding for that student, with the local school system often being able to keep at least 20% of that students funding, even if that student is no longer requiring any more support from that sending district.

VLACS-like models. Given the extraordinary success of VLACS, in not only providing offerings such as AP classes but also more innovative opportunities such as community-embedded courses and profession-based pathways, why not allow for any variety of groups to apply for the provision of offerings also not typically offered across many school systems? Perhaps they are designed around differing learning paradigms or focused on particular professions or themes. Or focused on facilitating learning in communities.

The power of VLACS is that (1) it is offering learning opportunities not offered across all systems and (2) the district or local system loses no money, and (3) a local school board cannot nix or block the offering for youth across the state. There is the question, of course, about accumulating the number of state-required credits for a student to be able to "graduate" from that school system. In this case, it is up to the state to either dictate acceptance of those credits for the student, if concerned about an application to a higher ed institution, to provide a transcript of learning from any one or more of the learning organizations the student has participated in.

But this kind of thinking is in direct alignment with the work toward credentialing learning across systems, something learning institutions at both the k12 and higher ed level and in industry are all working toward.

Note, that these offerings do not necessarily have to be virtual or online as well. And these offerings do not have to fit within the unfortunate currently prescribed structures of schooling as we now know it.

Interestingly, these alternatives have taken root here and there by the sheer will of educators, parents, and communities and continue to pop up despite the system. Pods, for example, were created early on in the pandemic. Those innovating under charter school expectations. Even districts with courageous leadership. And

A select few other examples of what I reference as "cool schools": learner-centered, agency-oriented, out of the box, future-focused, community-embedded

Homegrown, local learner-centered private schools
- The Verdi EcoSchool (Melbourne FL)
- Brightworks (San Francisco)
- City of Bridges High School (Pittsburgh)
- Embark Education (Denver)
- Nautilus School (Chicago)
- Sweetland School (Hope ME)
- Village Free School (Portland OR)

Private School Networks
- Acton Academy Schools (120+ in over 30 countries; in the US, such locations as Austin, Grand Rapids, Nashville, Durham, Rockford IL, and Verona NJ)
- Wildflower Montessori Schools (over 80 in the US)

Innovative, Learner-Centered Charter Schools
- Da Vinci Schools (Hawthorne CA)
- Minnesota New Country School (one of the originals, teacher-powered, Henderson MN)
- High School for the Recording Arts (St. Paul MN)
- Odyssey STEM Academy (Lakewood CA)
- Urban Montessori Charter School (Oakland CA)
- City Neighbors School (Baltimore MD)

Innovative District Schools
- Latitude High School (Oakland CA)
- Northwest Passage High School (Coon Rapids MN)
- Innovations High School (Sparks NV)
- Workshop School (Philadelphia)
- 5280 High School (Denver)

Districts (agency and learner-focused)
- Lindsay (CA) Unified
- Barrington (RI)
- Northern Cass School District
- Cajon Valley School District (El Cajon CA)
- St. Vrain Valley School District (Longmont CO)
- Albermarle County Schools

Regional Endeavors
- Remake Learning (Pittsburgh area)
- The Real World Learning Initiative (Kansas City area)

regional efforts, spurred on by a network of interested parties and stakeholders galvanized by local leadership.

But parents and educators (within and outside the public education ecosystem) are having to figure out other means of funding which often relies heavily on philanthropy or families themselves (although the families themselves are having to pay taxes for education, whether it be through property, state, and federal taxes). In this sense, families are having to pay twice. These individuals and families paying taxes throughout their lifetime are having to pay for these alternative learning environments on top of what they are already paying for in their taxes. At some point, someone (the populace, families, and politicians) have to start to think about how the choice of learning environments should be an option for all.

The unfortunate reality is that while states should be ones to incentivize and support this work, most states don't (period) or do so but badly. State governments are not very good at providing such services, so what states need to do is find organizations, districts, and community partners to do the work.

Getting funds to engage in an initiative that extends beyond the local school system and endeavors to stretch across multiple other parties and school communities can go a long way to buffering criticism and potential undermining.

Districts do undertake their own initiatives, such as the start-up of new schools. And there are a great many service providers (non-profit and for-profit) that can assist districts and schools in their efforts. But the additional costs and political debate can get in the way of pursuing many of these efforts. Hence, state-initiated, supported, and funded endeavors can go a long way in assisting others to develop new schools and new programs side-stepping the direct attack on local leaders and stakeholders.

This is why the state should step in and fund a variety of efforts with the support of incredibly savvy service providers to get a hundred new school designs and programs up and running and spend less time hamstringing those who wish to do better by youth, their families, and their communities.

Next ... I will present how such efforts could be incentivized and supported by the federal government, states, and local communities to start, grow, and proliferate learning environments that could serve all youth foregrounding their agency and opportunity for all across the country.

– 9 –
A Model for Change

So, how do we make sense of and use all of this information and these stories of success and stories of challenges to help MOBILIZE a new array of possible educational opportunities for all students across the country? What does this look like in reality? How do we go from hundreds of non-engaging, underperforming, and factory-model schools and bring options to our youth that adheres to our knowledge of learning and communities in keeping with the 21st century? How do we get our system to stop perpetuating old paradigms of teaching and learning in order to create a new cultural, political, and social ecosystem of vibrant communities? How do we prioritize student-centered, 21st century learning opportunities that support the ongoing development of new schools and allows for the closure of schools that do not serve our children well?

Going beyond Charter Schools

Over 20 years ago, everyone thought that charter schools would become the vehicle for experimentation and innovation that would result in the proliferation of better practices, better school designs, and greater outcomes for kids. It was believed this would happen in two ways: (1) charter schools would develop new and supposedly better schooling practices that other public schools would want to pursue and emulate, and (2) this would be driven by a sense of competition – if we don't, we might lose our students and subsequently our school. Neither of these things have happened. Yes, *some* charter schools have created some amazing school designs and practices that other schools should want to emulate. But for the most part, we've seen "other" public schools (and I say "other" public schools because I want to remind everyone that charter schools ARE public schools) simply portray charter schools out to be the "bad guys." Instead of looking at what they are doing well and looking to them for inspiration and insight as to how they could be doing school differently, they have simply berated charter schools for taking resources and skimming the best kids from their shared populations, using their political weight and social media to castigate their existence. "They are taking students from our schools, leaving us with less" is the idea they propagate.

But I must speak to the funding claim that has been made by most charter school adversaries, that they take funding and resources away from public schools. I vehemently oppose this view as it makes no sense to me. If you have half the students, and thus are getting half the funds to run your school, how are you losing funding? You still have the same funds per student (and, in fact, more than most as charter schools typically get only 80-85% of the same funding per student). So, in fact most charter schools are getting less funding. But you don't need the same amount of money to educate 80%, 70%, or 60% of your students. You don't need the same number of staff. You only need X% of the funds to serve X% of your students. So you are not, in reality, losing any resources per student.

This kind of argument is used to draw the ire of a school's constituency and fuel their community's vocal opposition to charter schools without fully explaining the actual situation. The ability for individuals and groups to sway others' views with only partial, skewed, and biased information drives me crazy! Which is what happens through social media all of the time. Many adversaries make easily codified statements without providing all of the details to gain support of their desired views and achieve their desired outcomes. Again, which drives me crazy. Particularly when it inhibits the possibilities for youth.

I make this point (other than just to give myself the space to vent), to spotlight how the stated intentions of policy makers to transform education through charter schools has in fact not worked. Rather, those who have been bold and savvy enough to pursue new designs of schooling have done so (see for example such schools as Latitude High School in Oakland, Da Vinci Schools in Hawthorne CA, and City Neighbors School in Baltimore). But when you look across the country many of these progressive, innovative charter schools have faced opposition when they started. And even if they do get up and running, continue to gather criticism for drawing resources from their local school community. My beef with all of this is that these schools are actually providing a better educational alternative. And are NOT using more money. They are simply taking the monies that would be used for each of their students to educate them. Yet states and districts limit their proliferation through the policies that stranglehold their growth and the rhetoric given by those who see them as draining resources (financial) rather than embracing them as providing a beneficial resource to their community.

The additional challenge is the continued focus on the outdated metrics of state standardized test scores to assess the efficacy of these schools. While there are some great charter schools, they are too few and far between because many of them, possibly despite their focus on the holistic development of their youth, are often redirected in their efforts to focus on their ELA and math scores because of their state's outdated expectations. In many of these cases, the charter school's energy is diverted, and the schools struggle in how to focus on ensuring their students perform well on the tests while also pursuing more learner-centered pedagogies.

This is a struggle for many who, with the best of intentions, have entered into the charter school world to create an alternative learning environment for youth, but find themselves handcuffed by the performance expectations of standardized test scores. These communities need help.

Despite this crazy bifurcation of goals, there are several communities that have been able to pursue a vision and mission that puts students first in a far more learner-centered efficacious manner, such as, City Neighbors School in Baltimore, Pathways High in Milwaukee WI, and Urban Montessori Charter School in Oakland CA. But these, just like traditional K12 schools, are still too far and few between.

As much as I would like to say that charter schools are the way to go, the reality is that charter schools are a mixed bag. Just like any public school, there are the good, the bad, and the ugly. Lesson: Just because a group comes forth with an idea of a school does not mean that they have a great idea or can run a great school! This is partially the result of the fact that, in most cases, charter schools are approved by fulfilling certain state checklists but are rarely approved based on the *quality* of their ideas, design, or the talent of the individuals proposing them. I know, because I was on one of these panels reviewing charter school applications for a state, and it came down to the most basic criteria (such as if you had a facility) which did not include a smart, intelligent assessment of the school's mission and pedagogy or the talent to run the school. This seems to be a big problem, don't you think? Hence, the mixed-bag results of charter schools. They are not all great!

So ... what to do?

Press Districts to be Cauldrons of School Innovation

If states had the courage to do so, we could re-invent and re-cast the charter school idea into a new mold, and here's how:

> *Districts should be institutions whose primary activity is to foster, seed, perpetuate, and support the development and operation of GREAT schools in their communities.*

This would be a first step, instead of what we have now, which is in most cases a central office bureaucratizing curriculum, hiring, and instruction. That should not be the role of a district office. What should be the role of a district office is the "flourishing" of educational opportunities for the youth and families in their community in keeping with what we now know about learning and human development. Districts should not be about franchising McDonalds – you get the point. They should be looking at how to support the active development of new educational opportunities for the youth in their community, borrowing from proven models that have evidenced success elsewhere. The role of the district then should be working proactively to provide such multiple offerings to families and youth who can then make choices amongst these options. If the ecosystem was designed to allow for such choice, then that would far better ensure that no youth would be left without an option that would best support their growth.

The idea of an "ecosystem" is important here. Used by Ken Robinson as well as others, the framing of our education systems as an "ecosystem" invites all kinds of associations that I believe are useful when considering the design of a system that actively supports our communities to thrive. With choice, schools not serving students well could and should be closed – either by a district or the attrition of their student body. Not to go too far off the deep end, but metaphors like the sun, climate, rain, and soil, can easily be connected to the idea of a "thriving educational ecosystem" for youth, the adults serving them, families, and our communities. There needs to be an ecosystem that supports the flourishing of schools, learning environments, and learning opportunities that are serving youth well – no small matter.

Again we can point to specific schools that do this and districts should be looking to develop mechanisms and systems to incentivize educators and local community partners to create such schools. The Tacoma Schools, for example, were behind Jon Ketler to start his

School of the Arts in downtown Tacoma, in partnership with several local artists and art institutions. Followed by his development of the Science and Math Institute situated in the middle of Point Defiance Park, where students could make use of the Park, Zoo, and Puget Sound. Followed then by their development of the School of Industrial Design, Engineering and Art wherein students take on local industry projects and intern with partners throughout the city.

The Highline Schools too, just south of Seattle, building on the success of their Big Picture School and Aviation High School, just opened Maritime High School. Why and how? An analysis of local industry needs pointed to the following:

- The maritime industry is huge in the Seattle area with over 800 maritime businesses in the county alone
- While there are currently 19,500 jobs in the industry to date with an average pay of $83,000, it is projected that there will be a job shortage of 150,000 mariners by 2025.
- Job growth is expected to be over 6% each year

Apart from these employment opportunities, the founding school team wanted to increase their students' engagement in authentic research and issues of sustainability.

Galvanized around common interests and concerns, Maritime launched in partnership with multiple organizations, including the Port of Seattle, Northwest Maritime Center, and Duwamish River Community Coalition. Partnerships such as these can feed resources and expertise into a school as well as create opportunities for students to learn in authentic contexts and contribute back to their community.

Such examples are just too far and few between. But they exist. And school systems should be looking to learn from these examples and incentivize, support, and establish such schools in their communities – grounded in local needs, students' interests, and potential future pursuits.

Incentivize Specific Practices

P-Tech. In 2011, IBM partnered with the City University of New York and the New York City Public Schools to create a new high school/community college/industry hybrid program that would prepare youth in Brooklyn for employment in "new-collar" (i.e., STEM and computer science) fields. Over time, the P-Tech model has grown to over 240 schools across 26 countries.

The purpose of the model was to give youth, typically youth growing up in low socio-economic contexts, a leg up in successfully pursuing gainful employment while contributing to the needs of a local community. The fact is, in many low socioeconomic contexts, youth are *not* graduating because they see no purpose to their high school education. And then those entering community college rarely successfully complete their programs.[75] Of course, for these young men and women, not having a high school degree or some post-secondary education greatly limits their opportunity for employment in gainful employment fields – those fields where one can make a living wage. More importantly, they are not gaining the specific skills needed by industry in their communities. Having a degree from a high school, community college, or four-year college in and of itself does not automatically get you into a highly desired professional trade or vocation. Only having direct experience in the field will get you that!

The designers of P-Tech recognized the significant shortcoming of an education model that worked as a series of escalators for youth to take, going from one grade to the next to graduation and beyond, broken in so many ways. There isn't a clear vocational/professional pathway. Educators say that you need an education. But to what end? Jumping from escalator to escalator without a clear end in mind doesn't land you work you love or that can sustain you.

Even for those graduating high school, pursuing higher education is not automatically the next step for millions of our youth. In some middle-to-upper income communities, going to an elite college or university is a clear expectation. Assumption really. It's baked into family and local social culture. But for many more, youth are going on to a local state school or community college. And for many more, close to half, youth are simply going to work, grabbing any job they can by whatever means they have. And even if you go to a local state school or community college or 4-year institution for that matter, the pathway to a high-need industry profession is a crapshoot. Hence, the escalator problem. Youth are told that they need to do well in high school so that they can then go to a good college. And then they need to go to a good college so that they can then get a good job. And then they need to get a good job so that they can then pursue a good career. Hence, jumping from one escalator to the other. But reality is ... these escalators don't all line up. And jumping from one thing to the next (school, job, career) is actually very tricky – and not easy to navigate. One thing does not necessarily line up and lead to the next. Actually, for most youth, the jump is significant, and youth jump from one escalator to the next crossing their fingers that the destination will be good. But they have to jump from one escalator to the next. And, unfortunately, without a clear pathway that can land them in a vocation or profession they actually want, they land somewhere as a result due more to chance than by design.

It's very sad, really. And what P-Tech did was to close the gaps from escalator to escalator. They created clear pathways for youth, for them to choose. The students enter a single program that gives them their high school degree, associate's degree, and the kind of real world experience that makes them employable in the industry of their choice.

That is the P-Tech model.

Now, back to you legislators and policy actors. What can *you* do?

Several years ago I went to the P-Tech website to find out where P-Techs had taken root (knowing they had grown in number) and saw that a great number of them were in New York State. I wondered why. Why so many in New York State and not elsewhere? Well, turns out that the state legislature, having seen the results of the P-Tech in Brooklyn, came to realize the model as an opportunity to impact local workforce needs across the state. The need for a pipeline of skilled labor was not just in Brooklyn, but all over the state, in such places as Rochester, Buffalo, Utica, Newburgh, etc. New York state has numerous urban centers where there is a need to re-invigorate industry with an infusion of skilled labor and give kids purpose in their education. They quickly saw that supporting the development and proliferation of P-Techs in these communities could be a solution to many needs – economic and educational. Why not create opportunity for thousands of youth in these communities and create employee pipelines to local industry where it was sorely needed?

With this recognition, the NY state legislature incentivized the start-up of a dozen partnerships across the state in a dozen low-socioeconomic communities so that there was greater potential for industry to grow and youth to be engaged in purposeful education. Now in its 6th year, a local school district with a local community college and local industry partners could apply to co-create their own local P-Tech.[76] Through this funding stream, there are now 48 P-Techs alone in NY State, across 37 communities impacting thousands of students' lives, involving 100+ industry and 35+

college partners, supporting skill-based employment pipelines across the state for youth.[77] These profession-based pathways support employment pipelines in such needed areas as:

- Mechanical engineering
- Advanced manufacturing
- Networking technology
- Advanced manufacturing
- Cybersecurity
- Computer science
- Business
- Health care
- Drafting & design technology
- Automotive technology
- Computer information systems

This is not to say that the P-Tech model is the only model of such innovative practice across the US or the world. Several other examples home-grown also exist. For example, in RI, Rhode Island Community College partners with the Rhode Island Nurses Institute Middle College to create a nursing pathway for youth in the greater Providence area,[78] in direct response to the forecasted need of 4,000 nurses in the state in 2024. And in Seattle, the Highline Public Schools developed Maritime High School.

Imagine that. Giving students a purpose to their education (toward gainful employment) and creating a pipeline to that employment, gaining the skills and work experience AT NO COST TO THEM, serving a real employment need in their community.

States can incentivize such partnerships through funding but ALSO through direct support of the programs.

Microschool the Possibility

More recently, Tom Vander Ark among many others[79] have ventured the potential benefits of microschooling – starting small schools with a small group of pioneers, building a learning environment from the ground up. I'm a big fan of this idea for a variety of reasons as well. First, it is a LOT easier if you start with a small group of amazing educators, learners, and families to get something off the ground, working out the kinks and nimbly adapting and pivoting as needed than it is to build something in a large system with the typical constraints of a bureaucracy and too many stakeholders. Second, you are far more likely to have success because you start at a scale (small) that allows you to iterate on the idea and revise, refine, and adapt as you build the school over time.

Microschools allow a small group of educators to put something down on paper (or whiteboard, or google doc, or in whatever format) and play out a new school design that is unlike what has been done before. Having a small number of individuals at the table allows the "imagineers" (as I like to call them) to quickly connect, design, iterate, and ultimately put their design into action. Large systems tend to slow down the design and implementation of new ideas and the iterative process necessary to bring those ideas into reality. Large systems tend to slow down the process through too many ornery communication needs, the press for shared expectations, and the debate over practices. One is far better off putting their money on a small, smart, and highly innovative and creative group of individuals than creating some formula that engages everyone and hoping that the different entities will follow through on the vision.

In this way, policy actors should be creating legislation that affords particular groups of individuals both within and outside of district systems to *microschool* a design with a small group of stakeholders, which can be inclusive of parents, students, and community members. But not too big. And not overlaid with bureaucratic nonsense.

Sounds a lot like charter schools, right? Well, in some ways it is but without all the red tape and typical machinations that stall and inhibit innovation – including funding.

With charter schools, funding becomes an issue. Charter school founders have to figure out a way with minimal and reduced funding to pursue innovation and are hamstrung by states' expectations rather than allowing for new expectations.

State legislatures should devise ways to fund innovation and protect innovators from the usual backlash. Would that mean there would be no oversight? No, I am not recommending that. I don't want to say specifically how this oversight should be given. But if it were me, I would appoint a small 5-person committee well aware of and highly knowledgeable of innovative practices and put it upon them to afford access to the funding and policy relief. Then appoint a larger team to semi-annually spot-check and review the activities and outcomes of the school the first three years. The spot-check would be comprised of a 2-3 day site visit with the engagement of staff, parents, partners, and students.

If the state were super-smart about growing and supporting innovation and transformation, then it would create its own innovation network. Schools could visit one another to share transformative practices and convene annually to share identified practices with others. In this way, the state could start and support its own in-state innovation network, with the hope of inspiring and supporting potential transformative practices across the state.

Scale the Model through a Network

We know from experience that there are specific models that have made a significant impact on student experience and student outcomes. And the best of these have figured out a way to scale their model. This is no small thing, since we have found that lots of individuals and groups, including districts themselves, have attempted to create new models of schooling with limited success. In some ways this recommendation stands antithetical to my previous recommendation as what I am saying in this recommendation is that it is far better to start anew with a model that has been well-crafted through multiple iterations across contexts and proven efficacious for learners.

However, if we only allow for innovation through scaling then there is no room for the initial innovations to be developed in the first place. There needs to be a policy environment that supports innovation from the ground up with close attention to impact that can – from its initial stages of success – offer itself up as a model that can serve youth in other contexts.

This is how many of the schools I point to have started – by a confluence of conditions that allowed for the initial innovation to take hold through the savvy work of those starting the innovation and the alignment of interest and resources in starting the innovation in their contexts. This is so true in the multiple examples I have referred to in the book, including the startup of the first Big Picture school, BVCAPS, the first New Tech school, EL schools, and the first P-Tech for that matter.

If it weren't for the right people being in the right place at the right time with a "perfect storm" of conditions – the need apparent, the right people in the mix, and a confluence of support – these innovations would have never happened.

Engage Stakeholders & Build a New Operational Ecosystem

Another pursuit with potential significant and long-term impact is convening multiple stakeholders in a local ecosystem, for example, Cedar Rapids IA, Indianapolis IN, Newport RI, Dallas, Chicago, or the Rosebud Reservation in North Dakota. I mention these localities specifically because this is exactly what Education Reimagined is doing in these localities, giving voice to parents, students, and local community entities such as Cedar Rapids (who are starting a new high school), Newport RI (working with FabNewport), and Chicago (with the Chicago Cooperative), listening first and then supporting them to imagine what education ecosystem they would like to have. Then asking, what is getting in the way.

Alin Bennett is one of the leads of this work at Education Reimagined, along with Bobbi Macdonald and several others. Recently he shared some central questions for their community partners in the work:

> If you had full policy, freedom, and significant investment, what would you build? Then what are your current barriers? What are your current opportunities? What do you see as possible?

From this inquiry, they engage community members in "rapid prototyping": What could be? And how could it work?

When challenges arise, such a funding or policy constraints (such as required seat time or content coverage), the group engages potential local funders and importantly, state policy actors that could potentially provide more funding but certainly, at no cost, waive some of the policies that get in the way of innovative school and learning designs. For example, youth pursuing competency-based learning rather than seat-time based learning.

In Indianapolis, for example, the work is proceeding with great promise because there are several educational stakeholders that can collaborate to design and pursue their design. First, there is a school model that is already evidencing great success, initiated by a strong partner in Purdue University, that wanted to provide an innovative educational program to help youth (particularly youth in under-resourced communities. Purdue Polytechnic High School, started in 2017, is now three charter schools in Indianapolis with strong support of the city, Mayor's office, and several other local community members.

The vision was to create a network of high schools that would build on Purdue's expertise in engineering, technology, and applied

Purdue Polytechnic High School Beliefs
Competency Education. Students learn more than just content knowledge at PPHS. The school focuses on the competency skills that employers and colleges identify as the most important skills to be successful in the real world.
Empowering Students. Students are given control over which projects they participate in. Industry Projects give students the opportunity to come up with creative solutions. Student voice and choice are an important part of EVERYTHING done at the school.
Pathways to Success. Students will be prepared for college or careers after PPHS. If they meet requirements, they have a direct admit to Purdue's Polytechnic Institute. Students get internships, certifications, & more!
Authentic Learning. Students work on authentic projects with local industry partners to solve REAL problems using the design thinking process. They create their own prototypes and pitch their ideas to industry experts.

sciences with hands-on, project-based learning experiences for students in Indianapolis.

The model has been widely recognized for pushing the boundaries where they need to be pushed in education today: project-based, hands-on learning; voice and choice in projects; self-paced curriculum; personalized schedule to a student's individual learning goals; internships; dual-credit courses; technical certifications; job shadowing; professional mentoring; etc. And if they fulfill all Purdue admission criteria, automatic enrollment into the university.

Finally, students learn at the school through projects. Immersion Projects where they problem-solve and solution-build with the help of coaches, gaining content knowledge where useful and applicable. Passion Projects where students can pursue a project of their interest related to what they want to learn and their future aspirations. And, finally, Personal Learning Time, where students can pursue independent learning, whether that is related to their Immersion Projects or Passion Project.

The value of of having this working model in place is that the community can see the impact on youth. Now the work of Education Reimagined and their partners is to further their image of what is possible growing from this model and potentially creating several more of these learning communities throughout Indianapolis utilizing current industry partner spaces or other available spaces, which then releases the district from having to build or upkeep currently outdated facilities.

It is no small thing that Purdue wanted to support the school and that President Daniels was keen on supporting a new kind of school. As Scott Bess, the founding Executive Director asked the founding board: "Are you going to create a STEM high school, or do you want to fundamentally reinvent what high school looks like."

It helps too that Scott is on the Indiana Education Board, where he can work with policy actors to re-evaluate policy in the state that might hinder the innovation they want to undertake.

So too in Cedar Rapids. Given the success of Iowa Big in engaging youth in real-world projects and hence real-world learning and learning of value, the district embarked on a journey to reimagine high school with the support of Iowa BIG, Education Reimagined, and other partners. They will be creating a new model of high school in keeping with models like Iowa BIG that have proven successful with youth, such as youth being out in the community and undertaking meaningful, real-world projects with the support if not collaboration with community partners. Fun fact, the building is even purposefully designed not to be able to house all students at any one time, with spaces for student work being identified throughout the community, such as the local library, YMCA, and other community partners.

As Alin says, the current system "is designed for efficiency, standardization, and compliance." And it is the policies and funding systems that work toward these outcomes where in reality it is the ecosystem – funding and policy stems – that should be oriented toward innovation and divergent practices that serve youth far better dependent on who they are, where they want to go, and what each community aspires to give their youth.

As Bobbi Macdonald, Alin's partner in the ecosystem work at Education Reimagined, shares:

> So it's kind of like there's top down work, and then there is grassroots work. But also when people begin to experience the kind of learning that we've been talking about, then they begin to demand it in a new way, too. So I just want to say we're kind of hitting it at every level, because you can't just wait for the grassroots demand, you also have to do the top down work of advocacy. The grassroots part makes a difference because there's like a feedback loop that emerges. You know, like, Hey,

these are the things that are limiting us. These are the things that are holding us back from doing it full out. So we want this changed. You know, so that's part of this effort, I think.

But for this to take off, district leaders are going to need to step up to the plate to support the incorporation of new practices and creation of new learning environments. And state policy actors are going to need to re-orient their position from ensuring standardization to incentivizing, creating, and supporting opportunity for innovation. Innovation within the ecosystem grounded in student, family, and community aspirations and new visions of learning and opportunity for their youth.

The Challenge Then

The challenge is to revisit our perspective on the purpose of education and the ways we can engage youth towards those purposes. The current ecosystem foregrounds test scores in ELA and math, the accumulation of credits, and a view of learning that is counter-productive to actual learning, meaning actionable learning.

The impact of *funding* and *policy* has come up again and again as significant instruments contributing to the outcomes we have today in our education systems – and I don't mean this in the best of ways.

Awful policy. Take the reallocation of Title I monies toward specific models of school turnaround with the punitive overarching expectation that the school will raise their students' ELA and math scores, or else. The provision of smaller learning community grants with the expectations that large high schools would break up into several smaller learning communities to foster better student-teacher relationships without the requisite adoption of practices that create purpose and opportunity for youth. The continued siloing of knowledge, skills, and know-how into discipline fields unconnected to real-world, meaningful application. The focus on content knowledge without the more significant frames of thinking and acting that impacts students' life course as well as their ability to contribute back to their communities and the world.

In my mind, as well as many others', Urie Bronfenbrenner's theory of ecological systems is extremely useful in considering how multiple stakeholders and actors in our education ecosystem should be engaged in revisioning our education ecosystem in support of agency and possibility for all. In short, Bronfenbrenner's theory highlights how the activity of our larger systems (such as policy and funding as well as implicit and explicit values at each level of the system) impacts how we experience and grow at more local systems.[80]

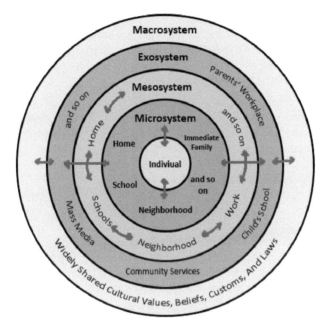

For example, in our current education ecosystem, the mandate by actors at the macrosystem level (policy actors) results in expectations and mandates of those who exist at the exosystem level (district and school leaders) who then feel compelled to direct classroom educators and staff who exist at the mesosystem to act in accordance with their own set of expectations as they believe is necessary given the expectations and directives of those at the macrosystem level (policy actors).

Unfortunately, at the end, it is the students and collaterally the families who are victim to this design, being acted upon by this waterfall of expectations and directives from our state legislature down to district leadership down to school leaders and ultimately classroom educators.

I point to the state ultimately for the origin of cascading expectations and resultant outcomes for youth, the experiences of their families, and the impact on our communities, as in the end it is the state who is responsible for the provision of education in each state. Which doesn't mean the feds have no say. In reality, they can and have play a significant role in what the states do and how they do it, as they hold the purse strings for a significant amount of funding, which each state wants. Dependent on what each state does and how they do it can result in the provision of more or less funding, as is clearly the case how the feds afforded each state ARRA and Title I monies from 2009-2014. And states will play good in order to receive federal dollars, as there is always a need for more funding to support education in every state.

To clearly illustrate how this cascading set of directives, expectations, and policy impacts each child, and collaterally each family, each community, and the state as a result of a state system of education, consider the current design of most high schools. In most states, districts are expected that each high school student will have covered specific content (such as biology, chemistry, physics, algebra, and US History) as indicated by seat time or the student cannot receive a high school degree. This expectation and directive is pressed by the policy actors in a state's education system who decided and reinforce these expectations which forces district and school leadership to develop, expect, and sustain the model of high school we now have. The unfortunate victims given these mandates are then (1) the classroom educators who are then expected to fall in line with this purpose and expectations of school as mandated by policy, whose behaviors then impact (2) the student, who is at the center of this circle, and collaterally, the family, the community, and the state.   In such ways as graduating youth without clearly identified personal and professional aspirations and skills that could (1) benefit them, and (2) their communities and (3) the state itself.

The other example that clearly illustrates the unfortunate outcomes of current state ecosystem directives is the press to raise student proficiency scores in ELA and math, which has caused some elementary and middle schools to double-down on reading, writing, and math with a skills focus offered through a variety of curriculum and online platforms that zero in on the skills disconnected from any real student interest or meaningful engagement.

How is our $$ being used? As for the impact of funding, we can see where some forms of funding can incentivize districts and schools to pursue new structures and practices, such as the small learning community grants provided between 2004-2010. While the intent was admirable, the outcomes were mixed as many districts wanted the money but were less serious about impactful follow-through.[81] Alternatively, the threat of withholding money can also mobilize activity. But history has equally shown that this form of press for change does not result in any truly significant and long-term impact.[82]

What does work? Inspiring and then supporting others who want to do something that will benefit others, such as one's teachers, their students, their families, and their community. And we have seen this again and again and again in the numerous stories throughout this book (such as the start of High Tech High, Big Picture, Charlotte Lab School, or Iowa Big) and the work of some district leaders (such as Lynne Moody, Pat DeKlotz, or Cory Steiner) or the individual effort of hundreds of educators and parents who have gone out of their way to start new independent microschools. It is in this mixture of individuals wanting to do good and harnessing relationships and resources where we see transformational change and new beginnings happen. So support such endeavors. Look for ways to inspire others about the possibilities, and then support those who wish to mobilize new activity and new schools that can far better serve our youth, their families, their communities, and the world.

Unfortunately, funding streams that mobilize such activity typically happens OUTSIDE federal and state support. Federal and state funding continues to support schools as they now operate. And state policies, even under the guise of innovation by way of charter schools, do not inherently engender the potential creative possibilities in education because they remain shackled by the same policy directives of our conventional school model, such as high school transcript expectations, seat time, and the focus on ELA and math proficiency scores by way of standardized tests.

I would be remiss not to reference some efforts by states to support if not incentivize innovative educational designs, such as Massachusetts with its "Innovation Schools Initiative" (https://www.doe.mass.edu/redesign/innovation), Colorado's "Innovation Schools Act" (https://www.cde.state.co.us/choice/innovationschools), and Indiana's "Innovation Network Schools" (https://www.themindtrust.org/innovation-network-schools), all initiatives which are intended to support schools and organizations to play out new designs and new models of school.

However, If one looks at the two most significant funding streams for public schooling – see an overview of the current streams of funding per student in the two tables below – there is no reason why a state and/or local district couldn't set aside a very small set of funds (even as little as .05%) to incentivize, support, and grow new schools and programs that are in keeping with our current needs today. And not just need, but in keeping with what we now know can truly give each youth a leg up in life. That helps them find purpose, and far better prepares them to be able to pursue the lives they wish to live and work they would like to pursue.

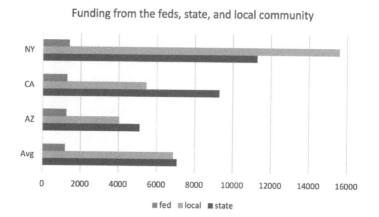

Funding from the feds, state, and local community

Unfortunately, as can be seen in the next table, too often philanthropic entities, such as the MacArthur Foundation, Walton Family Foundation, Gates Foundation amongst several others, inclusive of the very (relatively) small, for example, the Vela Foundation, Barr Foundation, One8 Foundation, etc., are the ones who have had to pick up where our public institutions have not. It was the Gates Foundation that had to initiate and support the small schools initiative in the early 2000s. The Walton Family Foundation supporting alternative schools that serve youth better, sometimes even OUTSIDE our public school system (such as One Stone). And the XQ Superschool initiative, basically an endeavor launched and almost entirely supported by Lauren Powell Jobs (Steve Jobs' wife), to support communities to reimagine high school.

One could argue the Charter School movement was and continues to be the way states support innovation, but the design of charter schools neglected and continues to neglect the upfront resources necessary to start something from scratch, as well as the policy dynamics that in many cases pit the local public school system against the start-up of a local charter school (except in those very few cases where districts are the ones initiating and supporting the charter school).

Current K12 Funding Sources[83]

Public (mix of federal, state, and local funds; includes traditional public and charter schools; funds can be supplemented through parent outreach, donations, and philanthropic funding)

Public School funding

- **Total funding:** $15,120 per student, ranging from $8,770 per student in AZ to $24,881 per student in NY State, with the greater majority spending between $11,000-$18,000.
- **Federal funding:** The federal govt. provides on average $1,193 per student, ranging from $1,100 in MO to $6,128 in HI, with the greater majority of states receiving between $1,800 to $3,500.
- **State funding:** State governments provide on average $5,098 per student, ranging from $7,058 in AZ to $11,273 in NY State State.
- **Local community funding:** On average, local communities provide on average $6,868 per student across the US, but this can vary greatly across states and local districts. For example, in Westport CT (where I went to high school), the total state and local funds provided per student in 2020-21 was $24,292. In Hartford CT (where I worked for several years), it was $17,939. But these discrepancies are even greater across other states.

Private (consumer)

- **Independent Private Schools** (typical, can range from traditional to progressive; primarily funded by families), now serving roughly 5 million students across the United States
- **Private school networks** (paid for by families and supplemented through donations and philanthropic funds)
- **Microschools** (at this time, entire family funded and possibly supplemented through grants, donations, and philanthropic funds)
- **Homeschooling** (primarily self-funded by parents)

Grants

Federal, state, and philanthropic, ranging from incentivizing the pursuit of new designs to implementation and assessment of specific practices. At the federal or state level, rarely funds the start-up and proliferation of innovative learner-centered progressive schools, leaving it to the beneficence of various foundations, such as the Vela Education Fund, to do.

Philanthropic giving

- The MacArthur Foundation has awarded hundreds of millions of dollars to schools and districts to improve schooling with mixed results from 1980-2004, leading them to focus on connected learning

- The Walton Family Foundation has awarded billions of dollars in the last 10 years to charter schools, school choice advocacy, research on education reform, and initiatives to improve educational outcomes
- The Gates Foundation from 2000-2009, contributed $1 billion to start and support the transformation of schools into small schools, with some significant results)
- The New Schools Venture fund has contributed more than $350 million from its start in 1998 in support of entrepreneurs and the start-up of schools with a focus on creating greater equity for learners
- XQ Superschool is an initiative launched by Lauren Powell Jobs funding new high school designs across the country, providing over $100 million since 2015
- The Vela Education Fund has provided over $23 million to support the startup and scaling of "permissionless innovation," supporting over 500 individuals and communities in the development of their learning environments

Yes, the feds have done what they thought and felt would best incentivize and support new practices and new designs in schools, for example, the small learning community initiative, turnaround schools work, even the i3 grants. And as mentioned before, some states are attempting to do the same with such efforts as Colorado's Innovation Schools Act, Massachusetts' Innovation School Initiative, and Indiana's Innovation Network Schools. But when you look across the educational landscape, many of these efforts have not yielded the transformational shifts we need in school designs, inclusive of re-orienting the purpose of school.

In most cases, these innovation efforts still hold schools accountable to the old metrics of schooling and do not entirely give them a whiteboard to re-imagine all of the possibilities. There are boxes to fill, and checkmarks to fill in. Some of the more innovative schools, such as Iowa BIG or Highline Big Picture school, have been able to create new means of evidencing learning that appeases the old guard while pushing the envelope toward more valuable, meaningful learning.

When you look at true innovation – new school designs that foreground student agency and opportunity – these are too far and few between, and typically created by a few individuals who have been able to break the mold, through their imagination and determination. The current ecosystem with the inculcated expectations, policies, and use of resources as they are and have been remains fairly fixed. So to pursue a revolution it will take many of us to bring the significant shortcomings of this reality to light, and then engage others in the idea that we can redesign school and redesign school in ways that far better serves our youth, our communities, and the world. Then inspire them with the "images of possibility" that will "feed the imagination." Then deliberately rally the relationships and resources we need to start a new wave of schools.

So now what? How is this going to actually happen beyond these few examples, these few schools?

I propose some ideas in the next Chapter.

– 10 –
What YOU Can Do

"If not you, who?" "If not now, when?"

The question then becomes: What can I do?

Good question. Dependent on where we are in relationship to the school system, we can feel completely at a loss as to what one can actually do. I'm a parent, what can I do to engage my school in considering new practices. Or the district to consider starting a new kind of school?

I'm a teacher in the system, what can I do to engage district leadership in considering the potential start-up of new kinds of schools? It doesn't matter whether the district is small or large. There are school and district leaders in the system that have attained their positions to either maintain the status quo or improve the schools – but nothing too outrageous or out of the norm. That could get the school board or parents concerned. Doing something new typically gets others anxious. What is this thing? What will it do? What happens if it doesn't work?

Even as a school or district leader, there could be roadblocks to change. Change is not easy for most, particularly when it involves their livelihood. Or one's children.

I don't have all the answers, but I have learned over the years that there are certain actions different stakeholders can take to potentially engage others in imagining new possibilities.

District Leader

Let's start at the top.

As a superintendent, the spotlight is on you. You have primary responsibility for the health and well-being of the district. And with that comes a great deal of public attention, expectations, and scrutiny. This is where the challenge can be incredibly difficult. So many stakeholders at play, each with different kinds of needs, and everyone wanting you to act and enact in a variety of ways, for the most part benefiting them specifically in their particular role.

There are only a handful who have been able to venture forth and create a system *with support* to push the envelope and do something out of the norm from other systems.

Here are a few.

Lynn Moody. Former superintendent of the Rowan-Salisbury Schools in semi-rural North Carolina. Just retired, I caught wind of Lynn Moody through my friend Kelly Young, who heads up Education Reimagined. She told me how Moody, in a way, was able to do an end run around the typical constrictions of state mandates and policies put in place when pursuing new practices in schooling. Recognizing that she would not be able to empower her educators to pursue new school practices without a waiver to do so from the state (North Carolina), she took a chance in a meeting with North Carolina State Senator Michael Lee, who was co-chairing a finance committee for education at the time. The committee was trying to figure out how to streamline the finance expectations for districts so that it was not so cumbersome to fill out and present their rationale for expenditures.

Lynn with a host of other superintendents was invited to speak to this issue at the state capitol and serendipitously ended up having lunch with the Senator. At this lunch (I was told), Mike ended up sharing this with Lynn (not directly a quote, but something like this): We have all this money we would like to give schools, but we just don't know how best to give it to them so that they would be better outcomes for our youth. Seeing an opportunity, Lynn said (again, not a direct quote), something like: Well, I know how I would use the money, but you have all these policy restrictions and funding expectations that limit us from doing what we could to help us serve our youth far better. The policies get in the way. And handcuff us from exploring new practices and pursuing new ideas. In short, she told the Senator that it would be far easier if districts were able to take control of how they spent their monies to serve their youth best. Of course, she added, it would take a great deal of deliberation and thought on the part of districts on how to best use their monies, but with this freedom they would be able to pursue initiatives and efforts that were now off the table.

As it so happens, the Senator took that information under advisement, and 18 months later, new legislation was created on district and school spending and Lynn, and her district in particular, were afforded the opportunity to use their monies as they saw fit. In short, the Rowan-Salisbury schools were identified as a "school renewal district," affording them the freedom to innovate around not only around their use of funding, but also their calendar, personnel, state testing, and curriculum With this freedom as well as the inspiration and careful deliberation Lynn took, which included conferring with and learning from a great number of organizations she knew were on the leading edge of schooling – Education Reimagined, Next Generation Learning Challenges, Transcend, Mastery Transcript, amongst many others – she was able to incentivize and support educators throughout the district to reimagine and pursue new visions of teaching, learning, and schooling.

But this story is unusual. It is a superintendent who put herself in a position to press the thinking of a legislature and engage other organizations in the process of re-envisioning possibilities in her district. As big if not a bigger point – she engaged her community with the possibilities of redesign, "feeding the imagination" I like to say, with visits to other districts, schools, and organizations across the country that could help them envision new possibilities.

As she said,

Not only do we now have this opportunity to transform as a renewal district, we have a moral obligation to do it well. Most school districts would dream for this scenario, so for them, we need to go big or go home. We have to be bold and show what a school district could really look like with the kind of flexibility we have.

We've spent the last 18 months getting clear on the direction we want to go. And, we have found great partners that are ready to work with us in moving it forward. We needed to find people who could speak our language and we have.

Now we're trying to figure out how to put the meat on the bones. How do you put the processes, procedures, and policies in place that sustain this kind of thinking and energy over a long period of time? As we flesh that out, we are ready to take this to the next level and be an example for the rest of North Carolina and the nation, as a whole.[84]

In reality, there are very few superintendents, central office administrators, school leaders and educators who will go out of their way to do something different for students, particularly when it comes to learner-centered, progressive practices, and new school designs. Doing something different means putting a spotlight on them. And the job is hard enough without adding the challenge of galvanizing a community to reimagine school and pursue those designs which lead to new opportunities for youth.

But there are more examples, of how this can be done.

Pat DeKlotz.   In 2006, Pat DeKlotz was appointed Superintendent of the Kettle-Moraine School District, which serves 10 municipalities between Milwaukee and Madison, Wisconsin. As a former marketing director and manager of technical support, DeKlotz decided to enter the teaching profession at the age of 42. As a middle school science teacher, she very quickly found that, "There was a sharp contrast between the work environment I had experienced in the private sector versus what I saw in public education." She added, "This highly qualified workforce was basically waiting to be told what to teach, how to teach, when to teach. There wasn't as much collaborative problem solving." And soon she wanted to challenge "some of the artificial boundaries that we have in place in education." Sound familiar?

After serving as Principal for two years, she became Assistant Superintendent, then Superintendent of the district. In keeping with other ideas in this book, she took advantage of an opportunity to grow something new in the district. And to engage her community members in reimagining how they do school.

Faced with a significant budget shortage as a result of a change in state funding and given a new opportunity to break away from typical school expectations, such as credit based on seat time, she was able to rally a small number of fellow educators, along with board support, to start two schools from the ground up two new schools. One focused on the performing arts and another on Global Education, which have since served as models of potential redesign through the district.

As I have recommended throughout this book, she started small and with the willing and interested. She didn't attempt to upend the entire school system, which for many would have been difficult. But rather sought out to empower a small group of individuals who would embrace change, embrace being part of a design process, and embrace learning, innovating, and pivoting as they go.

As she said, "We started with a handful who were excited, who were willing, who were risk takers, who were able to, you know, be very reflective and evaluate their successes as well as where they needed to improve." And this is not a small point, "One of the things that starting small allows you is the ability to be nimble. If you are learning something that isn't working as well as you want, you can change it very quickly. So we learned a great deal, and we did make modifications and changes along the way in order to best meet those student needs and best support the staff in doing so."

She also added, "There's a verse in Ecclesiastes that says, if you wait for perfect conditions, you will never get anything done." And later, "You know, I think about large-scale reform. You can spend all your energy trying to get people ready to go where you could be using that time to learn from the beginning. And, you know, knowing that people need models and that there are differences, if I can show teachers that maybe haven't experienced personalized learning themselves, what it looks like and the impact it has, they're much more willing to take it on. Because ultimately, all teachers want to do what's best for students."

I share this story because it is entirely illustrative of what could happen in *any* district across the country. There is no reason to have just *one* kind of school. One kind of high school. One kind of middle school. One kind of elementary. And typically, in the mold of what we have been doing in those models of schooling for a long time.

We need to give educators ownership of what they do and how they do it in the best interest of *their* students. And they need the space to go out of the box, and to innovate, and to learn and pivot as they go. To say it is not possible in your district means only that one has not rallied the various stakeholders to commit to doing something better for their kids.

Not saying it is easy, but it is going to take courageous superintendents, school boards, and educators to pursue these endeavors by galvanizing the opportunity, resources, and relationships that can make it happen. At least at some scale. Starting small and with the passionate and creative first.[85]

Susan Enfield.   Dr. Enfield was the Superintendent of the Highline (WA) Public Schools from 2012-2022. Two schools had been started in Highline prior to her hiring, but Dr. Enfield saw the value of having two schools in the district that served their students differently. And then based on the success of those two schools, was more than happy to support the start-up of yet another school in the district attentive to local needs and student interest.

Highline is home to the first Big Picture school in the Northwest (Big Picture is discussed elsewhere in the book). And under Dr. Enfield's leadership, not only did she fully support the high school but she supported the school's desire to incorporate middle school students in 2020.

Similarly, although Aviation High School started before her tenure, she acted as a staunch supporter of the school as it moved to Boeing field and expanded the opportunity for youth in the Highline Schools to attend. It is now regarded as one of the best STEM schools in the country, focusing on the aviation industry utilizing project-based learning, real-world work opportunities, internships, and mentoring from aviation experts. Not unlike many of the other schools I spotlight in the book.

Finally, she supported the development of Maritime Academy, which opened in 2021. Discussed earlier in the book, Maritime Academy was founded on the need of the local maritime industry with the opportunity to engage youth in real-world problem-solving and research in partnership with local industry and non-profits.

While this was only a part of Dr. Enfield's work – she instituted several other initiatives that expanded opportunity and support for youth throughout the district while Superintendent – it is worthwhile to note that the other needs and work of the district did not distract her or withdraw her attention and energies to support the alternative learning environments already established and even continue expanding those options.

While the work of being a superintendent is hard – navigating multiple stakeholders' needs while ensuring the health and well-being of the district – that doesn't mean that a superintendent cannot go out on a limb and actively work to create alternative learning environments for students and the community that want them.

The Importance of District Leadership. The instrumental role district leadership can play in the start-up and support of new learning environments is clear in the stories above, as well as the start-up of the three Tacoma schools and numerous CAPS programs discussed elsewhere. In such cases, district leadership saw the need

A Story of Change: the Northern Cass School District (ND)

When Corey Steiner became Superintendent of the Northern Cass School District, a very small district 30 miles Northwest of Fargo ND, serving a total of 630 students, he wanted to revolutionize how they did school, and empower students to pursue the learning they wanted. While the district was doing well on traditional metrics, they wanted to pursue the possibilities of personalized learning given the shifting landscape of work and opportunity for their youth. Inspired by visits to the Harrisburg School District in South Dakota and the Lindsay Unified School District in California, the conversations solidified their vision, that "Every learner can change the world; therefore, we must provide a world-class education."

Driven by this powerful belief, they focused on fostering learner agency by creating transparent and adaptable learning targets while at the same time supporting students to pursue their interests and passions, from a young learner composing her own music to an aspiring engineer building intricate models. Their innovation also extended beyond the classroom. Acknowledging that learning can happen anywhere and anytime, they explored the accreditation of open-walled experiences, from camping trips to community service and internships, students were encouraged to learn through their reflection on these experiences. Collaboration and communication became the pillars of this transformative journey, engaging educators, parents, and students in the journey. Through parent task forces and community forums, they ensured that everyone was part of the conversation. Parents became advocates for their children's education, and educators felt empowered to design personalized learning plans.

As they pursued these new designs, assessment practices underwent a profound shift, moving beyond the traditional to authentic assessments that allowed students to showcase their learning through projects, portfolios, and real-world applications.

The result? Teachers, once bound by rigid curriculum frameworks, now find joy and fulfillment in guiding their students' individual paths. They have embraced the role of facilitators, creating a nurturing and supportive environment where students feel empowered to explore, take risks, and pursue their interests. Given this, they have:

Increased Student Agency – The learner-centered approach has empowered students to take ownership of their learning. Students are actively involved in setting their learning targets, exploring their interests, and making connections between different subjects. They have a voice in their education and are encouraged to advocate for themselves, which has led to increased motivation, deeper engagement, and a sense of responsibility for their own learning.

Personalized Learning – By tailoring instruction to individual student needs, interests, and learning styles, the district has created a more personalized learning environment. Students have the opportunity to progress at their own pace, explore their passions, and pursue their interests. This approach acknowledges the diverse strengths and abilities of each student, ensuring that they receive the support and challenges they need to thrive.

Collaboration and Professional Growth – The district has fostered a culture of collaboration, sharing best practices, resources, and ideas, resulting in increased job satisfaction, professional growth, and a sense of ownership among educators.

Enhanced Parent Engagement – Through community forums, task forces, and open dialogue, the district has actively engaged parents and community members in the transformation process. By providing clear explanations, concrete examples, and opportunities for input, the district has built trust and understanding among parents. This engagement has led to increased support for the learner-centered model and a deeper appreciation of the impact it has on student learning.

Redefining Assessment and Transcripts – The district has challenged traditional assessment practices by shifting towards a standards-based assessment system. This change has moved the focus from grades and compliance to a more comprehensive understanding of student learning and assessments that represent the richness of student experiences, skills, and achievements, ensuring that colleges and universities can understand and evaluate the holistic development of students beyond traditional metrics.

and/or embraced an opportunity, when needed going out on a limb and forging ahead with what was needed to actively support the development of new learning environments across the system, as Pat DeKlotz and Lynn Moody did. In some other cases, it might simply mean pursuing an identified opportunity to start one or more alternatives in alignment with other models across the country (such as a Big Picture school or CAPS program) or take advantage of a vision and local interest to start a brand-new school (such as happened in the Tacoma schools, discussed earlier, or Highline schools, discussed above).

Either way, there is precedent for such progressive efforts, and my suggestion would be for any superintendent who wishes to do the same to reach out to others who can help them think through the particular challenges and possibilities in their community. Such work is not easy, and challenges may easily arise in attempting to pursue such activity. But that doesn't mean it shouldn't be done and pursued. It just means, I think, you need to find others that can offer you counsel and serve as a sounding board on how to successfully navigate the tensions and realize the possibilities.

School Leader

So, you have risen through the ranks. Initially a teacher, then assistant principal and now principal, in charge of the whole ship. First and foremost, there's a lot you need to do to keep the trains running on time, such as staffing, scheduling, student enrollment, curriculum, PD, teacher evaluation, parent engagement, general oversight of SPED and ELL programs and supports, etc. That's a lot.

You might feel good about it. In the best of all worlds, you are creating a community. You are a well-respected and beloved school leader. Better, you create a feeling of enthusiasm and sense of community where everyone is happy to be a part of the school and feel they are making a significant contribution to it. Teachers feel supported in their efforts.

Worst case scenario, there is a LOT going on and the job just feels too big. Too many staff. Too many issues. The district is breathing down your throat to ensure some form of quality instruction is happening in each classroom. And more importantly, that ELA and math scores are at or above expectations.

This is the reality for most. The district (leaders and personnel), in its industrial model of functioning as a system, worries itself with each of the schools and how they are running, and they expect each principal to run that school so that it is not under fire. In some cases, principals get individual attention when "the district" feels they need it. In some (many?) cases, the district decides what they think is in the best interest of the entire district and might purchase wholesale curriculum and PD that they entrust will have the impact of raising student scores on the state test.

Do I mean to imply this is the case in every school and district? Of course not. There are many schools (and districts) who have – through careful, cognizant, and attentive efforts – been able to develop a positive, collaborative, collegial culture that staff enjoy and thrive in. It is devoid of the pressure cooker ethos that can pervade school environments when leadership fails to create individuals in a community together around a shared purpose and sense of ownership to the endeavor. And this is far too much the case, I believe, because of the frequent turnover of leadership throughout the system at both the district and school level. It is also a byproduct of our current system where individuals are not brought on board to steer and nurture a school with its own identity and meaningful vision and purpose. Schools feel like part of an industrial complex where the paramount intent is to push curriculum and in some cases the achievement of test scores.

If you look at the "cool schools" list I have compiled – in the Resource section of this book and on my website (youcanchangeeducation.org) or highlighted on our Revolution podcast series – and access their profiles, related articles, and websites, you will see that they each have a specific focus to their work. Many of these foreground the development of student agency, support of student interests, engagement in meaningful (to the student) work, access to real-world experiences in support of their interests, and skill-building. All of these schools clearly center themselves around a shared community focus that everyone believes in, embraces, and actively works on with their colleagues and leadership.

The Big Picture Schools are a good example of this. Because of their focus and the clarity of their purpose, they have been embraced by many communities across the country. It is not hard to argue for youth getting out in the real world and exploring what it really entails, either professionally or in terms of societal needs and opportunity. It is also not hard to argue that getting kids side-by-side with adults in various professions could help them understand what the professions really are and the skills and knowledge needed to engage in those professions. The Big Picture schools have developed and refined the structures and practices that support such endeavors. For example, such simple things as: Tuesdays and Thursdays being internship days; having an advisor that knows you well and supports you; and public exhibitions of learning which evidence what you have learned in your efforts.

Iowa BIG takes this a step further and rather than focus on internships, they focus on teams of students working on real-world, authentic projects for others (non-profits, for-profits, government agencies and religious institutions). They do this by reaching out to community entities and asking if they have any projects they need done but can't get to right away. They then ask if they don't mind a team of students taking a crack at it. These then get dumped into a "project pool" where students can then look into the pool and decide on what they would like to work on, which is important because students are *choosing* what they want to work on rather than being *told* what they have to work on. This ensures student agency and intrinsic motivation for pursuing the work.

Today, Iowa BIG has become so well known for their work with youth and how they operate that community members now come to the school to pitch projects to the kids.

Finally, and perhaps aligned more to the typical structures and practices of traditional school, Olympic High School has taken their charge to create opportunity for the youth they serve in Southeast Charlotte and with time has built over 700 industry partnerships that offer over 500 internships to youth each year and provide over 24 million dollars' worth of time, technologies, and support.

Not unlike many other career academies and vocational schools across the country, they have five specific career academies wherein youth learn about the profession and develop the skills associated with that profession, supported by interaction with professionals in each field, job shadowing, and most importantly internships. But Olympic has moved the bar in what can be and how rich such programs can be in partnership with industry in their community through the concerted effort of one individual in particular, Mike Realon, who has from inception embraced the possibilities and grown the invaluable network and opportunity for their students over time.

Now the kids in their community, many from families making $24,000 or less, are gaining the hands-on and minds-on skills they need to pursue professions with expected incomes that will allow them to thrive. These students are making money through their internships in the summer (as much as $25/hour) and securing employment at a place of interest making as much as $50,000/year (if not more). And in many cases, their employer is paying for their post-secondary education which benefits both of them.

Classroom Educator

As detailed earlier, the first thing you can do is to "get in the know." You most likely have been subjected to lots of district and organizational rhetoric about how to move your teaching forward. Worst-case scenario, you have been and continue to be relegated to district and/or school-specific PD or mandates that are tantamount to pacing-guides and recipe curriculum because the school and/or district can't figure out a way to get out of their own way and create means for teachers to be creative and collaboratively work towards pedagogy, classroom and school practices that focus on being learner-centered rather than standard-, curriculum-, and content-centered.

This is because most districts do not know how to create communities of creativity and innovation. And this in some ways is not their fault. I don't necessarily want to point my finger at them, since it is the "system," as I have been arguing throughout the book, that is cause for most of what we see. The system, including putting the press on school and district leaders to achieve certain scores on standardized tests or else fall under the microscopic scrutiny of the state, has instigated this response.

In many ways, school and district leaders are in just the same bind as you– pursuing actions you may in fact not be comfortable with. The difference is that it is school and district leaders who should be figuring out how to do an end run around, if not through, the system. There are a very few school and district leaders across the country who have done this. But again, they are very few. Very few. Like .01% of district and school leaders across the country.

Most, when faced with the challenge of pursuing more learner-centered practices rather than state-mandated expectations to raise standardized test scores, follow the lead of most other districts and adopt similar practices.   This may include the purchase of curriculum programs, software, and wholesale PD that zeroes in on the challenge of raising math and ELA scores at the expense of more holistic approaches to learning.

But YOU have a different opportunity. In YOUR classroom and with YOUR students, you can seek out new practices, tools, and resources that you most likely can pursue within the context of YOUR classroom. Whether it is pursuing a new pedagogical practice like PBL, a new tool, like Flipgrid or Nearpod, or a new strategy, for example, 1st and 2nd drafts rather than just final drafts of work.

To find these, read and seek out new ideas in any one of the resources I have offered (more in Part V and the Appendix) and pursue suggestions provided by those mentioned throughout the book.

Beyond this, bring to light some of these new practices and tools to your community. The trick is to bring these to light --not by telling others "you/we should be doing this – and you/we are stupid for not" – but by finding a way that invites others into careful considera-tion of the ideas. No small feat. How do you say, when the time is right, "Hey, I was reading about ..." or "Hey, I've started to try and do this." It's a dance. But it's a change agent dance. It's a dance where you are not telling others YOU need to do this. But somehow bringing to light the issue as you see it in a way that they also can voice their concern for the issue, and then share the tool, practice, or strategy to light in a way that invites them to see the opportunity of their use to address the shared issue or inspiration.

This is real change agent work. And not always easy. But if you want to see change, you need to BE the change. And this is the thing you need to think about. How to engage others so that THEY want to try new ideas, pedagogies, and strategies out themselves as well.

School Board Member

This is probably a no brainer. But don't mistake that for being easy. It's definitely not.

As any of the cases above and below for any stakeholder, getting a bead on where your various stakeholders are at is critical, so that you can strategize and engage them in ways that facilitate the consideration of new learning environments.

It is hard to recommend any particular strategy as it is hyper-dependent on the perspectives of the stakeholders and their stance to change. Perhaps paramount above all is to find a way to engage them around their particular interests taking into account their vantage point. If you are a school board member, this means getting to know your other board members and finding a way to connect with them and build a relationship that can sustain the opportunity to explore and potentially mobilize support for more learner-centered initiatives if not schools.

Remember the story of how Iowa BIG came to be. Mary Meisterling, chair of the Cedar Rapids (IA) School Board at the time, got wind of Trace Pickering and Shawn Cornally starting a new school in the community, private to start. But having heard a bit about how the school would operate and its intention to engage youth in meaningful projects in the community led her to tell Trace and Shawn: I want that school in our district. Of course, Mary most likely had a great deal of respect on the board and in the community, so everyone supported the idea.

In some cases, a board can direct the superintendent and all district personnel to explore and pursue new ventures. In the case of Blue Valley, once Superintendent Trigg told them about the idea for a Center for Professional Studies supported by their focus group responses of parents, they were enthusiastic about the idea. Then after telling them it would take over a year to plan and get underway with a new building, they were so enthusiastic they asked him to get it up and running within the next few months.

Boards can play an extremely influential role, directing district leaders to undertake and pursue a number of initiatives. Unfortunately, boards are not typically made of educators "in the know." Of course, each school board member is well-intentioned, want to contribute to the health and improvement of the district. But many, if not most, school board members are not aware of the alternative, more progressive, learner-centered school designs that are possible.

As I have made note elsewhere, if one does not go out of their way to find and learn about alternative ways to do school, it is easy for one to assume that school should look like and operate the way that they have experienced school. So probably one of the most important things school board members should do is "to get in the know." For me, it would be learning about many of the schools I spotlight in this book. But also look to network with other educators across the country who are forward thinking – future-oriented. Educators who are helping other districts to move in this direction and district and school leaders leading such endeavors.

There is nothing like talking with those who are doing the work. Then you can ask them, how are you doing it? Like Ben Owens and Adam Haigler, my friends at Open Way Learning[86] who are assisting numerous districts in pursuit of their own visions for learner-centered communities. Or Devin Vodicka and Katie Martin who run the Learner-Centered Collaborative.[87] Or Transcend Education,[88] whose focus is to assist schools to be "extraordinary, equitable learning environments." And, interestingly, Transcend even hosts an innovative models exchange, [89] where a variety of learner-centered and equity-focused school and program models are showcased.

Of course, it is one thing to learn about these various models, including cataloging the impact on students, and another in being able to galvanize a school board around a shared vision for what they want to support and direct. And another on how a school board can most effectively direct and support the district in pursuing such endeavors.

I think this too is where organizations like the ones I have mentioned could go a long way in assisting board members and school boards in moving a district forward.

Community Member

I think much of my commentary and recommendations for school board members is appropriate for any community member as well. Although community members may have no formal power in their local system of education, such as a school or district leader or school board member might have, that does not mean you cannot gather information from others regarding what is and isn't working in the system and gather as much information regarding alternative environments and the benefit to students and the community as possible, if not also who could assist in the development of these endeavors.

Knowing alternatives and being able to point to them with evidence of impact can go a long way when talking with others. The idea is to remain curious and inquisitive and ask questions pertinent to what you see as the need. Coming in like a bull in a china shop rarely works in any context. But asking questions and finding out where others stand on issues and asking for their recommendations invites them into conversation, and can help build the relationships you need to pursue new designs.

In asking questions you are in a far better position to offer ideas and thoughts in direct response to what others are seeing and thinking, as well as offer additional thoughts directly related to what they value.

Being a change agent takes a great deal of savvy thought, being incredibly mindful of how you engage with others and finding ways you can engage them so they consider new possibilities. Being attentive to what they care about and value is central.

Not unlike the school board member, investigating and then reaching out to others that can inform you of alternative learner-centered environments can greatly help you communicate the possibilities to others. So not unlike my recommendation to classroom educators, school and district leaders, and school board members, it is advantageous to any community member to seek out and learn about the possibilities. Then consider how you can share those possibilities with others hoping that this might inspire them to consider those possibilities themselves.

Industry Leader

Much of what I have said before is pertinent as well here, except potential industry partners should not only reach out to the organizations and educators I have mentioned in this book, they should reach out to suggested industry partners working with those schools. For example, Olympic and now Palisades HS in Charlotte NC work with a great number of industry partners, and the educators there could connect you with industry partners that might be most advantageous for you to talk with, to learn more about how they partner with the school. The same is true with the CAPS Network. They now have over a hundred affiliates all working with industry partners across the country. And many other schools across the country are working with industry partners in a variety of ways.

Most important is to seek out the various ways that different schools collaborate with their partners and to consider how you might want to be involved, not just for the benefit of students but also your own company, organization, or non-profit. Learning more about how this could work could help you think about what you might want to do, and then aid you in talking with local schools and/or the district about how you would like to be involved and contribute.

Of course, if the school or district is not involved in the kinds of activity you would like to contribute to, that means you will be in a position to share with the school and/or district what you have learned and consider with them the possibilities for creating something programmatic that would be advantageous to the school and its students as well.

The first place to start, however, is to "get in the know." Then it is up to you who you should approach and how you might like to approach them with the ways you might like to partner with the district or school. Even use your newfound connection to other schools and/or organizations to facilitate an inquiry between your local school and/or district and the other educators you yourself have reached out to.

Policy Actor

I'm not saying this would be easy. There are certainly a great deal of political and social machinations that would need to take place to engage the necessary stakeholders to get innovative legislation off the ground.

The most promising actions policy actors can take to move education in their systems forward are:
- financially incentivizing innovation or particular practices
- providing policy conditions that allow for innovation and transformation

Failures in this realm, at least at the federal level, includes:
- grants that do not hold system and system leaders accountable for their actions or fulfillment of expectations
- not identifying external partners that can artfully and effectively help others to design and then mobilize their improvement/transformation effort

Areas that are definitely a mixed bag include:
- punitive actions to force the hand of systems and system leadership
- the lack of clear models *with* effective guidance and support to mobilize the effort to be successful

What is missing more than anything is (1) granting those who know what to do vs. those who do not know what to do and (2) not building in systems of expectations with the proper guidance and support to enable the successful development of new practices.

Rather than go into numerous examples under each of these categories, let me give a cursory overview some cases that serve to illustrate the central points above.

The failure of SLCs and the Need to assist Communities deeply invested in New Designs. I was part of the federal small learning community (SLC) initiative from 2004-2008 when I acted as a small learning community coach employed at Brown University serving over a dozen districts in their SLC work. Based on research of small school practices that seemed to have an impact on student persistence, success, and college-going rates the previous ten years, the intent was to (1) create smaller communities where students could be better known and better served with a smaller group of educators concerned for the well-being. This came with such practices as advisories, teaming structures, and the provision of career academies, which could create more purpose for student engagement. However, it proved to be a struggle in many ways, with the schools and districts charged with how they would pursue their SLC work, running up against challenges as scheduling, staffing, advisory designs, etc.

Most notable to me was the degree to which schools, when they received the funds, were whole-heartedly invested in the spirit of the work and willing and able to change their school design in the best interest of the students. And up against challenges in reconstructing their systems and practices, school communities tended to pursue those practices in ways that did not fully realize the vision.

In my mind, the promise of monies indeed incentivized districts to pursue the grants, but in reality the school systems and leadership were not fully invested in the ideas enough to pursue the new designs nor did they have the capacity to galvanize their communities in pursuit of the new designs.

There are two lessons here, I believe. When incentivizing new designs, ensure that you are affording communities with a specific and earnest interest in creating a new design that can truly benefit their youth and the communities. And ensure that the community is invested in bringing the new design to fruition.

P-Tech and the value of Scaling Models with Clear Guidance and Support. P-Tech is probably the best example of how a state can functionally scale a model that can have significant impact across communities. With the evidence of impact in hand from the first P-Tech in Brooklyn NY, the state legislature created an application and funding stream to incentivize and proliferate P-Techs across the state. [90] One thing that makes this work is the clear guidelines expected of the grant awardees as well as a clear model of what is expected with a provider that can effectively guide the grantees in enacting the model as proven successful across contexts.

All of these are very important elements, as has been borne out in other pursuits to create new model schools within states and across the country, no matter the funding agency (federal, state, or philanthropic), such as the New Tech Network,[91] ConnectED,[92] and EL Education Schools.[93] These networks have learned over time where to begin with the stakeholders in the district and how those district leaders can engage their stakeholders in the enterprise, galvanizing support. And then gaining the counsel and tools and processes for building out and eventually implementing the model.

All of these steps are very important. So as a state or local policy actor, pay significant attention to the process of engagement and facilitation toward eventual success.

Fund Districts that want to Partner with Exceptional School Designers. Which leads me to this potential effort. Fund districts to engage with exceptional school designers, developers, and facilitators. I am in favor of supporting small groups of individuals with a compelling design and identified capacity to build out the design. But there are several individuals and organizations who have, through experience, learned how to assist and support the development and early build out of particular school designs.

Many of these have already been mentioned before:

- P-Tech
- New Tech Network
- CAPS Network
- NAF (formerly the National Academy Foundation), which has helped scale over 650 career academies across the country
- Big Picture Learning
- EL Education
- Transcend Education
- Building 21

The above are established organizations who have a great deal of experience in supporting others to grow their model in a district. But there are also some exceptional educators who have developed local school models that have had a significant impact on their youth and community. And I often recommend that educators go out of their way to seek out such models and when one catches their attention in design and outcomes, to reach out to those educators to learn more about the model, how it started, and if they could be of assistance in helping them build out an iteration of their model in their own system.

Examples of such places with educators willing to help include:

- The educators who founded the SOTA, SAMI, and IDEA schools in Tacoma[94]
- Mike Realon and colleagues formerly of Olympic HS and now at Palisades HS in Charlotte NC
- Educators at One Stone who are developing a suite of tools and practices for other schools and school systems to use that puts student agency, design thinking, social entrepreneurship, and making a difference in the world front and center
- High Tech High
- the Da Vinci Schools

- Design39

This is not a complete list, but a start.

Policy actors at the federal, state, regional, or local level would do well to investigate and come to know each of these models and then consider mechanisms in their purview to offer funds to districts to investigate and then pursue any of these models with the specific assistance of any of these individuals and organizations.

Fund Ecosystem Development. Finally, I believe the effort that may have the greatest local, regional, and state impact is funding to support a coalition of entities that can build out an ecosystem of learning and support that directly impacts student vocational opportunity.

The best example I have of this is the ecosystem of supports, partnerships, and activities that students at Olympic HS and now at Palisades HS have in the Charlotte NC area. Over time, Mike Realon and the school has developed a network of industry partners that co-design and collaborate with the school to develop their courses, internship opportunities, and potential pathways into their industry. It is an amazing story, and some of it is captured in some of the videos I have recorded over the past several years.[95]

While this is a singular case of ecosystem development, state, regional, and local policy actors should take note of California's Linked Learning endeavor started in 2009 with nine demonstration districts serving over 275,000 high school students, 75% who were economically disadvantaged, and since has included an additional 20 districts and served over 85,000 students in more than 290 college and career pathways. The work has increased student engagement, student success and college readiness. It has closed the achievement gap, increased students' professional skills, led to more college enrollment, and students were more likely to be employed in a desired job.[96] Since then, the Linked Learning initiative in CA has grown to become a national organization – ConnectED, who are now working with over 300 high schools employing 1,000+ pathways in 40+ districts serving over 85,000 students.

These are just two examples – Olympic and Palisades in Charlotte and ConnectED in CA – of how an initiative, not unlike the P-Tech model, can work to serve an entire region while also considering local workforce opportunities and potential professional pathways that could give economically disadvantaged youth a leg up in possibilities.

As my friend Mike Realon often points out, creating such ecosystems can go a long way to breaking generational poverty, particularly for Black and Brown youth. Generational poverty is a very real thing and it is very difficult to break this ongoing cycle unless there is an intervention that can directly impact the employment trajectory of a student. This is one of the most telling stories in Charlotte, which was ranked 50th out of 50 the largest cities in the country for economic mobility. Many of their graduates have been afforded employment and apprenticeship opportunities at $40,000+ per year right out of high school with the potential of making $85,000 per year within eight years in a community where the median family income is less than $25,000. Many of these graduates then go on to become the breadwinners for their families just out of high school. And who doesn't want that.

This new model of education with purposeful professional pursuit is the new wave of secondary education, debunking the assumption that going to college is the only and necessary next step to getting ahead.

Policy actors should be taking a real close look at this reality and begin to consider ways that their K12 systems could lift youth out of generational poverty and contribute back to their communities.

Parent

This is probably the most challenging recommendation I can give as parents are typically cut out of the input equation. Unless a strong and vocal parent body can rally and come together as one and force the issue, not much will happen with the voice of a single parent.

Are battles what we want? No, not really. But districts will often give name to parent input but they are not really looking for significant evolution in their school district no less a revolution of their systems and practices. If you read the above under educator, school leader and district leader, you can see the squeeze they are having to attend to. You would hope that their work would be to imagine the possibilities and pursue innovation and transformation for the benefit of youth. But, sadly, as much as some school and district leaders wish to do this, when and where it happens is an anomaly.

This is true also of myself. I am equally challenged to engage local districts to take notice of ways they could do school differently.

In 2007, for example, the Newton Public Schools (where I lived at the time) received a federal small learning community grant, which afforded them the opportunity to reimagine how they might re-engage youth in smaller groups around areas of greater interest, at the same time supporting better relationships with their teachers. I received an invitation, as did all parents, to come give counsel to if not collaborate with the design team at the school. At the time, I was at Brown University, part of a group that was helping districts throughout New England, NY, and NJ design and pursue their own plans for small learning communities. And prior to the four years when I was doing that, I had been a high school redesign coach for eleven of the high schools in Seattle. Suffice it to say, I knew a few things about what was possible based on the intent of the grant (with the ultimate goal being what would be best for kids).

About eight parents showed up (including me) with 3 or 4 teachers. We listened as the teachers shared with us about the grant, along with a short handout, and described what they were thinking. I was polite. Listened. Let some of the parents ask some questions. And then started to probe. I asked a lot about how students might explore what they were interested in. How they might form small groups of students with faculty mentors in their explorations.

I stayed a bit longer, listening to what they wanted to do and asked few more questions just to see how far they were willing to go in the interest of their students rather than the ease for them to follow-through on.

I left and didn't go to the next meeting, emailing them that I was thankful to have been invited but disappointed that they were not willing to take the extra step for what would truly benefit their students.

Student

Well, this is a toughie, as students are typically the "receiver" of their education system and rarely asked what they would like to learn or how they would like to learn it. Thus, students are typically left unaware that there are choices being made about how they will be served and in reality know little of how those choices are actually being made. The resultant impact means that what they are learning and how they are learning it may have very little impact on the development of the skills and opportunity that can contribute to their future well-being.

So what can a student do? Well, it's tricky. Most students feel there is very little if anything that they can do. But there has been a history where students have risen and made their interests known.

The question is whether at least one individual, if not many in the system, will pay attention to and respect student's thoughts, questions, concerns, considerations, and aspirations.

In 2009, Sam, a then-11th grader at Monument Mountain High School in Great Barrington, MA, came home yet again disappointed in his school experience. And at the dinner table, yet again, he complained to his parents about it. Having heard his complaints all too often, his mother then said: "So why don't you do something about it and create your own school." Initially, Sam laughed at the thought and shrugged it off. But then later thought to himself, well, why not?

The account of Sam starting his own school within a school became known widely as "the independent project," as a result of a YouTube video created by Charles Tsai (youtu.be/RElUmGI5gLc) and subsequently a few follow-up videos and eventually a book Sam wrote with his mother about the start-up of the school.

I learned about the school within a school in this way, having viewed the YouTube video and, wanting to know more, ended up emailing the principal to inquire about it. Was it still up and running? Long story short, yes! She said it changes from year-to-year depending on the students that run it (which makes sense, as it is up to their design), but it was still running. I ended up driving out with a good friend of mine to visit with the current students running the school-within-a-school and learn more about how it started, ran, and was currently running today.

The visit was remarkable. I forget the students' names, but I do remember a few things about the visit that struck me:
- At the beginning of each week, each student chose a topic to learn more about and then taught their peers about it at the end of the week. Hence, they were learning a lot of good things.
- The group selected books to read together and discuss.
- Each student designed a learning project of their own where they learned by creating, making, or doing something to learn what they want to learn. In one case, a young man was learning how to play the electric guitar so was creating a studio album. A young woman wanted to learn Latin, so decided to write a play in Latin to force her hand at learning Latin.

- The group also decided to participate in group projects, identifying a process and an outcome they felt could drive their learning.

I remember walking into their "room" – which was a very small space in the middle of the school – hung with all kinds of posters, lights, and decorations. But it was theirs. And they had made it their own.

Interesting to me was the principal's comment that the school ran only if there were kids interested in running each year. And so far, 8-11 students each year had stepped up wanting to do it. To design their own school.

As I was quite taken by this amazing thing taking place in the middle of a typical, traditional high school and how a single student had made it come to life, I wanted to meet Sam and see years later what he was up to and the impact his starting the school had made in his life. Finding him was not easy, so I took to finding his mom and emailing her. (I found out that she was a professor at Williams College, which made it easier.) I mentioned having just read about the book and being completely bummed that I had missed them when she and Sam had just been at reading in a bookstore near me. (Bummer!)

It took a little work – back and forth via email – but eventually I was able to connect with Sam and arrange a time for some of my doctoral students to meet him (online).

I remember it distinctly. We were to connect with him at 2PM Boston time because that would be 7PM his time ... in Oxford, England!

(The conversation is available here: youtu.be/K4TofpjVDPM).

Two things struck me about this conversation.

1. Upon hearing he was at Oxford (no slouch of a school) I asked Sam: Why are you at Oxford? Upon which he replied: Well, when I wanted to go to college I wanted to go to a school where I could design my own learning. And after much investigation, found out that Oxford was the only school in the world that allowed you do that! (You can learn more about that elsewhere).

2. Upon humorously responding to that answer, I then asked: What are you studying? In which he replied: I am getting

my Doctorate in Zoology! What? I said. Why zoology?
Because it is the study of living systems, he said.

And there you have it.

I tracked Sam down because I wanted to see what became of a student who went out of his way to start his own school. And to see, if given the very "different" nature of this school to see if it had compromised him in any way in future pursuits: further education or otherwise. To which, I guess we must agree, it did not.

The trouble is millions of students are in a system that is making decisions for them. Not just about what they are learning but how they are learning it. They are just like "fish in water," not knowing they are in the water. And when feeling ill, or put off, or unhappy or angry ... or dumb or lost or panicked or anxious ... they typically turn the mirror onto themselves and see the problem as having to do with them, not the system. No one has even said or helped them to consider that the problem may lie with the system, not them. That the problem lies not with you (the student), but the system as it operates.

What Will It Take

In this chapter, I presented a number of examples of innovation, entrepreneurial activity, and ideas for "going to scale." I am borrowing from these examples and ideas to suggest some actions that could help us move forward, suggesting how you, no matter where you sit in the ecosystem, could take action toward a revolution in education.

This is no small task. The system is underway and many educators, community members, and policy actors sit comfortably in the system dependent on their role and history in the system. But I also know that there are many of you who are either new to the system or have worked in it for a long time, and also feel uncomfortable about it. I know, because I have talked with hundreds of you and you have said so. I think we could do a better job serving our youth. I don't think we are serving our youth well. I wish things could be different. Isn't there a way we could do this differently?

As we have seen so far, our current system of education is not engendering schools that support the development of our youth's skills or competencies, the development of their sense of agency and opportunity, or supporting them to pursue desired gainful employment. Yes, perhaps ten percent of our youth are born into a network of social capital – support and guidance, ways of thinking, and relationships – that gives them an incredible leg up. I was one of them, by the mere purchase of my family's new home in a very wealthy community with a highly regarded school system.

But I am not one to sit complacently. I recognize that I was afforded the privilege to excel at "school," in communities that created greater opportunity for me going forward. I recognize that much of this was luck – luck that my parents moved into an affluent community with a highly regarded school system. Luck, so to speak, that I was predisposed to do well and do well in the context of an "academic" culture, school.

For a revolution to occur, we need to speak up when we think we are not serving youth well. And we need to engage others in seeing the need to do things differently, but also the opportunity to do "school" differently. When we see school not serving our youth or our communities, we need to find ways to proactively engage others in considering this challenge. Beyond that, we can engage others in this conversation about what is and is not working and what *could* be by sharing some examples of what others are doing elsewhere, supporting them to also "imagine the possibilities," such as presented in this book. Then we each need to figure out in what ways we would like to engage ourselves toward new possibilities. And a place to start is connecting with others who are engaged in the revolution.

A year ago, after listening to story after story of change, of innovation, and of how of amazing new schools and programs started up gained traction (many of these stories which I have shared in this book), the observation of how many of these endeavors were simply the result of serendipity rose to the surface.

To most, and as told, others see these schools and programs as the result of incredible serendipity. Which is true. When you listen to and read these stories of start-ups, it always sounds like this or that person just happened to be in the right place at the right time. Larry Rosenstock was asked to speak to a large audience of business leaders in Washington DC and when the original speaker didn't show up, which then resulted in Sol Price (the founder of Price Club which later became Costco) asking Larry, "How much do you make?" To which, in reply, he said, "That isn't enough. Let's talk." Larry then became the head of his foundation. Which then led Sol asking Larry to speak to the San Diego Business roundtable. In which Larry then shared his idea for a school. Which then led the roundtable telling Larry, "We want that school here!"[97] And the rest is history.

So too, Trace meeting with Chuck Peters, the owner of the Cedar Rapids Gazette, who was trying to find a way to assist in a reimagining of education in Cedar Rapids, whereupon he hired Trace to be a community builder. Whereupon Trace was afforded the opportunity to proactively reach out to community members across Cedar Rapids and hold conversations about what they wanted for their children and for education in Cedar Rapids. Which led then to Trace meeting Shawn, who himself for years as a very young teacher was trying to find his way in making a dent in education, through his blog and constant messaging around competency-based teaching and learning.

Jon, through the Gates Foundation getting wind of his pursuit of starting a small Arts school embedded in the community, receiving a $500,000 grant in support of that vision, along with his longstanding and persistent outreach to artists and art organizations in the city.

Finally, the details of Dennis Littky ending up in the office of the Commissioner as a result of direct encouragement of the great late Ted Sizer, Dean of School of Education at Brown University. Which then led to Dennis and Elliot's proposal for a "new kind of vocational school," leading them to a provision of being a district unto themselves to jumpstart their school. This eventually led to the visit by Tom Vander Ark (who was then the Education Director for the Gates Foundation), who upon seeing what they were doing said, "I want you to start a bunch of these schools across the country."

You would think that in the days of bureaucracy and order, any if not all of these would have been the result of meticulous planning and formal proposals. Was meticulous planning involved? For sure. Were formal proposals made? For sure. But that is not what happens often "behind the curtain," as I like to say. When one uncovers how much the start of these endeavors arose from the serendipitous meeting of one person and another, the relationships of one to another, and the personal faith of individuals to create something awesome, it feels to me like pulling back the curtain on the Wizard of Oz. Behind the curtain are passionate individuals wearing their passions on their shirt sleeves. This in turn leads to others recognizing the potential for a new vision of schooling, with those others wielding the social and political clout to create the space for the seed of a good idea to grow.

As I thought about this, it became clear that one could *design for serendipity*, which sounds like an oxymoron. Doesn't serendipity just happen and happen by chance. Well, as I thought about it, in these cases yes and no. No in that there definitely was a bit of fortune involved in each endeavor. It was fortunate for Jon Ketler that the Gates Foundation got wind of what he was up to in Tacoma and wanted to learn more. Indeed it was fortune that Sol Price just happened to be in a room with Larry Rosenstock when he was talking about what a school could be. But it is also true that these individuals went out of their way to pursue their ideas and their vision by talking about both with lots of people, seeking out support and looking for alliances. And that is actually how you can design for serendipity, but getting out there and clearly sharing what you would like to do, what matters to you, and the need for change as you see it. When you do this enough, you never know when this passion and vision might inspire someone to join you in your effort and/or support you. As I have said, "Serendipity won't find you if you are sitting on the couch." Rather, you need to be active in your sharing your passion and interest and keep an eye and ear out for the connections, relationships, and resources that could help you pursue that vision, which means reaching out to other educators and organizations beyond your community and gaining some guidance and support beyond your system. Well, indeed, seek out and find allies and support within your community and outside of your community.

The Final Say

For me and many of my colleagues, education in the United States and the world is a social justice issue. If we believe in our *humanity* – that is the collective pursuit of well-being for all – then our systems are failing us.

I have been working in the field of education for over 35 years as a researcher, educational designer, and educator, and so have arrived at a perspective that pinpoints the numerous ways our systems are failing our youth, communities, and society. But I am also a parent and grandfather and have experienced the failings of our education system from that perspective as well.

I have two images seared in my mind that illustrate this point.

Fifteen years ago, I remember picking my daughter up from high school on one particularly warm, sunny spring day. I had the sunroof and windows rolled down. Music blaring. Excited to see my daughter and spend some time together. As I rolled in, all of the students were escaping out to their cars and rides. I could tell everyone was excited to get outside and capture some of the great light and warm weather. It was spring!

As my daughter approached the car and got in I noticed that she had scribbled a large maze in dark black ink high on her thigh (she was wearing shorts, too short I thought to myself – typical Dad). So I asked her "What happened?" She replied: "Math class."

Twelve years later, similar scenario, but fall. And my Grandson.

It was one of those crisp, brightly sunny fall days. The same scenario, but K through 5th graders pouring out from the school and onto the playground where a number of us parents, grandparents, and others happily met their kids. My grandson in particular loved to run out of school, dump off his backpack and jacket with me, and run onto the playground to play with the other 30-40 kids who typically stayed after to play before going home.

I remember at that time his mother and I were a bit anxious about how Bub (my grandson) would take to 1st grade in his new school. We lived close and I loved being able to pick him up and watch him play with the enthusiasm of a bright, lively, rambunctious kiddo that he was.

So there is the image. He is running out. Happy to escape. And ready to rock 'n roll! Shouting, with arms high up in the air, jumping:

"I'm freeeeeeee!!!!"

Ugh.

These two school systems are not bad. The first one (which all three of my daughters attended and my grandson too in Kindergarten) is touted as one of the best in Massachusetts. Students regularly go to the top colleges and universities. Score high on their SATs. Take plenty of AP courses. And participate in an array of extracurriculars. But apart from my middle daughter, my oldest and youngest basically survived. They liked the opportunity to be with friends. But apart from that, they were bored, went through the motions (minimal at best), and struggled. Got good grades. But just did what they had to do.

They were not motivated by any academic brass ring – being academically successful for its own sake and/or to be able to go to the best college or make their parents proud. My oldest's concern was her relationships with peers, and peers who were similarly disconnected from school. And my youngest it turned out had and continues to have a text-processing issue which meant reading was hard. In short, it was laborious for her. So much so that it zapped her energy and motivation to be engaged in any way when reading was the primary modality of learning in any class, which was far too often. (When a teacher said that it shouldn't take more than a half hour to read, for her that meant 2½ hours; so no wonder she gave up.)

I know that I am not the only parent who has struggled with this. Hoping that our kids will enjoy school and be engaged and feel like they are getting something out of it is something we all want, right? But how many of us have seen our kids become disenchanted with school (even at a very early age), if not angry, depressed, or deflated. And then we, as parents, end up disappointed and at a loss and not knowing what to do because we feel it is our responsibility to make sure our kids go to school. It is expected they go, right? And if they don't want to go, is it our responsibility to make sure they do? Because they have to. It's state law. And if they don't go, what then? What will happen to them? What will become of them? So what can I do to get this kid to school?

But should it be this way? Should we (as parents) be in a position where we have to rationalize to our kid why they *need* to go to school? Tell them it's in their best interest. Tell them that they *have* to go.

I think about my own grandson, whose teacher is well-meaning, and doing what she is told. She is teaching the prescribed curriculum. Teaching to the standards. Using the resources the district expects her to use.

But my kiddo likes to run and play. He likes to be active – moving, talking, trying things out. He likes to DO things – build things (think legos and sofa forts). Learn – he learns a lot through YouTube about things *he* wants to learn about (think fishing and basketball). And he likes to figure things out (think Fortnite, Roblox, and NBA2K).

Does learning look like *that* in his classroom? In his school?

No.

Hence, his mother and I have to do what we can to get him out of bed, get dressed, have breakfast, grab his backpack, and get to school. To a place he doesn't want to go. To a place where what he is really saying is: I don't want to be here.

Recently he told me: "I'd rather drink my own blood than to go to school."

As discussed previously, and as presented throughout this book, learning can be grounded in youth's authentic interests and toward a greater purpose above and beyond standardized test measures in ELA and math and the accumulation of traditional, antiquated high school credits. Learning can be designed through meaningful engagement and valuable experience. Learning can be purposeful, experiential, and personal.

Succumbing to the way we have always done school has led to the outcomes we have today – short on student agency and expanding students' real-world opportunity. Our youth are now graduating not knowing what their interests, strengths, and skills are and arriving at an endpoint untethered from their own clear aspirations, dreams, and visions of a future.

If, as a society, we value the well-being of our youth and likewise their opportunity to give back to our communities and our society, each of us must, in our own way, find a way to push back and inspire others to reconsider the purpose of school and reimagine what teaching, learning, and schooling can look like. In short, we need to join forces in pursuit of a revolution, and connect with, lean on, and support one another as fellow revolutionaries.

We know better. We know that cognitive engagement propelled by authentic student interest supported by the astute guidance of others helps one to build one's competency. Yet, the current design of schools does not actively foster such practices. We are so embedded in the way we currently do schools, it's like being a fish in water we can't even see the poisonous waters we swim in. And we are blind to how our values as exhibited in these systems are perpetuating the disenfranchisement of youth. This is school today.

Back to our measures of success. I am not going to refer to those measures the feds and states use now. ELA & math standardized test scores, graduation rates, etc. Rather, I am going to measure success by the intellectual and emotional engagement of our youth, and the potential pathways we are affording them. Evidence of their competencies through their work and reflection. Evidence that they find their learning meaningful and relevant. Evidence that they are gaining agency and possibility. And evidence to which they feel their school, and all of its members, have helped them to identify their aspirations and are working to help them pursue their desired future.

If I can hear a student tell me about what they are interested in, what they love to do, and what they hope to do with their life moving forward ... then THAT is success. As we have read here, this means far more progressive activities in schools that engage youth through authentic work. This means contexts and relationships where a student feels fully supported in being successful. Moreso, it means that educators and others have decided to step out of the status quo and decided to reimagine education for the benefit of youth. Working hard to inspire and pursue a revolution in education.

Resources

People, Books, Web Sites, Blogs, and Social Media to draw From

Books

Pedagogy of the Oppressed. Paulo Friere.

Creative Schools: The Grassroots Revolution That's Transforming Education. Ken Robinson & Lou Aronica.

The Underground History of American Education, Volume I: An Intimate Investigation Into the Prison of Modern Schooling. John Taylor Gatto.

Dumbing Us Down. John Taylor Gatto.

A Different Kind of Teacher: Solving the Crisis of American Schooling. John Taylor Gatto.

Most Likely to Succeed: Preparing Our Kids for the Innovation Era. Tony Wagner & Ted Dintersmtih.

What School Could Be: Insights and Inspiration from Teachers Across America. Ted Dintersmith.

An Education Crisis Is a Terrible Thing to Waste: How Radical Changes Can Spark Student Excitement and Success. Yong Zhao, Trina E. Emler, Anthony Snethen, & Danqing Yin.

Creating Innovators: The Making of Young People Who Will Change the World. Tony Wagner.

Savage Inequalities: Children in America's Schools. Jonathon Kozol.

The Shame of the Nation: The Restoration of Apartheid Schooling in America. Jonathon Kozol.

Free to Learn. Peter Gray.

Teaching to Transgress: Education as the Practice of Freedom. bell hooks.

Experience and Education. John Dewey.

Democracy & Education. John Dewey.

Difference Making at the Heart of Learning: Students, Schools, and Communities Alive With Possibility. Tom Vander Ark & Emily Liebtag.

Better Together: How to Leverage School Networks For Smarter Personalized and Project Based Learning. Tom Vander Ark & Lydia Dobyns.

Dark Horse: Achieving Success Through the Pursuit of Fulfillment. Todd Rose & Ogi Ogas.

The End of Average: How We Succeed in a World That Values Sameness. Todd Rose.

Beyond Reform: Systemic Shifts Toward Personalized Learning -Shift from a Traditional Time-Based Education System to a Learner-Centered Performance-Based System. Lindsay Unified School District.

The Future of Smart: How Our Education System Needs to Change to Help All Young People Thrive. Ulcca Joshi Hansen.

In Search of Deeper Learning: The Quest to Remake the American High School. Jal Mehta & Sarah Fine.

From Reopen to Reinvent: (Re)Creating School for Every Child. Michael B. Horn.

The Power of Place: Authentic Learning Through Place-Based Education. Tom Vander Ark, Emily Liebtag, & Nate McClennen.

Open Up, Education!: How Open Way Learning Can Transform Schools. Ben Owens & Adam Haigler.

Learner-Centered Innovation: Spark Curiosity, Ignite Passion and Unleash Genius. Katie Martin.

Evolving Education: Shifting to a Learner-Centered Paradigm. Katie Martin.

One Kid at a Time: Big Lessons from a Small School. Eliot Levine, Tom Peters, & Ted Sizer.

The Big Picture: Education Is Everyone's Business. Dennis Littky & Samantha Grabelle.

Leaving to Learn: How Out-of-School Learning Increases Student Engagement and Reduces Dropout Rates. Elliot Washor & Charles Mojkowski.

World Class Learners: Educating Creative and Entrepreneurial Students. Yong Zhao.

Unschooled: Raising Curious, Well-Educated Children Outside the Conventional Classroom. Kerry McDonald & Peter Gray.

You, Your Child, and School: Navigate Your Way to the Best Education. Ken Robinson & Lou Aronica.

The Innovator's Mindset: Empower Learning, Unleash Talent, and Lead a Culture of Creativity. George Couros.

How to Navigate Life: The New Science of Finding Your Way in School, Career, and Beyond. Belle Liang & Timothy Klein.

Making Learning Whole: How Seven Principles of Teaching Can Transform Education. David Perkins.

Future Wise: Educating Our Children for a Changing World. David Perkins.

Designing Your Life: How to Build a Well-Lived, Joyful Life. Bill Burnett & Dave Evans.

The Human Side of Changing Education: How to Lead Change with Clarity, Conviction, and Courage. Julie Wilson (Jungalwala)

Articles

What Happens when you Launch Students' Interests into the World?
https://www.gettingsmart.com/2021/07/08/what-happens-when-you-launch-students-interests-into-the-world

The Perfect Storm: A Focus on Students' Future
https://www.gettingsmart.com/2022/01/27/the-perfect-storm-a-focus-on-students-future

J-term at Lyndon Institute: Engaging in Interest- and Passion-driven Learning
https://www.gettingsmart.com/2020/05/02/j-term-lyndon-institute-engaging-interest-passion-driven-learning

Web Sites/Blogs

A Revolution in Education:
https://www.arevolutionineducation.org

You Can Change Education:
https://www.youcanchangeeducation.org

Getting Smart
https://www.gettingsmart.com

Education Reimagined:
https://education-reimagined.org

The 74 Million
https://www.the74million.org

What School Could Be
https://whatschoolcouldbe.org

What School Could Be Innovation playlist
https://whatschoolcouldbe.org/innovation-playlist

The Human Restoration Project
https://www.humanrestorationproject.org

Rebel Educator
https://www.rebeleducator.com

Podcasts

A Revolution in Education (Season 1):
https://arevolutionineducation.buzzsprout.com

A Revolution in Education (Season 2):
https://arevolutionineducation2.buzzsprout.com

RethinkingEDU
https://rethinkingedu.podbean.com

The Iowa BIG podcast:
http://iowabigpodcast.com

The CAPS Network podcast:
https://capsnetwork.buzzsprout.com

DivingDeepEDU
https://podcasts.apple.com/us/podcast/divingdeepedu/id1527156724

Rebel Educator
https://podcasts.apple.com/us/podcast/rebel-educator/id1576581544

Videos

Do schools kill creativity? Ken Robinson
https://www.ted.com/talks/sir_ken_robinson_do_schools_kill_creativity/no-comments

Organizations

Getting Smart
https://www.gettingsmart.com/work-with-us

Open Way Learning
https://www.openwaylearning.org

Learner-centered Collaborative
https://learnercentered.org/

Transcend Education
https://transcendeducation.org

Building 21
https://building21.org

Education Reimagined
https://education-reimagined.org

CAPS Network
https://yourcapsnetwork.org

Schools

Discussed in the Book

Big Picture Schools
https://www.bigpicture.org

CAPS Network
https://yourcapsnetwork.org

BVCAPS (Blue Valley Center for Professional Studies)
https://bvcaps.yourcapsnetwork.org

Building 21
https://building21.org

One Stone
https://onestone.org

The Tacoma School of the Arts
https://sota.tacomaschools.org

The Tacoma Science and Math Institute
https://sami.tacomaschools.org

The Tacoma School of Industrial Arts, Design, and Engineering
https://sami.tacomaschools.org

Aviation High School (Highline Schools)
https://rahs.highlineschools.org

Olympic High School (Charlotte NC)
Read and hear about it here:
https://www.gettingsmart.com/2021/07/08/what-happens-when-you-launch-students-interests-into-the-world

Design 39
https://design39campus.com

Others mentioned in the Book

Embark Education

Workshop School

Da Vinci Schools

Verdi EcoSchool

Polytechnic High School (Purdue)

Pathways High

High School for the Recording Arts

Northern Cass School District

Others useful as inspiration for Possibilities

U School

With Appreciation & Gratitude

To my friends and fellow revolutionaries

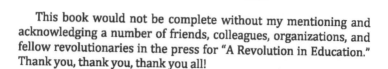

This book would not be complete without my mentioning and acknowledging a number of friends, colleagues, organizations, and fellow revolutionaries in the press for "A Revolution in Education." Thank you, thank you, thank you all!

In no particular order except for when they impacted me to think and see as I do.

To my mentor, David Perkins, at the Harvard Graduate School of Education, who took me (and a number of us) under his wing and treated us as colleagues and collaborators in how to think, see, invent, and do good in the world.

To a great number of exceptional educators I learned about early on that expanded my thinking of what is possible: Dennis Littky & Elliot Washor who started the Big Picture Schools. Meeting Andy Smallman & Melinda Shaw who started a very small learning community of students who learned in community spaces in Seattle, now the Puget Sound Community School. Mike McMann, who gave me the opportunity to work with eleven of the high schools in Seattle from 2002-2004. Nova High School, you amazed me during that time. Eric Muhs, physics teacher, loved how you engaged kids.

I learned the hard way at Brown University, attempting to help high schools transform themselves. I learned a lot about how much folks are stuck in the system. From Brett Lane while there, how the system operates and how intractable it all is given our policy environment.

Then fast forward, at Northeastern University, the opportunity to reach out to and learn about all the cool schools and cool people out there pushing the envelope in what teaching, learning, and schooling can look like through our NExT initative there. Here are a BUNCH of folks, who still inspire me and fuel my passion to do the work, many of them my fellow revolutionaries: Chad Carlson at One Stone, and the story of Joel & Teresa Poppen that started it all; Jon Ketler and what he has been able to do with his colleagues in Tacoma WA; Mike

Realon and all he does and all his community has been able to do for the kids in the southeast corner of Charlotte NC; Sheila Harrity and what she did at Worcester Tech and then Monty Tech; Corey Mohn and his crew, and the others I have been able to get to know and become good friends with in the CAPS Network, Ethan Wiechmann & Nate Clayberg at Cedar Falls CAPS, in particular; Jeff Petty and all he has stood for and been able to do in Highline Public Schools and beyond; Ben Owens and more recently Adam Haigler and Ben Pardavis of Open Way Learning; Ricky Singh (thanks for just jumping in) and Mary Moss and their colleagues at the Charlotte Lab School; my friends in the Worcester Public Schools, who show me what it takes every day.

And then there are those running the incredible organizations that fuel the possibilities of education: Tom Vander Ark and his crew who run Getting Smart; Kelly Young and Education Reimagined; and although I don't know them personally, am incredibly thankful to the74million.org and how they shine a spotlight on the issues in public education.

To my good friend Jim McCue, who jumped right in to help me with the second season of the A Revolution in Education podcast, and who continues to be a good friend beyond the usual. And I must thank all of you who contributed to that and from who I learned as well.

Then thanks to my numerous Northeastern University colleagues who work hard to inspire and empower all of our EdD students to be change agents in the world. And speaking of ... the amazing students we have in our program that I continue to learn from all the time.

Then there are those special few I have gained wisdom and inspiration from. My good friend Cath Fraise, for her pursuits and all that she is. As well as my good friend Alan Stoskopf.

Of course, I am blessed with my family, who are the center of my universe.

And, finally, to my mother, who believed in me and only expected that I would make the most of my life. Which I hope I have done and will continue to do, not just for myself, but for others too, as evidenced in this book and all of my work.

Finally, a special thanks to Kristin Lizotte, Cara Zimon, Ben Owens, Adam Haigler, Corey Mohn, Kate McCaffery-Pomerlea, and Sophia Paffenroth for giving a good critical read of the text with numerous suggestions.

Endnotes

1   Chris Dede, Yong Zhao, Curt Bonk, and Punya Mishra have been
    producing this great podcast on the future of learning with
    educators across the globe since the onset of COVID. Really great
    stuff. And definitely worth checking out.
    https://silverliningforlearning.org

2   For those not in schools, advisories are when groups of students
    work with a teacher on such things as academic guidance, social
    emotional learning, or other topics the school decides is worthy of
    an advisory.

3   See: https://nces.ed.gov/programs/coe/indicator/cba/annual-
    earnings

4   See: https://www.literacymidsouth.org/news/the-relationship-
    between-incarceration-and-low-literacy. This page provides a good
    overview of the relationship between education level and
    incarceration, with data for each state, which varies a great deal:
    https://blog.batchgeo.com/does-education-influence-incarceration

5   New York Times, October 9, 2009, p. A12, citing a study conducted
    by researchers at the Center for Labor Market Studies at
    Northeastern University.

6   https://www.nccp.org/publication/child-poverty-and-
    intergenerational-mobility

7   See Yong Zhao's *Learners Without Borders* and *An Education Crisis is
    a Terrible Thing to Waste*, Tony Wagner and Ted Dintersmith's *Most
    Likely to Succeed*, Ken Robinson's *Creative Schools*,

8   See Paulo Friere's *Pedagogy of the Oppressed*

9   See Monica Martinez and Dennis McGrath's *Deeper Learning* and Jal
    Mehta and Sarah Fine's *In Search of Deeper Learning*, and the *Deeper
    Learning: Beyond 21st Century Skills* anthology edited by James
    Bellanca.

10 See this excellent article by Tom Vander Ark in Getting Smart,
    www.gettingsmart.com/2021/07/students-as-coauthors-of-
    learning-a-resources-guide, to see what I mean by this with the
    wide-variety of examples across learning communities where this is
    at play.

11 See Julie Wilsons books, *The Human Side of Changing Education*

12 The past 2 years of catalyst grants have focused on such things,
    granting as much as $50,000 seed money to pursue ideas in keeping
    with these ideas and as much as $500,000 to grow and proliferate
    such endeavors. See:
    https://www.barrafoundation.org/grants/catalyst-fund

13 To learn more about High Tech High, you can visit their website here: https://www.hightechhigh.org. But you can also learn more about it by watch in the documentary *Most Likely to Succeed* (https://teddintersmith.com/mltsfilm), as well as several videos available on YouTube.

14 To learn more about Tacoma's Next Move Internship program, see here: https://www.tacomaschools.org/departments/cte/internships/next-move

15 To hear more about this event and the outcomes, you can listen to the first episode of the Iowa BIG podcast: https://open.spotify.com/episode/5qXEc74I6ndZOmktVMqKmG

16 There is a plethora of research on this fact grounded in the literature on experiential learning, situated learning and cognition, intrinsic motivation, etc.

17 You can read about his adventure in his own penned book, *Don't Tell Me I Can't: An Ambitious Homeschooler's Journey.*

18 For more on this, feel free to review *21ˢᵗ Century Skills* by Bernie Trilling & Charles Fadel, *21ˢᵗ Century Skills* edited by James Bellanca & Ron Brandt, and *The Global Achievement Gap: Why Even Our Best Schools Don't Teach the New Survival Skills Our Children Need—and What We Can Do About It* by Tony Wagner.

19 There is in fact a large body of theory and research that points to the need for "situated learning." First propose by Jean Lave and Etienne Wenger in their seminal text *Situated Learning*, many of used the theory and related research to clearly point out the shortcomings of our education system in affording learners with the experiences that yield the ability to actually think and act in a domain, with guidance and support of mentors with learners as apprentices, first observing and then taking over some of the work of the mentor.

20 From https://money.cnn.com/infographic/economy/education-vs-prison-costs

21 Clayton Christensen's Theory of Disruption is widely acknowledged as one of the most influential theories of innovation of all time. The theory, grounded in several business and other industry cases, points to how disruptive technologies and businesses come to be by offering a service or product more desired and readily available than what is currently available. In the private sector, entire companies can go under as a result of holding on to old products or practices, with new industry providing an innovation more desired and accessible.
I make the point in this book that this theory, as much as I like it, doesn't seem to hold in our public education system because (1) the opportunity to innovate is limited and (2) current schools and school systems don't fold because there is no alternative offered

from which the user can choose. Hence, schools and their systems continue to access students and get funded as the district model of public schooling ensures that all students attend as they are required to do so, thus maintaining their users and reaping the financial reward of their enrollment, independent of the quality of what is provided.

A free market education ecosystem might result in better schools if the money were able to follow the child and new schools could be created. Something that is sharply criticized or supported depending on the stakeholder.

22   And, in fact, it turns out that students growing up in lower SES communities tend to choose their local school over any other choice, which some have argued maintains lower quality schools continuing to be well attended despite their lesser academic output. (See *The Paradox of Choice: How School Choice Divides New York City Elementary Schools*, by The Center for New York City Affairs at The New School, *High School Choice in New York City: A Report on the School Choices and Placements of Low-Achieving Student* by the Research Alliance for New York City Schools, and https://www.nytimes.com/2017/05/05/nyregion/school-choice-new-york-city-high-school-admissions.html in the New York Times for more on this.)

23   To this day I sit in disbelief that there is a 3,000-student, primarily concrete four-story high school in Brooklyn with very few windows called Dewey High School. Really?

24   I personally was at a brand new vocational school that happily shared they were offering vocational strands in carpentry, food services, beauty school, early childhood care, and automotive. Now, I am not against any of these options, but as they told me this, I thought to myself, this is all that you think your students can aspire to do?

25   See the Denver Public Schools' School Choice website here (https://schoolchoice.dpsk12.org) and several examples of alternative schools available to students in Denver here: the Denver School of Innovation & Sustainable Design (https://dsisd.dpsk12.org) and the Denver School of the Arts (http://dsa.dpsk12.org). In addition, the Denver Charter School Network is supports and advocates for charter schools in Denver, providing insights into the charter school landscape in the city: https://www.dcsdk12.org. Finally, the Denver Innovation Lab Schools are a network of schools that focus on personalized learning, student-centered approaches, and innovative practices (see here: https://www.denverinnovationlab.org)

26   You can read more about the new small schools effort starting in the early 2000s in New York City in this report: https://www.newvisions.org/pages/small-schools-study. And

more about this effort can be found here as well:
https://www.newvisions.org/pages/new-school-phase-in. It is
interesting to note that at one point very recently the NYC Dept. of
Education had an Office of New Schools under Bloomberg, but no
longer exists. Question is: Why?

27 If you wish to investigate some of these arguments, you can look at
the highlights of a recent report here
(https://www.educationnext.org/charter-schools-show-steeper-
upward-trend-student-achievement-first-nationwide-study),
commentary here
(https://www.publicschoolreview.com/blog/charter-schools-vs-
traditional-public-schools-which-one-is-under-performing), and a
good review of Charter School impact here
(https://futureofchildren.princeton.edu/sites/g/files/toruqf2411/f
iles/resource-links/charter_schools_compiled.pdf)

28 With the expectation to meet proficiency levels in math and ELA,
many schools are saddled with the expectation of proficiency and
growth that sometimes takes precedent over other activities and
foci that could better serve youth. In many charter school
communities serving youth growing up in socio-economically
depressed communities, youth are not surrounded by the kinds of
support and rich literate contexts that give them a leg-up in these
measures. So often these schools, in search of ways to tackle this
problem, defer to more traditional means of raising student
achievement such as double-dosing (students spending an
inordinate amount of time in math or literacy programs). And
admin and teachers quickly resort to focusing on these measures at
the expense of potentially more holistic responses.

29 Kaleb Rashad, current interim CEO of High Tech High, referred to
these schools as employing a "militaristic" version of schooling,
foregrounding routines for the purpose of increasing ELA and math
scores.

30 See Julie Wilson (Jungalwala's) book *The Human Side of Changing
Education* and *The Human Side of School Change* by Robert Evans.

31 These are but just a few and ones I familiar with, but if you go to
https://education-reimagined.org/map/ you can investigate and
learn about so many more, and inquire as to how these school got
up and running.

32 Indeed, I wrote an article in Getting Smart, published January 27
'22, under this title to showcase how many of such school
transformations are the result of "a perfect storm." See:
www.gettingsmart.com/2022/01/27/the-perfect-storm-a-focus-
on-students-future

33 Olympic has received a wealth of accolades for its efforts, including
being only 1 of 3 high schools in the country to received 5
distinguished awards for their career academies. See:

https://schools.cms.k12.nc.us/olympicHS/Pages/AboutOurSchool.a
spx.

[34] As told by them in the 2nd episode of Season 1 of their Iowa BIG
podcast:
https://open.spotify.com/show/0OMMYog49ht2fmXJYBt45A

[35] Design thinking is a process for designing that has evolved since the
'50s and most notably used by designed but later applied to solving
problems and creating designs in business and education. It
became more popular with such institutions as Stanford creating
the dschool (https://dschool.stanford.edu) and engaging others in
the process, as well as the highly regarded IDEO
(https://designthinking.ideo.com), a global design and innovation
organization.

[36] Grant Lichtman was one of these individuals, who had just
completed a 3 month road trip visiting over 60 innovative schools in
his Prius, bringing his insights, examples, and stories to bear in their
design. You can read about his trip and insights gained in his book
#EdJourney: A Roadmap to the Future of Education.
He has a wealth of great stories and insights gained over time in his
other books and website: https://www.grantlichtman.com

[37] To learn more about the iSchool visit https://www.nycischool.org.

[38] See more here about Building 21: https://building21.org

[39] Montessori schools have grown rapidly around the world and
comprise over 22,000 schools globally. I myself am a partial
product of a Montessori school, up until ½ way through 3rd grade
(as written elsewhere in this book). You can learn more about the
growth of the Montessori schools here
(https://www.forbes.com/sites/emilylanghorne/2019/03/27/the-
montessori-comeback/?sh=343227c44648), here
(https://amshq.org/About-Montessori/History-of-Montessori), and
what they are here (https://www.public-
montessori.org/montessori).

[40] The story of Reggio Emilia is an amazing one. Amidst WWII, the
Italian govt. decided to shut down all public schooling but in
response, the families of Reggio Emilia wanted to create their own
school for their children. You can learn more about this history
here (https://45conversations.com/reggio-emilia-approach), and
the Reggio Emilia approach here
(https://www.rasmussen.edu/degrees/education/blog/what-is-
reggio-emilia), and here.

[41] Take your pick: One Stone (see Project Good and Solution Lab, as
just two examples), High Tech High (High Tech High project
examples), and the numerous projects at Iowa BIG
(www.cedarrapids.org/about-us/news/2019/11/iowa-big-
students-work-innovative-projects-economic-alliance-members).

42 There are a plethora of reports clearly indicating these needs by
    employers, dating as far back as 30 years ago. For example, *21st
    Century Skills* by James Bellanca & Ron Brandt and, *21*ˢᵗ *Century
    Skills* by Bernie Trilling and Charles Fadel. And a brief on the need
    as it is playing out in some districts
    (https://www.panoramaed.com/blog/comprehensive-guide-21st-
    century-skills).

43 To learn more about the shortcomings of this reality, feel free to dig
    in deeper by reviewing the work of academics on situated learning
    and situated cognition.

44 These examples come from a variety of schools across the country,
    including One Stone, BVCAPS, High Tech High, Da Vinci Schools,,
    amongst man others.

45 More of this can be perused and considered in Tom Vander Ark and
    Emily Liebtag's book *Difference Making at the Heart of Learning:
    Students, Schools, and Communities Alive With Possibility*

46 A number of reports have pointed out the significance of intellectual
    agility in future work and our future world. Some of these include:
    The Future of Jobs Report and the *Future of Work* series produced by
    the World Economic Forum; the *Skill Shift: Automation and the
    Future of the Workforce* and *Jobs Lost, Jobs Gained: Workforce
    Transitions in a Time of Automation* reports by the McKinsey Global
    Institute; the *The Path to Prosperity: Why the Future of Work is
    Human* report by Deloitte; and the *Skills for a Digital World* and *The
    Future of Education and Skills: Education 2030* report by OECD.

47 For a start, one can review: *Cultivating Intellectual Agility: A
    Multidimensional Framework for Talent Development* by Mark Runco
    and Kathryn Tucker; *Fostering Intellectual Agility in the Classroom:
    The Role of Problem-Based Learning* by Steven J. Corbett and Teck-
    Hua Ho; *Promoting Intellectual Agility: The Role of Teachers and
    Classroom Practices* by Carol C. Bann and Mark A. Runco; *Supporting
    Intellectual Development: The Role of Parenting and Family Context*
    by Eva M. Pomerantz and Qian Wang.

48 For more on this need, see: *Intellectual Character: What it Is, Why It
    Matters, and How to Get It*, by Ron Ritchart; *Teaching for Critical
    Thinking: Tools and Techniques to Help Students Question Their
    Assumption*" by Stephen D. Brookfield; *How to Think: A Survival
    Guide for a World at Odds*, by Alan Jacobs; "Fostering Intellectual
    Agility through Project-Based Learning" by Suzie Boss; "Developing
    Intellectual Agility: Insights from Longitudinal Studies" by Robert J.
    Sternberg.

49 Julia Freeland Fisher has written a lot about this, most recently
    about how such social connections and networks can benefit youth.
    See, for example, https://www.christenseninstitute.org/blog/what-
    schools-miss-when-theyre-missing-relationship-data,
    https://www.christenseninstitute.org/blog/how-do-you-talk-to-

students-about-their-networks,
https://www.christenseninstitute.org/publications/relationship-mapping, her website (https://whoyouknow.org) and her book
Who You Know.

50   A great deal of research has clearly evidenced how relationships
benefit personal well-being. One book summarizes these findings in
the Harvard happiness study started in 1930, called *The Good Life:
Lessons from the World's Longest Scientific Study of Happiness.*

51   A few places to start: Explore the CASEL (Collaborative for
Academic, Social, and Emotional Learning) website for multiple
insights and reports: https://casel.org; in addition, a wealth of
research and recommendations can be found on Penn State's
Prevention Research Center's site on human flourishing:
https://prevention.psu.edu/focus-areas/promoting-human-flourishing

52   Fore on the need to focus on the development of social acuity in
youth: "The Role of Social Skills in the Transition to Adulthood" by
Emily A. Greenfield and Emily E. Tanner-Smith (2011); "The Social
Brain and Its Superpowers: The Mentalizing Brain, Empathy, and
Social Change" by Marco Iacoboni (2009); "The Social and
Emotional Learning Challenge: A Guide to Assessing and Managing
Emotional and Social Difficulties in Young People" by Tanya Byron
et al. (2010); "The Importance of Teaching Social Issues: A Meta-
Analysis" by Elifnaz Kabatas Yıldız and Özlem Türkdoğan (2020);
The Development of Social Competence in Childhood. by Kenneth H.
Rubin et al. (2006).

53   Here are just a few such reports and research related to the short-
and long-term benefits of personal agency: "Toward a psychology of
human agency. Perspectives on Psychological Science" by Albert
Bandura in *Perspectives on Psychological Science, 1*(2), 164-180; *The
path to purpose: How young people find their calling in life* by
William Damon; *The teen years explained: A guide to healthy
adolescent development* by Center for Adolescent Health at Johns
Hopkins Bloomberg School of Public Health; a host of research can
also be found here: https://searchinstitute.org

54   Here is a start for educators: *Teaching Students to Drive Their
Brains: Metacognitive Strategies, Activities, and Lesson Ideas* by
Donna Wilson and Marcus Conyers; *The Power of Agency: The 7
Principles to Conquer Obstacles, Make Effective Decisions, and Create
a Life on Your Own Terms* by Anthony Rao and Paul Napper; *Student
Agency: How to Encourage Ownership, Inquiry, and Personal Success*
by Vicki Davis; *Cultivating Habits of Agency in the Classroom* by Ron
Ritchhart; "Promoting Student Agency: A Report from the
Achievement Gap Initiative at Harvard University" by Sarah Fine.
For parents and families: *Parenting for Independence: Strategies for
Raising Responsible, Self-Confident Kids* by Maribeth Kuzmeski; *The*

Self-Driven Child: The Science and Sense of Giving Your Kids More Control Over Their Lives by William Stixrud and Ned Johnson; *The Art of Self-Directed Learning: 23 Tips for Giving Yourself an Unconventional Education* by Blake Boles

55 For more on this, one can review: "Personal Agency of Modern Adolescents: Research Results," T. Antopolskaya & A. Silakov (2021); "Adolescents' Development of Personal Agency: The Role of Self-efficacy Beliefs and Self-Regulator Skill," by B. Zimmerman & T. Clearly (2005); "Identity and Agency in Emerging Adulthood," by S. Schwartz, J. Côté, & J. Arnett.; "Navigating the Future: An Ecological Perspective on Agency in Emerging Adulthood," by W. Damon, A. Colby, and A. Pallas (2014).

56 For more on this, see: "The Emergin Study of Positive Empathy," by S Morelli, M. Lieberman, and J. Zaki; "Imaging Empathy and Prosocial Emotions," by C. Lamm, M. Rutgen, and I.C. Wagner (2019).

57 For more on this, see: "Fators influencing the development of empathy and pro-social behavior among adolescents: A systematic review," by C. Silke, B. Brady, C. Boylan, & P. Dolan (2018).

58 *Belatedly, Egypt Spots Flaws in Wiping Out Pigs.* New York Times article, published Sept. 19, 2009.

59 There is even more to this story and how systems thinking and political action takes a downward spiral in this story. See *Cleaning Cairo, but Taking a Livelihood.* New York Times article published May 24, 2009.

60 See, for example, "Systems Thinking to for Community Involvement I Policy Analysis, by G. Midgley & K. Richardson (2007).

61 See, for example, *The Flat World and Education: How America's Commitment to Equity will Determine our Future* by Linda Darling-Hammond, *Inside the Black Box of School Reform*, by Larry Cuban, and *Finnish Lessons: What can the World Learn from Educational Change in Finland?*, by Pasi Sahlberg.

62 Dave Lash and Grace Belfiore wrote two great reports about wayfinding for students for the Next Generation Learning Challenges group's *MyWays Student Success Series: What Learners Need to Thrive in a World of Change.* The first report is Opportunity, Work, and the Wayfinding Decade and second report is titled Wayfinding Abilities for Destinations Unknown. Each can be found at https://www.nextgenlearning.org/resources/opportunity-work-and-the-wayfinding-decade-myways-report-1 and https://www.nextgenlearning.org/resources/wayfinding-abilities-for-destinations-unknown-report-10, respectively.

63 Research has shown that rote learning is typically forgotten over time and not assimilated into one's active use or memory. But we don't have to rely on research to know this to be true. You yourself probably know this to be true if you try to remember any of the

"rote" information provided you in school. And if you ask any of
your family members or friends, you will find this to be true as well.
Not rocket science here.

64 There are several reports that point to this reality. For example,
"Are College Graduates Finding Good Jobs?" by Jaison R. Abel and
Richard Deitz, Federal Reserve Bank of New York, *Current Issues in
Economics and Finance*, Volume 20, Number 1, 2014
(https://www.newyorkfed.org/medialibrary/media/research/curr
ent_issues/ci20-1.pdf); *The Permanent Detour: Underemployment's
Long-term Effects on the Careers of College Graduates*, Burning Glass
Technologies, 2018 (https://www.burning-glass.com/wp-
content/uploads/permanent_detour_underemployment_report.pdf;
The Future of Work: The Good Jobs Challenge. Strada Education
Network. 2019 (https://www.stradaeducation.org/wp-
content/uploads/2019/03/GJC-Report-Final-3.26.19.pdf); *Three
educational pathways to good jobs: High school, middle skills, and
bachelor's degree*. by Carnevale, A. P., Smith, N., & Strohl, J.
Georgetown University Center on Education and the Workforce.
2019 (https://cew.georgetown.edu/cew-reports/three-pathways-
to-good-jobs)

65 Several reports point to this reality: A 2017 study titled *Assessing
Person-Job Fit: A Review of the Literature* published in the Journal of
Career Assessment by authors Lauren L. D'Innocenzo, John P.
Hausknecht, and Adam W. Meade; A 2015 study titled "Interest fit
and job satisfaction: The importance of person-environment fit"
published in the Journal of Vocational Behavior by authors Joris
Lammers, Jonatan Van Hiel, and Filip Lievens; and a 2013 study
titled *Person-Environment Fit and Burnout: Is Job Fit More Important
Than Organization Fit* published in the Journal of Career
Development by authors Laura M. Graves and Patricia P.
McDermott.

66 See, for example: the 2021 report by the Lumina Foundation,
Degree Attainment and Social Impact in the Workplace, found that
workers who earned a bachelor's degree in a field related to their
current job were more likely to report higher job satisfaction and
earnings (https://www.luminafoundation.org/resources/degree-
attainment-and-social-impact-in-the-workplace); a 2020 study, *Job
Satisfaction and Subjective Well-Being Among College Graduates*
published in the Journal of Happiness Studies, found that workers
who earned a degree in a field related to their job were more likely
to report higher job satisfaction and happiness, compared to those
who did not (https://link.springer.com/article/10.1007/s10902-
019-00154-6); a 2019 study by the Strada Education Network, *The
Value of Upskilling: Employer Perspectives on the Opportunities and
Barriers to Worker Upskilling*, reported that workers who earned a
degree in a high-demand field (such as healthcare or technology)

were more likely to report higher job satisfaction, earnings, and opportunities for advancement (https://www.stradaeducation.org/wp-content/uploads/2019/10/Strada-Gallup-Report-Final.pdf).

67 Here are a few of them: One Stone (https://onestone.org), Building 21 (https://building21.org), schools in the CAPS Network (https://yourcapsnetwork.org), Big Picture schools (https://www.bigpicture.org), and Road Trip Nation (https://roadtripnation.com) has been providing several resources related to wayfinding for years.

68 https://onestone.org

69 Born in China, Yong Zhao has taken to looking at education systems around the world, and his books are excellent, including *Learners Without Borders, An Education Crisis is a Terrible Thing to Waste, Counting What Counts, Who's Afraid of the Big Bad Dragon*, and *Reach for Greatness.* I highly recommend.

70 You can read more about our Dissertation in Practice here: https://files.eric.ed.gov/fulltext/EJ1331813.pdf

71 Over the last year, "durable skills" has become of greater focus and attention. To read more about the movement toward "durable skills" and the research that spotlights their need, see https://durableskills.org

72 Learn more here: https://www.verdiecoschool.org; and here: https://education-reimagined.org/verdi-ecoschool-a-conversation-with-ayana-verdi; and here: https://education-reimagined.org/map/verdi-ecoschool

73 This is in reference to a classic *I Love Lucy* clip where Lucy and her friend Edith try their hand at a job where over time more and more chocolates are being dispensed down a conveyor belt at such a speed they cannot handle carefully placing them in the boxes of chocolates and end up just throwing them down their blouses.

74 And at the time of this writing (August 2022), it was just projected that the state of Florida itself might fall short of 80,000 teaching positions as a result of the state of teaching today.

75 Many report that on average only about 13% of community college students graduate within 2 years, 22% within three years, and 28% in four, with the percentage much lower for those financially strapped. See https://www.communitycollegereview.com/blog/the-catch-22-of-community-college-graduation-rates for more.

76 See more here: http://www.nysed.gov/postsecondary-services/pathways-technology-nys-p-tech-program

77 For more on P-Tech, see: https://www.ptech.org https://www.ibm.org/initiatives/p-tech

In NY State: http://www.nysed.gov/postsecondary-services/pathways-technology-nys-p-tech-program

[78] See https://rinimc.org

[79] See https://www.forbes.com/sites/tomvanderark/2020/08/04/microschools-meet-the-moment, https://www.cato.org/commentary/how-microschool-networks-are-activating-education-entrepreneurs, https://www.christenseninstitute.org/blog/the-ecosystem-evolution-of-microschools.

[80] The diagram of Bronfenbrenner's ecological systems theory is taken from this website: https://psychology.fandom.com/wiki/Bioecological_model. More about Bronfenbrener's ecolocial systems theory can be reviewed here (https://www.simplypsychology.org/bronfenbrenner.html), here (https://dropoutprevention.org/wp-content/uploads/2015/07/paquetteryanwebquest_20091110.pdf), and here ("Bronfenbrenner's ecological theory" in *The encyclopedia of child and adolescent development*, by Tudge & Rosa).

[81] See "What We Know About Small Learning Communities" by the National High School Center published in 2009, "The Breakup: Understanding and Repairing Failed Small Learning Communities" by the American Youth Policy Forum published in 2007, and "Scaling Up Small Learning Communities: Lessons Learned from New American High Schools" by the National High School Center in 2006.

[82] See, for example: "Throwing Money at Schools" in *Journal of Policy Analysis and Management, 1*(1); "Threat Rigidity, School Reform, and How Teachers View Their Work Inside Current Education Policy Contexts" in *American Educational Research Journal, 46*(1); "The Limits of Sanctions in Low-Performing Schools" in *Education Policy Analysis Archives, 11*(3)

[83] A wealth of good information on education funding can be found here: https://educationdata.org/public-education-spending-statistics. In addition, there is a plethora of data that shows the disparity of education funding across the United States, as pointed out in this excellent piece: https://www.edweek.org/policy-politics/state-k-12-spending-is-inequitable-and-inadequate-see-where-yours-ranks/2021/10

[84] To learn more about what Lynn Moody did, see here: https://education-reimagined.org/rowan-salisbury-schools-a-conversation-with-dr-lynn-moody

[85] See https://www.gettingsmart.com/podcast/podcast-patricia-deklotz-on-high-school-transportation and https://www.nextgenlearning.org/articles/learning-without-boundaries-at-kettle-moraine-school-district for more.

[86] To learn more about Open Way Learning, go here: https://www.openwaylearning.org

87 To learn more about the Learner-Centered Collaborative, see here: https://learnercentered.org
88 To learn more about Transcend Education, read more here: https://transcendeducation.org
89 See here: https://exchange.transcendeducation.org
90 To see what they are actually doing, go here: http://www.nysed.gov/postsecondary-services/pathways-technology-nys-p-tech-program
91 See here: https://newtechnetwork.org. Also: https://www.gettingsmart.com/2017/04/18/new-tech-network-common-learning-model and https://www.gettingsmart.com/2020/07/21/how-new-tech-schools-jumpstarted-el-pasos-education-transformation,
92 See https://connectednational.org.
93 See https://eleducation.org.
94 Jon Ketler and his colleagues who started and run the three Tacoma school spotlighted in this book (SOTA, SAMI, and IDEA) have a non-profit specifically to showcase their school practices and, when of interest, support others' efforts. See here for more: https://www.elementsofed.org.
95 Over the years I have captured the work, stories, and impact of Olympic HS through interviews with staff, industry partners, students, and alum. To share these videos I have created a playlist of these videos on YouTube, which you can access here: https://www.youtube.com/playlist?list=PLlL6DBfRA7L7S3dVJqJ8D FV7KRbwVxHN9. Or here: https://bit.ly/41xI6If
96 See https://www.linkedlearning.org/impact/student-outcomes.
97 As told by told by the great Rob Riordan, co-founder of High Tech High.